Praise for *Prisoner of the State*

"Zhao speaks from beyond the grave . . . the up-close-and-personal tone [of the book] stands out. Scholars will mine *Prisoner of the State* for historical nuances."

—Perry Link, coeditor of *The Tiananmen Papers*

"Zhao Ziyang violated one of the central tenets of Communist Party doctrine: He spoke out. . . . [*Prisoner of the State*] marks the first time . . . that a senior Chinese leader has spoken out so directly against the party and its system. Reaching from the grave, Zhao pillories a conservative wing of the party for missteps that led to the bloody crackdown."

—John Pomfret, *The Washington Post*

"A rare first-person account of crisis politics at the highest levels of the Chinese Communist Party."

—Erik Eckholm, *The New York Times*

"Until the appearance of this posthumous work, not a single voice of dissent had ever emerged from the [Chinese Communist] party's inner circle . . . [*Prisoner of the State*] is fascinating for the way it conveys the flow of power in China at that time."

—*The Economist*

"This book will be of special importance to anyone interested in what happened during the spring of 1989, culminating in the Tiananmen killings of June 3 and 4."

—Jonathan Mirsky, *The New York Review of Books*

"An extremely rare first-hand account of elite Chinese politics."

—Geoff Dyer, *Financial Times*

"In this unique book we have the final verdict on the triumph of dictatorship in 1989 from the man who tried to stop it. . . . This is the highest-level memoir ever to come out of the People's Republic. . . . The enormous political value of this book, however, is that it makes a mature call for democracy in a distinctly Chinese voice."

—Michael Sheridan, *Sunday Times* (UK)

"Zhao Ziyang's book lifts the lid on discussions within the party that led to the brutal crushing of the protest movement."

—Michael Bristow, BBC News

"The Chinese leader ousted for opposing the crackdown has broken his silence in a posthumous memoir that gives a rare insight to the inner workings of the Communist Party during a critical time . . . the first-person account and intimate details of political bickering and machinations are new."

—Audra Ang, Associated Press

"A fascinating story (and a great scoop) . . . it will be a huge contribution to our understanding of the history of the period."

—Simon Elegant

"A rare and fascinating look today at how China's leaders viewed the 1989 Tiananmen Square protests and crackdown."

—Thomas Mucha, GlobalPost

PRISONER
OF THE
STATE

THE SECRET JOURNAL OF
ZHAO ZIYANG

Translated and Edited by
Bao Pu, Renee Chiang, and Adi Ignatius

Foreword by Roderick MacFarquhar

Simon & Schuster Paperbacks

NEW YORK LONDON TORONTO SYDNEY

Simon & Schuster Paperbacks
A Division of Simon & Schuster, Inc.
1230 Avenue of the Americas
New York, NY 10020

First Simon & Schuster hardcover edition May 2010

SIMON & SCHUSTER PAPERBACKS and colophon are
registered trademarks of Simon & Schuster, Inc.

For information about special discounts for bulk purchases,
please contact Simon & Schuster Special Sales at
1-866-506-1949 or business@simonandschuster.com.

The Simon & Schuster Speakers Bureau can bring authors to
your live event. For more information or to book an event,
contact the Simon & Schuster Speakers Bureau at
1-866-248-3049 or visit our website at www.simonspeakers.com.

Designed by C. Linda Dingler

Manufactured in the United States of America

3   5   7   9   10   8   6   4

The Library of Congress has cataloged the hardcover edition as follows:

Zhao, Ziyang.
Prisoner of the state : the secret journal of Zhao Ziyang /
translated and edited by Bao Pu, Renee Chiang, and Adi Ignatius;
foreword by Roderick MacFarquhar.
p. cm.
1. Zhao, Ziyang. 2. Prime ministers—China—Biography. 3. Political
prisoners—China—biography. 4. Statesmen—China—Biography.
5. China—Politics and government—1976–2002.
6. China—History—Tiananmen Square Incident, 1989.
I. Bao, Pu. II. Chiang, Renee. III. Ignatius, Adi. IV. MacFarquhar, Roderick. V. Title
DS779.29.Z467 A313 2009
951.058092—dc22   2009455606

ISBN 978-1-4391-4938-6
ISBN 978-1-4391-4939-3 (pbk)
ISBN 978-1-4391-5407-6 (ebook)

Contents

PRISONER OF THE STATE

Preface

Adi Ignatius

It was an exhilarating moment for China and the world. In late 1987, at the end of a spirited Communist Party Congress that seemed to propel China on a more progressive course, a new team of leaders emerged, led by a preternaturally tranquil man named Zhao Ziyang.

Zhao wasn't an unknown: after an impressive career in the provinces guiding the first, baby steps of China's recovery from Mao Zedong's lethally unsuccessful economic experiments, Zhao had been summoned to Beijing in 1980 and was soon named Premier, responsible for the economy.

Yet now he was being elevated to the most senior position in China's leadership: General Secretary of the Party. Since he was only sixty-eight years old—a mere child among China's leaders—he had to deal with an older generation of Party veterans who lacked official titles but nonetheless wielded ultimate authority. But the supreme leader of those octogenarians, Deng Xiaoping, had given Zhao the keys to the republic. It was his time to shine.

Zhao was unlike any previous Chinese leader. When the new inner core, the Standing Committee of the Politburo, appeared at the end of that Congress in 1987 for an unprecedented face-to-face with the international press corps at the Great Hall of the People, Zhao beamed with a relaxed confidence. He seemed to signal that China was ready to join the world, that it had begun a process of transforming not just its economy but also its tightfisted politics.

For the first time in memory, the entire Standing Committee appeared in Western attire, their Mao suits stashed away for this photo op aimed at telling the developed West that China was comfortable on stage. When a reporter commented on Zhao's impressive double-breasted pinstripe suit,

Zhao, with a big grin, playfully pulled open the jacket to show off a lapel that indicated: made in China. A new era seemed to be at hand.

Over the next two years, however, things would spin out of control, for China and for Zhao. Missteps on the economy led to a rampant inflation that unnerved China's citizens and opened the door for China's more cautious leaders to seize authority and reimpose central controls.

And then, in April 1989, the Tiananmen protests erupted. By the time they were suppressed, less than two months later, Zhao was out of power and under house arrest in his home on a quiet alley in Beijing. China's most promising change agent had been disgraced, along with the policies he stood for.

Zhao spent the last sixteen years of his life, up until his death in 2005, in seclusion. An occasional detail about his life would slip out: reports of a golf excursion, a photo of his aging visage, a leaked letter to China's leaders. But China scholars often lamented that Zhao never had his final say, that he didn't leave his take on what really happened behind the scenes during the tumultuous years that he was in Beijing and, in particular, in 1989 during the Tiananmen protests, when he stood up to China's conservative forces and lost.

The fact is, Zhao did produce such a memoir, in complete secrecy. This book is the first time it is being made public.

Zhao, it turns out, methodically recorded his thoughts and recollections on some of modern China's most critical moments. He talked of the Tiananmen crackdown, of his clashes behind the scenes with his powerful rivals, of the often petty bickering that lay behind policy making, of how China had to evolve politically to achieve long-term stability.

Somehow, under the nose of his captors, Zhao found a way to record about thirty tapes, each about sixty minutes long. Judging from their contents, they were made around the year 2000. Members of his family say they knew nothing about the project. Zhao produced these audio journals mostly by recording over some low-quality cassette tapes that were lying around the house: kids' music and Peking Opera. He indicated their order by numbering them with faint pencil markings. There were no titles or other notes. The first few recordings, covering Tiananmen and other topics he was eager to address—like allegations that Zhao had backstabbed his predecessor, Hu Yaobang, when Hu had been forced out of power in 1987—seem to have been made in discussion with friends. Their voices are heard on the tapes but have been edited out to protect them and their families' security.

When Zhao finished the recordings after about two years, he found a way to pass tapes to several trusted friends. Each was given only a portion of the total recordings, clearly an attempt to hedge the risk that the tapes might be lost or confiscated. When Zhao died in 2005, some of the people who knew of the recordings launched a complex, clandestine effort to gather the materials in one place and then transcribe them for publication. Later, another set of the tapes, perhaps the originals, was found, hidden in plain view among the grandchildren's toys in Zhao's study. The audio recordings themselves have been returned to Zhao's family, who will decide how they should be preserved. Clips of the recordings will be released to the public upon the release of this book.

Prisoner of the State is a nearly complete presentation of Zhao's recorded journal. The book does not follow Zhao's precise sequence. Some chunks were rearranged and others trimmed to eliminate repetition and for greater readability. For instance, we open with sections that deal with the Tiananmen protests and crackdown of 1989 and with Zhao's many years under house arrest. We begin each chapter with brief editors' notes, in italics, to help set the stage for readers who aren't familiar with what was happening in China at the time. We also have inserted material throughout the book in brackets and footnotes to provide added clarity. Wherever these appear, these are our words, not Zhao's.

Although Zhao gave no instructions as to how or when the materials might be published or otherwise used, he clearly wanted his story to survive. Here's what he says at the start of Part 1, which covers the events leading up to the Tiananmen Massacre of June 4, 1989: "I jotted down some notes about the events surrounding the June Fourth incident because I was worried that I might start forgetting some of the specifics. I hoped that it might serve as a kind of historical record."

What is the significance of this journal? Above all, it is the first time that a leader of Zhao's stature in China has spoken frankly about life at the top. He provides an intimate look at one of the world's most opaque regimes. We learn about the triumphs and failures, the boasts and insecurities, of the man who tried to bring liberal change to China, and who made every effort to stop the Tiananmen Massacre. This is Zhao's version of history, and he perhaps was making his arguments for a future generation of leaders who may revisit his case and decide whether he should be rehabilitated in the memory of the Party, and of the nation.

The power structure that Zhao describes is chaotic, often bumbling. Competing factions rush to win over paramount leader Deng Xiaoping, whose nods of assent or rejection resonate through society as if handed down from an oracle. In this narrative, Deng is a conflicted figure who urges Zhao to move quickly with economic reforms but consistently fights back against anything that seems to challenge the Party's supremacy.

He is at times portrayed not as the authority, but as a puppet, subject to manipulation by Zhao or his rivals, depending on who presents his case first. Zhao reflects on comments he made to Soviet leader Mikhail Gorbachev that upset Deng. His assumption, based on years in the inner circle, is that Deng could not have had such a reaction simply on his own: "I have yet to learn who it was or how that person managed to provoke Deng."

The China that Zhao portrays is not some long-lost dynasty. It is today's China, where the nation's leaders accept economic freedom but continue to intimidate and arrest anyone who tries to speak openly about political change. Although the central figures of Zhao's narrative have mostly passed from the scene, the system itself and its habits have not evolved. At the end of 2008, more than three hundred Chinese activists, marking the sixtieth anniversary of the Universal Declaration of Human Rights, jointly signed Charter 08, a document that called on the Party to reform its political system and allow freedom of expression and an independent judiciary. Beijing responded as it always has: by interrogating many of the signatories and arresting some, including prominent dissident Liu Xiaobo.

China is still a nation where the Party's obsession with self-perpetuation drives its public behavior, and where patriotic voices that don't narrowly conform are silenced. That has consequences far beyond the political sphere. In 2003, when the deadly SARs virus began to spread in China, officials initially resorted to form by trying to control the news and cover up the extent of the problem. That lack of candor may have exposed many thousands more to possible infection.

This journal isn't comprehensive. It doesn't deal with Zhao's long and productive career, only the tumultuous three years before he fell from power. Yet his impressive achievements and the reputation he developed are worth remembering.

Zhao's rise to power traces to his success running economic policy in the provinces. Though born in Henan Province, he built his career in Guangdong, where he became Party chief in 1965 at the remarkably tender age of forty-six. Like countless other officials, he was purged during the Cultural Revolution; he was assigned the relatively menial task of being a fitter at the Xiangzhong Mechanics Factory in Hunan Province. Zhao Wujun, the youngest of his four sons (there is also one daughter), worked with him. The family lived in a small apartment nearby with a suitcase in the middle of the living room that served as the dinner table.

Zhao's return from exile shows the high regard Beijing's leaders had for him. As Zhao once described it to friends, in April 1971 the Zhao family was suddenly roused in the middle of the night by a banging at the door. Without explanation, the factory's Party chief informed Zhao that he was to go at once to Changsha, the provincial capital. The factory's only means of transport was a three-wheeled motorcycle, which was quickly readied to take him.

Zhao was driven to Changsha's airport, where a plane had been prepared to fly him to Beijing. Still unaware of what was happening, he boarded the plane; it landed in Beijing, and he was driven to the well-appointed Beijing Hotel. Zhao said he didn't sleep all night; after his years in the political wilderness, the mattress was too soft.

In the morning, he was taken for a meeting with Premier Zhou Enlai at the Great Hall of the People. When they met, Zhao began a speech he had been preparing all night: "I have been rethinking the Cultural Revolution during these years as a laborer—" Zhou cut him off and told him, "You've been called to Beijing because the Central Committee has decided to name you as a deputy Party chief of Inner Mongolia."

Zhao later learned that Chairman Mao himself had been responsible for his return from political exile. Mao one day had suddenly asked an attendant, Whatever happened to Zhao Ziyang? When he was told that Zhao had been purged and sent to the countryside as a laborer, Mao expressed his displeasure with the excesses of the purification effort he had launched with the Cultural Revolution: "Purging every single person? That's not what I want . . ." With that, Zhao Ziyang was rehabilitated.

Zhao held top jobs in several provinces and won widespread praise for finding solutions to the economic paralysis left over from Mao's collectivization. He became the Party leader in Sichuan Province in 1975 and launched ambitious changes in the countryside that increased agricultural output and farmers' wealth. His success prompted locals to say "yao chi liang, zhao Ziyang," a wordplay on his name that translates roughly as "If you want to eat, look for Ziyang."

Unlike many other high-ranking officials, Zhao had a reputation for pragmatism, for taking care of business. He couldn't stand having people do things for him. Before he was purged for the final time in 1989, there was an evening when he was having trouble sleeping. The Party's service bureau sent over a doctor to give him massages to help him rest. After a few visits, Zhao had them stopped. Asked why, he said, "The first thing this doctor did each time he came was to kneel down on the floor and take off my shoes. I couldn't stand it." Zhao never seemed to warm to the isolation of Zhongnanhai, the Party's fortified compound in the center of Beijing. When he'd meet people from outside China's inner circle, he'd excitedly ask, "What's the latest news out there?"

But if Zhao was a rule breaker, he was also a man of discipline. Whereas his predecessor as Party chief, Hu Yaobang, was indiscreet (an incautious interview with a Hong Kong journalist may ultimately have cost him his job), Zhao was circumspect and mindful of the potential fall-out from every step he took. That rigor extended to his personal life as well. For years when he worked in the provinces, friends urged him to quit smoking. Finally, in 1980 when he was about to become Premier, he changed his mind. "Okay, it's time," he told friends. He never smoked again. (He did continue to drink, however, and had a reputation for being able to handle large quantities; a friend says Zhao had no trouble tossing back six mao-tais over a dinner.)

His years in the provinces were surely his happiest. In Beijing, Deng charged him with leading reforms—first in the economy, and later in politics. But China couldn't easily adapt to dramatic change, and when things got too shaky, Deng opted for stability. He sacrificed his two most liberal lieutenants: first Hu, then Zhao. Dreams of a broad political awakening in China were put on hold.

Zhao's account of his final years is dignified, yet sad. Under house arrest, he could do little but obsess over events, rewinding the clock to pore over the technicalities of the Party's official case against him. From the outside it could be argued that he was handled gently, at least compared with earlier, violent purges of communist officials. He wasn't put in jail, and the Party eventually lost interest in trying to tear him down. But his captors succeeded in keeping him out of view and making him irrelevant, throwing up enough obstacles to deter all but the most determined visitors. As Zhao says in this journal, "The entrance to my home is a cold, desolate place."

Scholars will no doubt wish to compare Zhao's memoir with other accounts of that era. For one thing, he contradicts the widely held belief that the decision in 1989 to call in the military to crack down on student demonstrators was put to a formal vote of the Politburo Standing Committee. Zhao attests otherwise: there was no vote. For Zhao it's a critical detail, since a proper vote could have lent the decision an air of procedural legitimacy. Zhao explains his own defiance in the clearest of terms: "I refused to become the General Secretary who mobilized the military to crack down on students."

Just after the decision was made to call in the army—and aware that his own political career was probably finished—Zhao made a remarkable

visit to the seething Tiananmen Square to speak with the student protesters. (Hearing that Zhao was making the trip, his rival, Premier Li Peng,
tagged along. Zhao says Li was "terrified" and quickly fled the scene.) Accompanied in the end by director of the General Office Wen Jiabao, who
would later become China's Premier, a teary Zhao spoke to students
through a bullhorn. "We have come too late," he said, urging students to
leave the square to avoid a violent outcome. They didn't heed his words.
Around two weeks later, the tanks were unleashed, and hundreds of demonstrators were killed.

Though he was the main voice at the top articulating a gentle response to the protests, Zhao is largely forgotten today. For three years
after Tiananmen, China stagnated under the repressive shadow of the
Massacre. But then Deng Xiaoping, mindful of his own legacy, made a
celebrated trip to China's vibrant southern region and sounded a call to
free up economic policy and let people get rich. The result is a China with
a booming economy and a repressive government. If Zhao had survived
politically—that is, if the hard line hadn't prevailed on Tiananmen—he
might have been able to steer China's political system toward more openness and tolerance. His ultimate aim was a strong economy, but he had
become convinced that this goal was inextricably linked to the development of democracy.

Zhao's call to begin lifting the Party's control over China's life—to let
a little freedom into the public square—is remarkable coming from a
man who had once dominated that square. Although Zhao now speaks
from the grave, his voice has the moral power to make China sit up and
listen.

Foreword

Roderick MacFarquhar

I met Zhao Ziyang only once, when I called on him in his hotel bedroom in London during his June 1979 trip as head of a Sichuan Province delegation. The room swarmed with his colleagues, all somewhat bemused at my sudden appearance among them. I was aware of Zhao's growing reputation as the Sichuan Province first secretary, since he was pioneering reforms in agriculture, and that this trip abroad was an opportunity to educate himself. But at that point my scholarly interests were more historical: If I came to Sichuan, would he talk to me about his experiences in running Guangdong Province in the 1960s? He would be happy to. I handed an aide my card and withdrew.

From that brief encounter, I formed a few, doubtless superficial but nevertheless firm impressions. This longtime Party cadre was open, good-humored, and energetic. Sadly, I was never able to consolidate those impressions. When I made my next research trip to China, Zhao Ziyang was the country's Premier and I knew better than to try to get past the barriers of Beijing's bureaucracy.

What we have in this book is Zhao's personal account of what it was like being Premier, and later Party General Secretary, and later still, what it was like living under house arrest. The documents give us a close-up of the vicious world of Beijing high politics as Deng Xiaoping's acolytes—Party General Secretary Hu Yaobang and Premier Zhao Ziyang—battled on behalf of Deng's reform program. Much of this has been documented

by Western scholars, but here we have an account of the internal struggles that underlay the vague turbulence visible on the surface.*

What clearly emerges is that Zhao greatly enjoyed his role as Premier,
including the research and thinking it required, the mistakes and disap-
pointments, and the satisfaction that came with China's accelerating expansion. He had his opponents among the Old Guard "elders," in
particular Chen Yun and Li Xiannian. Chen had been the voice of economic reason in the 1950s, whenever Mao Zedong went off the rails, and
he still believed that the Five-Year Plan system under strong central control would have worked even better but for the Chairman's errors; after
all, it had turned the Soviet Union into a superpower. Effectively, Chen
Yun proposed that China should go back to the future. He devised the
model of a "birdcage economy": the planned economy was the cage and
the birds were the market economy. This way the market could be prevented from getting out of control. Zhao respected Chen Yun—he is the
only one of the elders discussed in this book whom Zhao normally desig-
nates as "Comrade"—and always tried to visit with him to discuss new
policies and bring him around. If that proved impossible, there was always Deng to fall back on to keep Chen Yun in line.

Li Xiannian was a totally different personality, and Zhao seems to
have developed an active dislike for him early on. Li was the only senior
civilian official to serve alongside Zhou Enlai throughout the Cultural
Revolution. As Hua Guofeng rose to leadership during the last days of
Chairman Mao, Li became Hua's principal economic adviser and, had
Hua survived as leader, would have been a power in the land. Li never
got over this, nor his resentment that Zhao inherited his role. Li regularly
grumbled that his own achievements during the brief Hua interregnum
should be acknowledged as part of the basis for current progress. "The
economic successes are not all the result of reform. Weren't there successes in the past too? Weren't the foundations laid in the past?" In fact,
Hua's "great leap outwards"—the massive buying of plants from overseas—grossly overstretched the Chinese economy. But because Li was an
elder, nobody stuck it to him, certainly not Zhao, and so Li grumbled on
about Zhao's fixation with "foreign stuff," his willingness to learn from
what had been successful for the Asian Tiger economies, and even from
the West. Li, who later was consoled with the post of head of state, was
the most prominent opponent of reform and, according to Zhao, "he

---

*   For a comprehensive Western account of this period, see Richard Baum, *Burying
Mao: Chinese Politics in the Age of Deng Xiaoping* (Princeton, N.J.: Princeton University
Press, 1994).

hated me because I was implementing Deng Xiaoping's reforms, but since it was difficult for him to openly oppose Deng, he made me the target of his opposition."

Other than his problem with Li Xiannian, Zhao was fortunate that of Deng's two standard-bearers, it was Hu Yaobang who took most of the heat from the elders and the conservatives. According to Zhao, this was because as General Secretary, Hu was in charge of politics and ideology, and the conservatives found Hu decidedly uninterested in their concerns. Zhao, who writes warmly about Hu, suggests that in part it was because Hu sympathized with intellectuals and did not want to persecute them as had been done during the Cultural Revolution. Hu also had a tendency to shoot from the lip with little concern for the impression conveyed. In fact, one major divergence between Hu and Zhao was over Hu's tendency to press for faster economic progress, overriding Zhao's preference for slower but steady. Both were committed to introducing a market economy, but Hu seemed still to hanker after movement economics, Maoist-style. In 1983, Deng had to call them both in and expressly order Hu not to counteract the government's economic officials. Zhao believed that Deng had lost faith in Hu long before an outburst of student demonstrations at the end of 1986, which became the occasion for his dismissal as General Secretary; all in all, being allowed to retain membership on the Politburo was not too bad a fate for Hu under the circumstances.

And yet Hu had had one advantage that Zhao could never emulate. He had worked at the center for most of his political career, which meant he had a constituency, connections; indeed, Zhao tells us, Hu was accused by his many enemies of promoting a Communist Youth League faction, since he headed that organization during the 1950s. By contrast, Zhao had worked in provincial apparats in different parts of the country, and on being summoned to Beijing in 1980, he had no connections, or as he put it, "fewer channels. Therefore some of the behind-the-scenes dealings remain obscure to me, even now." Instead, Zhao had a constituency of just one: Deng Xiaoping. Of course, it was the best one-man constituency to have, but even Deng had occasionally to bob and weave when faced with strong opposition from his fellow elders. No wonder that Zhao begged Deng not to resign every time the latter had mentioned the possibility. For his part, Deng was assuring Zhao as late as April 1989—only a month before his career crashed in ruins—that he had secured the agreement of Chen Yun and Li Xiannian for Zhao to serve two more full terms as Party General Secretary, the job that Zhao had taken when Hu Yaobang was dismissed in January 1987. But before turning to that sad final phase of Zhao's career, it is worth pausing to consider his role in the reform program.

Deng is normally seen as the architect of reform. Certainly, without his strong initial push for it and for opening up to the outside world, there would have been no such program. Thereafter he remained among the elders the godfather of the effort, ready to sally forth from seclusion to defend it against all comers. But reading Zhao's unadorned and unboastful account of his stewardship, it becomes apparent that it was he rather than Deng who was the actual architect of reform. It was Zhao who, after countless inspection tours, finally realized that the commitment to rural collectivization was passé, a view that was reaffirmed when Deng came back to power in December 1978. Zhao supported a national household responsibility system as the way to develop agriculture and raise farm incomes. As Zhao acknowledges, without Deng's support it would never have been possible to proceed. But Deng did not make the conceptual breakthrough. Zhao did.

It was Zhao, too, who conceived of the hugely successful coastal development strategy. This was not the Special Economic Zone policy launched early in the reform era. Rather it was an effort to mobilize all the coastal provinces to develop an export-oriented economy, importing large quantities of raw materials, transforming them, and then exporting the results in equally large quantities. There were many different kinds of objections that Zhao overcame, but again, once he convinced Deng, it was relatively smooth sailing. Zhao devised the policy in 1987–88 and it outlasted his political demise, but thereafter it was no longer referred to as the coastal development strategy because that phrase was so closely linked to Zhao and no credit could be allowed to go to him.

Zhao takes responsibility for failures, too. One of the big issues in the late 1980s was price reform, but late in the debate Zhao agreed to postpone it because of the state of the economy. This was one of the few occasions that he and his principal opponents, Premier Li Peng and Vice Premier Yao Yilin, were on the same side. But Li and Yao took advantage of the economic problems to sideline Zhao. Deng had lain it down that Zhao would still be in overall charge of the economy even after he took over the general secretaryship, but Li and Yao now increasingly ignored Zhao's inputs. As veterans of the Chinese political system, they were quick to sense erosion of power.

Zhao's record remains impressive. What is even more impressive is that he was working virtually single-handedly at his level. He developed a loyal coterie of reform officials who worked for him, notably his aide Bao Tong who remains under house arrest till this day. But it was Zhao in the first instance who had to persuade or do battle with the elders. It was Zhao who had to watch his back for the slings and arrows of outraged "colleagues" such as Li Peng and Yao Yilin. It was Zhao who had to argue with the bureaucrats at the national and provincial levels, officials who probably had not had a new idea since well before the Cultural Revolution, but who were determined to protect their turf and their ways of managing it. And yet, throughout the 1980s, till he left office, Zhao was thinking, questioning, inspecting, discussing, and arguing over the next step forward. Deng had displayed excellent judgment in choosing Zhao as the architect of the reform program.

Zhao never wanted the formal promotion to the position of General Secretary. He loved what he was doing and didn't want to become involved in disputes over theory or politics. Had Deng come up with another candidate for the office, Zhao would have gladly stayed where he was. But the only suggestions of alternate names came from conservatives who were playing their own devious games, which Zhao naively took at face value, but which Deng saw through. So Zhao, duty-prone, was trapped.

He soon realized how lucky he had been to have had Hu Yaobang running interference all those years. Zhao now inherited two new nemeses: Hu Qiaomu and Deng Liqun ("little Deng," no relative of Deng Xiaoping). Hu Qiaomu was the prince of pens, Mao's onetime secretary and favorite ghostwriter. Deng Xiaoping had refused to have any dealings with him for some years. Deng Liqun was a longtime leftist theoretician with considerable contacts among the conservative elders. He ran a research office under the Central Party Secretariat that could be relied upon to produce the most anti-reform ideas and commentaries. According to Deng Xiaoping, "little Deng" was very stubborn, "like a Hunan mule." His supporters, on the other hand, doubtless thought he was admirably determined in standing up for the truth.

Zhao had displayed no interest in the ideological battles that Hu Yaobang had fought with Hu Qiaomu and little Deng, and they viewed him as neutral, concerned only with preventing ideological issues from disrupting economic development. But when Hu Yaobang was dismissed and they thought they could embark on an anti–bourgeois liberalization campaign, they ran up against Zhao's opposition. In short order Zhao achieved what Hu Yaobang had failed to do: he dissolved little Deng's power base by liquidating the research office of the central Secretariat, and he closed down left-wing magazines such as *Red Flag*.

As a quid pro quo, Zhao proposed that little Deng be given a seat on the Politburo at the next Party Congress so that he could air his views.

This was agreed to, but when the necessary first step had to be taken—
election to the Central Committee from which the members of the Politburo were drawn—little Deng failed to get elected. Despite his earlier
agreement to little Deng's promotion, Deng Xiaoping decided to let the
vote stand. Little Deng's supporters among the elders were furious and
began to regard Zhao as worse even than Hu Yaobang.

Yet Zhao was to have one more triumph. He decided to solve once
and for all the nagging problem that had underlain the whole reform era:
If China had completed a socialist revolution in the 1950s, why was it
adopting capitalist methods now? He decided to take a phrase that had
been around for some years—"the initial stage of socialism"—and assign
it a theoretical prominence it had so far lacked. This would not deny the
socialist achievements thus far but it would free China from rigid socialist
dogma. He also tried to please everyone by emphasizing the status of the
"Four Cardinal Principles," enunciated by Deng in 1979: upholding
the socialist road, the dictatorship of the proletariat, the leadership of the
Communist Party, and Marxism–Leninism–Mao Zedong Thought. Zhao
proposed that the Central Committee plenum that had brought Deng
back to power in December 1978 had implicitly meant to say that the
Four Cardinal Principles and reform and opening up were on an equal
level and that these were the two basic points, with economic development as the main focus. This was turned into a colloquial phrase by Bao
Tong and his colleagues as "one central focus, two basic points." Not everyone saluted it, but Deng Xiaoping loved it, and that was what mat-
tered. The idea became the theoretical centerpiece of Zhao's Political
Report to the 13th Party Congress in the fall of 1987.

When we come to the events of April–June 1989, when the students
began their marches to Tiananmen Square to show their respect for Hu
Yaobang, who died on April 15, it is possible that Western readers have
access to more knowledge than Zhao Ziyang had at the time. This is as a
result of the publication abroad of secret Communist documents on the
crisis,* some of which Zhao probably never saw, particularly the minutes
of the meetings of the elders who decided on Zhao's dismissal and the
selection of his successor. What Zhao provides here is his analysis of the
student movement and his policy for handling it.

Zhao infuriated his conservative colleagues, such as Li Peng, with his
relaxed attitude toward the student activities. He was convinced that after

---

*   Zhang Liang, Andrew J. Nathan, and Perry Link, *The Tiananmen Papers* (New
York: PublicAffairs, 2002).

their initial demonstrations, with persuasive handling the students could be induced to return to their campuses. With Li Peng promising to follow Zhao's line, the latter left on a long-scheduled visit to North Korea. Unfortunately for Zhao, Li Peng found a way to get around his promise. Shortly after Zhao's departure, Li Peng rushed the leaders of the Beijing Municipal Party Committee to report first to the Politburo Standing Committee and then to Deng. Their report was full of fire and brimstone, prophesizing that if control were not immediately restored, there could be a nationwide upheaval. Deng, with his memories of the Cultural Revolution—during which his son was crippled for life—was bound to be impressed by such a report, and he designated the events "anti-Party, anti-socialist turmoil." Zhao was contacted in North Korea and in the absence of any other information, perforce had to agree with Deng's analysis. Li Peng ensured that Deng's words and sentiments were immediately expressed in a *People's Daily* editorial on April 26. Contrary to Li Peng's expectations, however, the editorial, far from frightening the students into submission, infuriated them further because their patriotic actions were so misdescribed. On the 27th, the students marched again to the square, breaking through a police cordon. Li Peng, with Deng's help, had reignited the student movement.

Immediately on his return, Zhao saw that no matter how many placatory speeches were made, the offensive bits of the editorial would have to be withdrawn if the student movement were to be quieted again. But his inquiries indicated what he already knew: Deng had no intention of allowing the editorial to be disavowed. Li Peng's greatest triumph was that he had finally found an issue over which to divide the Deng-Zhao partnership. Zhao tried other ways of appeasing the students, but by mid-May he was out of options and faded from the policy scene. When his resistance to the imposition of martial law proved futile, the Zhao era was over and all that remained was to attend the Central Committee meeting and accept dismissal.*

Zhao, who died in 2005, was to spend more time under house arrest than he had spent trying to run the reform program. During this period, he was allowed to make occasional trips to carefully specified locations, play occasional rounds of golf, and have visitors as long as they were

---

* For Zhao's speech in his own defense, see Yang Jisheng, "Zhao Ziyang's Speech in His Own Defense at the Fourth Plenary Session of the 13th Central Committee of the Chinese Communist Party," *Chinese Law and Government* 38, no. 3 (May–June 2005), pp. 51–68.

heavily screened.* But much of Zhao's time was spent protesting the petty restrictions under which he was incarcerated. Ever the conscientious Party official, he quoted the state constitution and the Party rulebook to his jailers. To the end, he seems genuinely, if naively, to have believed that at some point his opponents might crack under the weight of his impeccable legalism. Of course, they didn't. Legality didn't figure at all in the handling of the Zhao case, only power and stability. It's almost as if Zhao had just arrived in Beijing from the sticks and didn't realize that law plays no real role in Chinese political life. But perhaps he took some slight consolation from the idea that the leadership had genuine fears of the turbulence that he might arouse if he were to be seen on the open street.

In captivity, Zhao thought about political reform, Deng's ideas, Hu Yaobang's, and his own. He concluded that Deng didn't really believe in political reform, only in tighter administration. Hu hadn't thought his ideas through, but his mildness in political campaigns and his insistence on pardoning all those wrongly arrested in previous campaigns led Zhao to speculate that if Hu had survived he would have "pushed China's political reform forward" toward democratization.

Zhao confesses that as of the mid-1980s, he was an economic reformer and a political conservative. Gradually he came to realize that without political reform, the economic reform program was in peril: for instance, the massive corruption would continue. By 1989, he was prepared to tell visiting Soviet leader Mikhail Gorbachev that the position of the Chinese Communist Party would not change, but its method of governing had to change: rule of law had to replace rule by men. He wanted to increase transparency and to establish multiple channels of dialogue with various social forces. Moreover, he felt the social forces should be allowed to organize themselves, rather than being required to submit to bodies led by the Party-state. Zhao wanted the possibility of choice, albeit limited, in elections to the national legislature.

Thereafter, Zhao's views evolved further. "In fact, it is the Western parliamentary democratic system that has demonstrated the most vitality. It seems that this system is currently the best one available." This modernizing involved both a market economy and a democratic political system. In China, this would mean a long period of transition, one requiring two breakthroughs by the Communist Party: allowing competition from

* One of his visitors, Zong Fengming, wrote down what Zhao had said immediately after he returned home after each visit (no note-taking was allowed in Zhao's home); out of this secretarial activity has come Zong Fengming, *Zhao Ziyang ruanjinzhong de tanhua* (Zhao Ziyang: Captive Conversations) (Hong Kong: Open Books, 2007). See Andrew Nathan's review in *China Perspectives*, no. 3 (2008), pp. 136–42.

other parties and a free press, and making the party itself more democratic. Reform of the legal system and the establishment of an independent judiciary would also take precedence. Zhao concludes with a brief
disquisition, based on experience, on how difficult it would be to introduce such reforms.

The story of Zhao's captivity prompts two reflections: If a patriotic official only came to the conclusion that democracy was needed for China
after years of nothing to do but think, what chance is there for a busy official today to have the leisure or the security to think such thoughts while
on the job? And if he did manage to come to such a conclusion, how
would he implement these ideas in the teeth of Party opposition at all
levels of society? It took a disaster of Cultural Revolution proportions to
shake China out of the Stalinist economic model. China doesn't need
another Cultural Revolution, but the Party would have to be shaken to its
roots for its leaders to contemplate following the final message of Zhao
Ziyang's testament.

Today in China, Zhao is a nonperson. In a less paranoid time in the
future, perhaps he will be seen as one in that honored line of Chinese officials down the ages who worked hard and well for their country, but fell
foul of the ruling authorities. Their names remain inspirational, long after
the names of their venal opponents have been forgotten.

THE TIANANMEN MASSACRE

I

The Student Protests Begin

The student movement of 1989 is one of the defining moments of Zhao Ziyang's career. On April 15, news of the death of Hu Yaobang, the liberal reformer who had been ousted from his position as Communist Party General Secretary two years earlier, sets off an outpouring of public mourning by college students in Beijing. It is a clear act of defiance against the decision made by paramount leader Deng Xiaoping and other Party elders to expel Hu.

The protests come at a time when China's citizens are already worried about rising prices and growing corruption in the country's half-reformed economy. As a result, hundreds of thousands of Chinese join in the demonstrations.

The Communist Party leadership is split. The conservatives who had supported the toppling of Hu argue for a crackdown. But Zhao, who had succeeded Hu as Party chief, worries about the political consequences of a severe response, and that a hard-line backlash could derail economic reforms. As the protests drag on, the power struggle intensifies.

Soon after the protests erupt, however, Zhao is due to travel to North Korea on an official visit, which limits his ability to influence the Party's response to the demonstrations. While he is away, on April 26, the government authorizes publication of an official verdict on the protests, in the form of an editorial in the People's Daily. *Its strident tone only makes things worse and diminishes Zhao's ability to manage the situation.*

Here Zhao speaks in depth for the first time about the source of the protests. He explains why he felt they didn't pose a direct threat to the government and how they could have been resolved long before the violent suppression of June 4.

Seven years ago [in 1992], I jotted down some notes about the events surrounding the June Fourth incident because I was worried that I might start forgetting some of the specifics. I hoped that it might serve as a kind of historical record.

Now I will talk about the incident according to these notes. Some of these issues were covered in the speech I delivered at the Fourth Plenum of the 13th Central Committee [held June 23–24, 1989, when Zhao, ousted from power, defended his role during the protests], but there are also other issues that I did not mention then. I will now talk about all of them.

First, I would like to talk about what initially triggered the student protests. All of the early incidences of student protests were related to the commemoration of [Hu] Yaobang.

Yaobang died on April 15, 1989. Immediately after the announcement was broadcast, some college students initiated commemoration activities. Soon thereafter, they took their activities onto the streets, and the number of participants grew and grew. Though at this point some students made some extreme statements because of piqued emotions, overall their activities were fairly orderly and nothing excessive took place.

On the nights of April 18 and 19, several hundred people gathered outside Xinhua Gate [outside the Party's headquarters]. I later called for and watched the video recordings made by the Ministry of Public Security. In the so-called "incident of students besieging Xinhua Gate," some of the students in the front were in fact shouting repeatedly, "We must maintain order! Don't do anything out of line!" There was a large crowd of spectators behind them. The students made verbal demands, including demands to meet certain members of the leadership. Then people pushed from behind and it got a little bit chaotic. The students then organized a team to act as guards to keep back the crowd of spectators.

On April 22, while the official memorial service for Hu Yaobang was taking place, tens of thousands of students were assembled in Tiananmen Square. This had been officially approved. The loudspeakers in the square broadcast the audio from the official memorial service inside the Great Hall of the People, so they could all listen in.

This was the situation before the publishing of the April 26 editorial in the *People's Daily*.

Why did the students react so strongly in commemorating the passing of Hu Yaobang? The reasons were complicated.

First, Hu Yaobang had always had a very good public image. He was responsible for reversing numerous cases of unjustified persecutions following the Mao years; he had always been a proponent of reform; most important, he was incorruptible while in power. There was a lot of dissatisfaction with corruption back then, so commemorating Hu Yaobang provided a chance to express this discontent.

Second, many people were displeased or even outraged by Hu Yaobang's demotion in 1987. Many people were averse to the Anti–Bourgeois Liberalization Campaign [launched in 1987] and continued to be opposed to it. In addition, people found unacceptable the way in which the leadership was changed. In general, people were expressing a feeling of indignation over how Hu Yaobang had been treated.

Third, when the government's reorganization was proposed in the fall of 1988, programs for reform had been cut back on all fronts. No action had been taken on political reform while economic reform had been brought to a standstill or even retracted. Students were dissatisfied with the general situation and were expressing their desire for advancing reforms through their commemoration of Hu Yaobang.

There were three kinds of people who took to the streets to protest: the vast majority of people belonged to the category I described above. There were also those who held grievances against our past policies and were taking the opportunity to make some noise. Of course, there was also a small number of people who opposed the Party and opposed socialism that were hoping to aggravate the situation.

At a Politburo Standing Committee [PSC] meeting [the date is unclear], I said that we should not forbid the activities of the students who were merely holding their own commemorations while the Central Committee was holding memorial services. There was no reason why we should reserve for ourselves exclusive rights to commemorate Hu, while forbidding the students to do so.

I suggested we punish according to law only those who engaged in the five type of behaviors: beating, smashing, looting, burning, or trespassing. In all other normal circumstances, there should be an attempt to reduce tensions.

After the official memorial service for Hu Yaobang, I proposed a course of action with three points:

1. With the memorial service now over, social activities should return to normal. Students need to be persuaded to discontinue their street demonstrations and return to their classes.

(At the time, I felt that whatever their motives, the students had in fact engaged in nothing more than commemorating Hu Yaobang. So with the memorial service over, and their having had a chance to participate by holding their own activities, there should have been no reason to continue the demonstrations. It was time to return to classes.)

2. According to the principal goal of reducing tensions, dialogue should be conducted at multiple levels, and through various channels and formats to establish mutual understanding and to seek a variety of opinions. Whatever opinions they held, all students, teachers, and intellectuals should be allowed to express themselves freely.
3. Bloodshed must be avoided, no matter what. However, those who engaged in the five kinds of behavior—beating, smashing, looting, burning, and trespassing—should be punished according to law.

My suggestions were all accepted by [Premier] Li Peng and every member of the Politburo Standing Committee and were officially documented.

The above assessment of the situation and the principles for action agreed upon were disseminated via various channels to local government branches. These were the three points that I proposed before my visit to North Korea. I spoke to key leaders of the Central Committee about them while taking the elevator down after the memorial service, and later expressed them again formally.

On the afternoon of April 23, as I was preparing to leave Beijing train station to head for North Korea, Li Peng came to send me off. He asked me if I had anything further to add. I said that my position had been summarized in those three points. I later heard that Li Peng reported the three points to Deng Xiaoping, who also expressed his agreement.

There were no disagreements from members of the Politburo Standing Committee, at least not openly. I can remember only one: on the evening of April 19, Li Peng called me unexpectedly and demanded accusingly, "The students are trying to break into Xinhua Gate! Why aren't any counteractions being taken?" I told him that [PSC member in charge of security] Qiao Shi was immediately responsible, and that he should be able to take care of any urgent situation that might arise using existing emergency plans.

I later informed Qiao Shi of Li Peng's call. In fact, by the morning of the 20th, most of the students had already left Xinhua Gate. The few who remained were cleared away by the police. They were ordered onto buses that drove them back to their schools.

This was the situation of the student demonstrations before I visited North Korea, and the policy of the Standing Committee at that time.

2

An Editorial Makes
Things Worse

*The Communist Party leadership doesn't know how to respond to
the growing student protests. When Zhao leaves on his trip to North
Korea, hard-liners opposed to his reforms take advantage of his
absence and maneuver supreme leader Deng Xiaoping to their side,
leading him to angrily denounce the demonstrations.*

*Any hope of calming things down is lost on April 26, when the
Party issues its official verdict on the protests in an editorial in the
People's Daily that reports Deng's harsh words. Deng is shocked to
learn that his comments have been published, but withdrawing the
piece would imply that China's supreme leader had made a mistake,
a path the Party doesn't wish to risk. The Party and the protesters
are now locked on a collision course. Zhao has failed to sense the
danger before leaving for Pyongyang.*

So why did the student demonstrations later turn into such a mess?
The crux of the situation was the April 26 editorial. The students
had feelings of dissatisfaction that, one way or the other, they were going
to express. If they had not held demonstrations then, they would have
held them later. They were truly discontented!

However, the scale of the demonstrations, the mess it turned into,
and why it happened when it did were all the results of the April 26 editorial. The situation before the publication of the editorial and the situation
afterward were different. If the right measures had been taken to direct
the situation, then there would not have been such dire results.

I visited Deng Xiaoping on April 19 to discuss my North Korea trip, to talk to him about the student demonstrations, and to give him my views on how the situation should be handled. At the time, Deng had expressed support for me. Yet things took a strange turn after that.

The very evening of the day that I left Beijing, Li Ximing and Chen Xitong of the Beijing Party Committee asked [chairman of the National People's Congress Standing Committee] Wan Li to call a meeting of the Politburo Standing Committee to listen to their report. Wan Li fell for their trick. (Wan Li and I had been in total agreement in our view of the student protests.) Wan Li directed their request to Li Peng, as Li Peng was temporarily in charge of Standing Committee* activities while I was abroad. The very next evening, Li Peng called for a Standing Committee meeting.

With Li Peng presiding, Li Ximing and Chen Xitong vigorously presented the student demonstrations as a grave situation. They disregarded the fact that the student demonstrations had already calmed down. In fact, student opinions had begun diverging.

Some of the students believed that they should resume classes and had already done so, while a minority opposed the return to classes. Internal friction had become apparent in some schools. Some of the students had attempted to resume classes, while other, more extreme students had blocked the entrances to the classrooms to prevent them from entering. This shows that for some students, the activities had not fully satisfied their need to vent their anger. If measures were to be taken to reduce tensions, to have dialogue, and to allow students the chance to propose certain reasonable requests, this was a good time to do so.

However, in their report, they [Li Ximing and Chen Xitong] went so far as to state, "Nationwide, large-scale demonstrations including the participation of high school students and workers are being organized and are fomenting." They also reported that "university students in Beijing have sent contacts to places around the country and have conducted fund-raising in the streets to prepare for activities on a larger scale." They denounced the extreme opinions of a few students, especially remarks directed specifically at Deng Xiaoping. They presented the demonstrations as opposing the Communist Party and targeting Deng Xiaoping personally.

With the onset of reform, students, especially college students, had been exposed to many Western ways. Remarks critical of political leaders were made casually and considered inconsequential; the intense climate

----

*   The author often shortens "Politburo Standing Committee" to "Standing Committee."

[of fear] that existed during the Cultural Revolution* and before no longer existed. Many of these student remarks targeted me, such as those that accused my children of making business deals utilizing official resources or those that claimed that trainloads of fertilizer had been sent to my hometown.

With hundreds of thousands of people involved, it's impossible for there to have been no extreme or one-sided comments. Things appear extremely grave if you select only the ten most extreme statements being expressed by all of the people involved. I am not sure what was behind Li Ximing and Chen Xitong's behavior: either their old mentality of class struggle was at work or they had other ulterior motives.

The student demonstration was deemed an "organized and carefully plotted political struggle," and was documented as such in the minutes of the meeting. Li Peng, Li Ximing, and Chen Xitong were the ones initially responsible for this.

On April 25, Li Peng and [President] Yang Shangkun reported to Deng Xiaoping about the Politburo Standing Committee meeting. Deng Xiaoping had always tended to prefer tough measures when dealing with student demonstrations because he believed that demonstrations undermined stability. After listening to their report, Deng immediately agreed to label the student demonstrations "anti-Party, anti-socialist turmoil" and proposed to resolve the situation quickly, in the manner of "using a sharp knife to cut through knotted hemp."

When I had visited him on April 19, he had agreed with my position. On the 25th, after being briefed by Li Peng and Yang Shangkun, he had changed his mind to agree with their assessment. After all, it coincided more closely with what he had really believed all along.

Deng's discussion with Li Peng and others on April 25 was supposed to be an internal affair. However, Li Peng decided to disseminate the contents of Deng's remarks that very evening to Party cadres of all levels, and paraphrased their talk in the editorial that he had the People's Daily publish on April 26, publicly designating the student demonstrations as "premeditated and organized turmoil with anti-Party and anti-socialist motives."

Before my visit to North Korea, neither Li Peng nor the cadres in Beijing mentioned these viewpoints to me. Immediately upon my leaving

---

* The Great Proletarian Cultural Revolution was a period of great upheaval in China that lasted from 1966 to 1976. Launched by Chairman Mao Zedong, who was frustrated by the passive resistance of his own bureaucracy to his radical economic policies, the ultraleftist campaign led to the persecution of millions, including purges of hundreds of thousands of Communist Party officials.

Beijing, they quickly held a Politburo Standing Committee meeting and gained support from Deng Xiaoping. This constituted a departure from the previous position and the principles adopted by the Standing Committee.

Deng was not happy about how Li Peng had made his remarks public. Deng's children were also displeased that Deng had been put in the position of being in direct confrontation with the public. As I was preparing a speech for the commemoration of the May Fourth Movement,* [Deng's daughter] Maomao called [Zhao adviser] Bao Tong, who was drafting the text, to suggest that the speech include remarks about how much Deng loved and protected young people.

Later, on May 17, at the meeting at Deng's home in which the decision was made to impose martial law, Deng demanded of Li Peng, "Don't repeat what you did before; don't reveal that it was I who made the decision to impose martial law!" Li Peng said repeatedly, "I won't! I won't!"

It was obvious that some people were attempting to use the extreme words of a few students to aggravate the situation and push the government to the point of direct confrontation. With the implementation of reform, it should not have been such a big deal that students criticized leaders. They were just expressions of frustration and were not a challenge to our entire political system.

However, selectively gathering all the personal criticisms and reading them aloud to Deng made for a tremendous insult to the old man. These people selected sporadic extreme opinions of a tiny minority of students and represented them as the major trend of the movement, which they claimed was directed specifically against Deng Xiaoping himself. Deng tended to think in a certain way that was formed during the years when class struggle was the primary objective, so as soon as he heard Li Peng's report, he reacted accordingly. I am afraid this is one of the major reasons for his decision.

While I was in North Korea, the minutes of the Standing Committee meeting of April 24 and Deng Xiaoping's remarks reached me through the embassy. I replied by telegram: "I completely agree with Comrade Deng Xiaoping's decision regarding the policy toward the current turmoil."

When I received these documents, I had to respond, and I was not in any position to express disagreement because I was abroad and had no

---

* The May Fourth Movement is the name given to nationwide demonstrations staged in 1919 that were provoked by the Treaty of Versailles, which was perceived as unfair to China. The demonstrations marked the shifting of the modern Chinese intellectual movement away from Western liberalism, toward the ideals of the Russian Revolution. China's Communist Party identifies the movement as its intellectual origin.

direct knowledge of the situation at home. However, I did not express my views on the minutes of the Standing Committee meeting. Upon reading Deng Xiaoping's remarks, I did not think that any immediate actions would be taken against the students. My first thought was that another campaign against liberalism might begin, possibly on an even greater scale than before (it hadn't occurred to me that the student protests would not subside, because I had not thought of them as a major problem). [A new campaign could] damage the momentum that the reforms had gained since the 13th Party Congress [held in October/November 1987], especially in political reform. That's because Deng believed that the student demonstrations were the long-term results of the lax execution of the Anti–Bourgeois Liberalization Campaign.

However, after the publication of the April 26 editorial, the situation immediately changed, and the confrontation escalated. Students were angered by the editorial's wording and political accusations. "Anti-Party," "anti-socialist," "premeditated plot," etc., were terms that had not been heard in years, so they provoked intense emotions. Those who were moderate before were then forced to take sides with the extremists.

After I returned from North Korea, I invited several people from universities over for discussions. All of them talked about this situation. Upon the publishing of the April 26 editorial, many people were highly displeased, including those in various government departments. Many exclaimed, "How did we end up with *that* thing?!"

The number of demonstrators on the streets on April 27 had swelled to ten thousand. The harsh words of the editorial made students feel that their actions might lead to a crackdown. Some even left wills and letters of farewell for their families before taking to the streets.

The April 26 editorial not only agitated the students, but also left those in various government departments, organizations, and other political parties in a general state of discontent. They found it incomprehensible and were displeased or even angered by it. They believed that the students had acted out of a sincere concern for important matters of state and the fate of reforms, and had expressed their views on some hot social issues, all out of goodwill and patriotism. The government not only failed to express support or provide guidance, but with the harshly worded editorial took a stand in opposition to the students, labeling them with the political tags "anti-Party" and "anti-socialist." The reaction from intellectuals was especially critical.

The government's response boosted popular sympathy and support for the students. Video recordings showed that wherever the students went, crowds lining their passage applauded and welcomed them. Some even joined in the protests. Even the police who had lined up to form a blockade made only superficial attempts to stop them, and then let everyone pass. Some of the prepared roadblocks were opened up as soon as the students arrived, as if they'd never meant to stop them in the first place.

Many senior cadres grew quite worried about the student demonstrations. After Deng Xiaoping's remarks, they were afraid that the escalating confrontation would result in bloodshed. Again and again, they warned the Central Committee to show restraint and to avoid using force. [Influential Party elder] Peng Zhen phoned the Central Committee's General Office directly several times to say that under no circumstances should force be used. He hoped the Central Committee would not aggravate tensions.

One exception was [Party elder and chairman of the Chinese People's Political Consultative Conference] Li Xiannian, who after hearing Deng's remarks, phoned Deng and said, "We must make the decision and be prepared to arrest hundreds of thousands of people!" I admit I can't attest to the accuracy of this. [Another Party elder and vice president of China] Wang Zhen also proposed arresting more people.

Faced with tens of thousands of demonstrators and the entreaties of all these senior cadres, those who had been determined to quell the demonstrations, such as the Beijing Party Committee and Li Peng, were suddenly at a loss as to how to proceed. This was certainly a positive thing. The students had anticipated a crackdown, but when it didn't happen they returned to their schools celebrating their victory and were left feeling more encouraged and fearless than ever.

Because Deng's remarks had been sent to school administrations and the editorial had been published, many members of Party organizations, university presidents, and teachers had initially made intensive efforts to prevent students from taking part in the demonstrations, pleading with them not to take to the streets. When the students returned unharmed, these people felt humiliated. They did not like feeling that they had been misled. They had put themselves out for nothing.

[Beijing mayor] Chen Xitong and many others like him shared this feeling. At the Politburo Standing Committee meeting on May 1, Chen Xitong was full of anger as he presented his report from the Beijing Party Committee. He said that the school officials all felt as though they'd been "sold out." I condemned his remarks and asked him, "Who has sold out whom?"

The large-scale demonstrations of April 27 made a few things clear. The original intention of the April 26 editorial's designations "anti-Party, anti-socialist" was to deter the students. The result, however, was the opposite: the demonstrations had grown bigger. This showed that the old ways of political labeling that had worked before were no longer effective.

Second, since Deng Xiaoping's internal remarks of April 25 had been disseminated widely, the students were aware that Deng was in support of the editorial. They went out to protest anyway, proving that even the symbol of the paramount leader had lost its effectiveness.

Third, the Beijing Municipal Government had just announced a new regulation for demonstrations that imposed strict limits and countermeasures, but this had also been ignored, making the new regulation as good as a piece of wastepaper. Even the police blockades had failed.

Once I'd grasped the circumstances after my return to Beijing, I realized that if the situation were to continue without a reduction in tensions, a violent solution was almost a certainty. The situation now was entirely different from what it was before April 27, because the students had grown fearless. They believed that the government had already used all the means at its disposal, all of which had proven ineffective, leaving only the mobilization of the military. Yet the students could not imagine that the government would actually mobilize the army against them.

When I passed through [the northeast city of] Shenyang on my way back from North Korea, I was given a report on the responses of Shenyang officials to Deng Xiaoping's remarks. They had expressed doubts: "Can measures of this kind still be used?" They told me that many people were critical of Deng after hearing his remarks.

Hence, upon my return from North Korea, the situation had grown perilous. Large-scale bloodshed had become all too possible.

3

Power Struggle

As the protests escalate, the political stakes get higher. Zhao returns to Beijing and tries to calm things down. Soviet leader Mikhail Gorbachev's pending visit to China gives protesters leeway, since the Party isn't likely to crack down violently on the eve of this trip. Hard-line Premier Li Peng opposes Zhao's effort to deal leniently with the situation, and both sides try to win over paramount leader Deng Xiaoping. Tensions escalate when Shanghai officials shut down a bold newspaper that they feel has gone too far in its reporting on the protests.

I have described above how, during my visit to North Korea, the guidelines laid out to deal with the student demonstrations were changed by Li Peng and others at home. Now I will address the struggle between the two sharply conflicting approaches to the student demonstrations that occurred after my return from North Korea.

Li Peng's decision to disseminate Deng Xiaoping's remarks on April 25 and 26 throughout Beijing and down to local administrative levels resulted in many criticisms of Deng. This really upset Deng and his family. Deng's family accused Li Peng of having abruptly pushed Deng to the front lines while he himself played the good guy.

Given the above situation, and because the editorial provoked large demonstrations on April 27 and widespread criticism, Li Peng felt pressured to ask [Political Secretary of the Politburo Standing Committee] Bao Tong to draft an editorial on April 29 and to request that [State Council spokesman] Yuan Mu and [State Education Commission Vice Minister] He Dongchang hold a dialogue with the students.

During the resulting dialogue session, they [Yuan Mu and He

Dongchang] responded positively to many of the students' pleas, conceded that many of the students' objectives were the same as those held by the Party and the government, and explained that the editorial was not directed against the students. They even declared that 99.9 percent of the students were good, with only a tiny minority being anti-Party and anti-socialist. These were the measures taken to calm the students.

At the same time, they were extremely worried that the April 26 editorial might be overturned, and were especially afraid that I would not support their actions upon my return. [Director of the United Front Work Department] Yan Mingfu reported to me that Li Peng had told him that if, upon my return, I did not support the April 26 editorial, Li would have no choice but to resign. Li Peng and [Politburo Standing Committee member] Yao Yilin colluded with each other to persuade me to express my support. They repeatedly requested that I add phrases such as "opposing turmoil" and "opposing bourgeois liberalization" into the speech I was preparing for the commemoration of the May Fourth Movement. When the draft was sent to them for comments, Li and Yao both requested the addition of remarks condemning bourgeois liberalization.

Furthermore, because of the wide dissemination of Deng Xiaoping's remarks, Deng felt that his image among young people had been damaged. Deng Rong [Deng's daughter, also known as Maomao] told me through Bao Tong that references to Deng loving and protecting youths must be added to the speech. Under the circumstances, I did indeed decide to add to the speech one paragraph dedicated to how much Deng loved and protected youths.

As soon as I had returned from North Korea, on the morning of April 30, Li Peng rushed over anxiously to get me to call a meeting so I could listen to the report of the Beijing Party Committee. His goal was to pressure me to express support for the actions they had already taken.

By May 1, at a gathering of Standing Committee members, I was already aware of the strong reactions against the April 26 editorial. However, since I myself still knew very little about the actual situation and also to avoid a sudden reversal in policy, I did have to express some kind of approval of Li Peng's work, at least in some vague way.

However, I emphasized that it was critical to win over the support of the mainstream. We had to distinguish the tiny minority from the mainstream, and not push the majority of people over to the opposing side. That is, we should not create a situation in which the bulk of the populace felt we were trying to repress them. No matter what the reason, we had to calmly acknowledge the fact that the view expressed by the April

26 editorial was widely divergent from the view held by the vast majority of people, especially students, intellectuals, and other political parties. I pointed out the need to conduct a wide range of dialogues. Not only should we meet with and seek the opinions of students, but also teachers and workers.

As for the designation of the nature of the events, I emphasized that we could give new explanations that built upon the wording of the April 26 editorial, by indicating that only a tiny minority was actually anti-Party, anti-socialist, and pushing for chaos. I hoped to mitigate the effects of the April 26 editorial. I also pointed out that we must advocate a return to classes because this was agreeable to the students' parents, their teachers, and most of society. So long as classes were resumed, the situation could be stabilized and emotions would have a chance to cool down. Then all other matters could eventually be resolved.

Once back from North Korea, I tried to garner information from all sides. I first called for the visual recordings of the demonstrations of April 27. On May 2, I responded to requests from leaders of other political parties—Fei Xiaotong, Sun Qimeng, and Lei Jieqiong—to convene a session to discuss the student demonstrations. On the morning of May 5, I asked the president of Peking University, Ding Shisun, and the vice president of Beijing Normal University, Xu Jialu, for a meeting. I asked them for a synopsis of the situation in their schools and for their assessments. In the afternoon, I invited myself to a discussion being held by the Central Committee of the China Democratic League for the university staff members within their organization.

After gathering information and assessing the situation, I believed even more strongly that the student demonstrations had gained widespread sympathy from all corners of society and that the April 26 editorial and the way that the Central Committee had handled the demonstrations were in contradiction to the wishes of the people. If no measures were taken to ease the tensions caused by the April 26 editorial, students would continue to fear that they were being threatened with retaliation, and tensions would continue unabated.

I also felt that if the student demonstrations could be resolved along the principles of democracy and law, through dialogue and an easing of tensions, it could possibly boost China's reform, including political reform. On the other hand, if we were to suppress the demonstrations with violence, another Anti–Bourgeois Liberalization Campaign would be sure to follow, on an even larger scale than before. Conservatives would make a comeback and reform programs would come to a standstill or even be reversed. Chinese history would go through another period of zigzagging. The two approaches promised to result in two totally different outcomes.

However, the crux of the issue was Deng Xiaoping himself. I hoped at the time that he could just relax things a little bit, for example, by saying something like "It seems that when Li Peng gave his report on April 25, we overreacted to the situation. It now appears that the student demonstrations are not such an overwhelming problem." With something like this to work with, I could turn the situation around without even putting any of the liability on Deng. The Politburo Standing Committee and I could take responsibility.

However, if Deng refused to relax his position, then there was no way for me to change the attitudes of the two hard-liners, Li Peng and Yao Yilin. If they did not change their view, it would be difficult for the Standing Committee to carry out the principles of reducing tensions and opening dialogue. I was very well aware that Deng had always taken a tough stance on these kinds of issues. In addition, he had been prejudiced by Li Peng's reports, so it would be extremely hard for me to make him change his position.

I was eager to have a talk with Deng and to gain his support. I phoned [Deng's secretary] Wang Ruilin asking for a meeting with Deng, but Wang said Deng had not been feeling well lately and he worried that his health problems might make him unable to receive Gorbachev, which would be a serious matter indeed. So he asked that I not report anything to him at that time. To this day, I still believe that what Wang said was the truth; Deng was indeed in bad health then.

On May 2, I explained my idea to Yan Mingfu and asked him to contact Deng via Yang Shangkun and others who were closer to Deng.

On May 3, I went to visit Yang Shangkun at his home. Yang said that he had already spoken with Wang Ruilin and Deng's children, and they believed it would be difficult to reverse the position taken in the April 26 editorial, but thought it could be downplayed by not mentioning it again while gradually turning away from it. They said that if I were to talk to Deng then, only to have him reaffirm his stand, it would make it even more difficult to turn things around in the future.

Yang said, "Those of you who are in the front lines can turn things around gradually." Yang Shangkun also indicated that he could appeal to the other members of the Standing Committee. That same day, Yan Mingfu came by my home and told me that Wang Ruilin and Deng's children said that those in charge of the Central Committee should deal with the student movement as they saw fit, according to the situation. If we talked to Deng then, only to have him disagree, then we would only have made matters worse.

In the days that followed, things progressed according to this idea of downplaying and gradually changing. My May Fourth speech was also based on this idea: the tone was distinctly different from the April 26 editorial, yet I used no phrasing that directly contradicted it.

After the May Fourth speech, Yang Shangkun told me the result of his discussions with other members of the Politburo Standing Committee: Hu Qili and Qiao Shi agreed with the new approach; Li Peng and Yao Yilin opposed it. Comrade Wan Li, whom I spoke to directly, was in complete agreement with the new approach. This would mean that among the Standing Committee members and those who had attended the Standing Committee meeting, a majority supported me.

Yang also told me that he had spoken with [influential Party elder] Peng Zhen, who was entirely supportive of my position. Peng told him that if Deng were later to look for someone to place the blame on, "Ziyang should not be left alone to bear the responsibility," that he and Yang should also share responsibility. This was his way of expressing his determination to support me.

Before my return, when the Beijing Party Committee had proposed imposing martial law, Yang Shangkun had responded with sharp criticism: "How could we justify to the rest of the world imposing martial law on our capital?" I believe that Yang Shangkun held a moderate view toward the student demonstrations before Deng decided to impose martial law.

On May 4, I delivered a speech to delegates of the Asian Development Bank regarding the student demonstrations. The speech was drafted by Bao Tong in accordance with my views.

In this speech, I conveyed the need to resolve the matter in a cool, reasonable, restrained, and orderly manner based on the principles of democracy and law. I also pointed out that the student demonstrators had expressed both approval of and dissatisfaction with the Party and the government, and that they were absolutely not against the basic foundations of our system. Instead they were merely asking us to correct some of our flaws. I also said that in demonstrations of this magnitude, one could not rule out the fact that some people might want to manipulate things according to their own interests, but that this would not result in a major upheaval in China.

After that speech, positive responses were received from a wide range of sources, both domestic and overseas.

After May 5 and in the days to follow, many universities in Beijing resumed classes. The director of the Xinhua News Agency in Hong Kong, Xu Jiatun, who was then in Beijing, sent me a handwritten note, in which he mentioned that when he had met with Yang Shangkun on May 4, Yang had expressed total agreement with my speech.

At this time of widespread support, Li Peng came to my house on the evening of May 4 and was forced to commend me for my speech. He said he would follow up with some of the issues I'd mentioned when he himself met with delegates of the Asian Development Bank. But when I pointed out that the April 26 editorial was problematic, he disagreed.

Because I could not meet with Deng himself, I discussed the matter with other comrades as mentioned above and attempted to turn the situation around gradually. Indeed, the situation was gradually turning around. When this approach was being taken, the situation became calmer and most of the students returned to their classes. However, they were waiting to see what happened next; that is, how the promises made in the May Fourth speech would be realized.

I thought it best to use the time of relative calm to take active measures to set up dialogue with students and all other social groups, to respond to the issues of deepest concern to the students, and to adopt some of the students' reasonable ideas. These would have been concrete steps in the direction of opening dialogue and reducing tensions.

While I and other members of the Politburo Standing Committee and those who had attended Standing Committee meetings were actively attempting to effect this turnaround, Li Peng and others in his group actively attempted to block, delay, and even sabotage the process, so that the proposed dialogue and methods to reduce tensions laid out in the May Fourth speech could not be carried out.

Meanwhile, on the topics of most concern to people and raised by the students—such as corruption, government transparency, democracy, rule of law, and public scrutiny of government—we needed to take active measures. I suggested establishing a Commission Against Corruption with real authority, under the National People's Congress [NPC], that would independently accept reports and conduct investigations into the unlawful activities of families of senior Party leaders; strengthening the public's ability to scrutinize the government; increasing government transparency and speeding up the process of establishing laws on the press and demonstrations; and adopting the practice common around the world of protecting the people's democratic rights by establishing specific laws.

I further proposed calling a meeting of the NPC Standing Committee to conduct public hearings on the auditing of several major corporations that were commonly believed to be plagued by corruption. All the arrangements and further investigations should be managed by the NPC, because in the minds of many people, the NPC was more transparent than the Party or the government.

My general approach was thus to carry out reform in the areas of concern to the people, so that we could reduce the level of dissatisfaction among the people and the students, so as to reduce and end the student demonstrations, and at the same time we could seize the opportunity to boost political reform. Tackling these specific issues would enable the NPC to play its rightful role as the highest authority in the nation while directing the students' attention toward furthering political reform.

On May 13, when Yang Shangkun and I went to Deng Xiaoping's residence to discuss issues pertaining to Gorbachev's forthcoming visit, I also talked to him about the recent situation with the student demonstrations. I expressed my views about open dialogue, tackling corruption, and transparency. In principle he agreed, and said that there was "a need to take the opportunity to tackle corruption, to make a concerted effort." He also mentioned that there was a need for increased transparency.

There had been many rumors circulating about the sons and daughters of senior leaders doing business by taking advantage of official government resources. Many of these rumors accused my own sons and daughters. Because of this, on the afternoon of May 1, I proposed at a Politburo Standing Committee meeting that the Politburo order the Central Discipline Correction Commission and the Ministry of Supervision to open an investigation of my family members. Later I sent a formal letter to the Politburo to request that it support my proposal.

Another issue that the students cared about was press freedom. On May 6, in a discussion about reforming press policy with comrades [PSC member] Hu Qili and [Central Committee Secretariat member] Rui Xingwen, I proposed that attention be paid when drafting new press laws to relaxing the restrictions on news reporting, editorials, and commentary.

On May 3, I went to [NPC Standing Committee chairman] Wan Li's home and talked with him about the student demonstrations. I commented that some of the leadership had overreacted to the student demonstrations, a result mainly of an outdated mentality formed by the prolonged focus on class struggle. Times had changed, and we needed to change this mentality to coincide with the trend of democracy and rule of law. He completely agreed with me, and said that many leaders from Tianjin and Beijing had complained to him that the Central Committee had been too soft on the student demonstrations, another example of this kind of old mentality at work. He also suggested that these problems needed to be resolved.

Either during the Politburo Standing Committee meeting of May 8 or the Politburo meeting of May 10 (I don't remember which), he [Wan Li] made some very good suggestions about following the worldwide trend toward democracy and properly addressing the issues that the students had taken up in their demonstrations. He expressed his full support of my Politburo proposal when he held the NPC Standing Committee meeting. He also set a date for another meeting of the NPC Standing Committee, to be held soon, and listed these issues on the meeting's agenda.

On May 9, Wan Li came to my house to tell me he was about to leave for an official visit to Canada and the United States. He had thought about speaking to Deng Xiaoping about the issue before leaving, but had not found the time to do so. On several occasions while in Canada and the United States, he called the student movement both patriotic and democratic, praising it highly.

The attitude that Wan Li adopted toward the student demonstrations was no accident. He had always believed in opening up to democracy and had always supported political reform. He had been opposed to the Anti-Liberalization Campaign of 1987 and had given speeches specifically about the democratization of decision making. Among senior leaders of the Central Committee, he was the one who most ardently supported reform.

Li Peng, Yao Yilin, and Beijing Municipality [Party Secretary] Li Ximing made fierce attempts to block, resist, and delay the carrying out of my proposals. They did not openly express opposition to my May Fourth speech in the few days following, and even voiced a few words of praise. But in fact they were working furiously to distort it.

They claimed that my speech was actually in line with their April 26 editorial but had just taken a slightly different angle. They then asked [State Education Commission Vice Minister] He Dongchang to spread a notion at a meeting held by the State Council with several university Party chiefs that Zhao's speech represented only his personal opinion and did not represent the Central Committee's. This message was quickly spread among the students.

They attempted even more furiously to resist and to delay any dialogue with the students. Originally the idea of the dialogue was to meet directly with the student demonstrators, but they not only denied the participation of any student organizations that had emerged during the demonstrations, they also prohibited the students from selecting their own representatives. They insisted on letting only students from official student organizations participate, which could not in any way have been representative of the student demonstrators. Wasn't conducting dialogue in this manner the same as completely rejecting dialogue altogether? Also, when they did hold dialogues, they did not discuss things openly or seek diverse opinions with an attitude of sincerity. Instead they were merely paying lip service, in the same way that they had always handled foreign reporters at press conferences, presenting an image that would benefit themselves politically. This left the students with the impression that the government's offer to hold dialogues with them was totally insincere.

I repeatedly criticized this behavior, but was ignored. On efforts to fight corruption and increase transparency, they were even more remiss. Li Peng even opposed listing these issues on the agenda of the NPC Standing Committee meeting. He called me specifically to object to putting these items on the agenda.

Because of that, after students had returned to their classes and several days had passed, they could not see how the government was taking any real actions. The dialogues that took place seemed aimed only at brushing them off, and of course no concrete steps were taken on reform; so in fact, doubts grew about my May Fourth speech. A more intense confrontation was therefore made inevitable.

Now we must answer the question "Why did the student movement continue for such a long time?"

They claim that my May Fourth speech had revealed a rift within the Central Committee, into the so-called "two voices." That is not true! The real reason was that the guidelines laid out after my return from North Korea—namely to defuse tensions, to open dialogue, to resolve the issue through democracy and law, and to start tackling hot issues by proceeding with political reform—had been blocked, resisted, and sabotaged by Li Peng and his associates.

Just before Gorbachev's arrival, Li Peng said to me, "You're not going to continue to use soft measures to deal with the student demonstrations, are you? After so much time has elapsed, haven't they already been proven useless?"

This comment fully revealed his hidden ill intentions. He used resistance and sabotage to ensure that efforts to resolve the student demonstrations on the basis of democracy and law would fail, with the intention of looking for an excuse to crush the student demonstrations using violent means.

An incident at the *World Economic Herald* in Shanghai also happened during my visit to North Korea. It started when the newspaper printed a report on the activities commemorating Hu Yaobang. The Shanghai Party Committee found the content inappropriate and ordered the paper to cut the report, but it refused to do so. The Shanghai Party Committee therefore decided to close down the paper for reorganization and suspended the chief editor, Qin Benli.

According to what I heard, [Shanghai Party chief] Jiang Zemin had phoned the office of Deng Xiaoping for a directive on handling this. The students and the masses were in a highly charged emotional state then. By doing what it did, it [the Shanghai Party Committee] not only angered the Herald's staff, but also provoked general opposition from the staff at other news agencies in Beijing, Shanghai, and other places around the country. Many [members of these staffs] took to the streets to voice their support of the Herald and demanded that the Shanghai Party Committee reverse its decision against the Herald. Their actions coincided with the student demonstrations and the two groups mutually reinforced one another.

When I'd returned to the country, I felt the Shanghai Party Committee had been too rigid and simplistic in dealing with the issue and had also chosen a bad time to do it. But since the matter had already passed, I didn't comment on it; it seemed inappropriate for me to admonish the Shanghai Party Committee and side with the staff of the news organization. The Central Committee therefore took the position of not intervening, allowing the Shanghai Party Committee to resolve the issue itself.

On May 2, when I was holding a talk with members of other political parties, Yan Mingfu reported that someone representing the local Shanghai United Front Work Department had told him that the Shanghai Party Committee wanted to back down from its previous position. They hoped the Central United Front Work Department would assist them. I replied, "Since the Shanghai Party Committee has made such a request, you should help them find a solution."

On May 10, Jiang Zemin came to Beijing and talked to me about plans to reduce tensions. I told him the matter should be resolved in Shanghai without the interference of the Central Committee, thereby avoiding creating suspicion that the Shanghai government was merely bowing to pressure from the Central Committee. Jiang Zemin was unhappy about this, and after June Fourth, listed this incident as one of the accusations against me.

4 | The Crackdown

Zhao's final attempts to soften the government's response to the protests fall short, as Deng lines up in support of Premier Li Peng's tough stance. At a tense meeting at Deng's home, which Zhao describes in some detail, the paramount leader authorizes the imposition of martial law. Zhao is opposed and refuses to carry out the policy; he is soon excluded from decision making. Zhao visits Tiananmen Square to urge the students to return to campus, but it's too late. He learns of the June Fourth crackdown when he hears gunshots from his home.

Having grown entirely disillusioned with the government dialogues, the students decided to use the occasion of Gorbachev's visit to stage large-scale street demonstrations and a hunger strike. They believed it was the best opportunity to exert pressure on the government, which would be compelled to show tolerance during the state visit. But the students were mistaken, for the more they pushed ahead, the more pretext Li Peng and his associates had to crack down on them using violent means.

When I got wind of this, I took the opportunity to deliver a speech on May 13 at a gathering of workers. Roughly, what I told them was that it would be unreasonable for the students to disturb international state talks and do damage to the Sino-Soviet Summit because their demands had not been satisfied. Moreover, it would not gain the support of most people. I hoped they would take the big picture into consideration, and not injure our friends while delighting our enemies.

My plea was printed in all the major papers. However, the students did not respond to it at all; they proceeded regardless. On the afternoon of May 13, more than two hundred students from more than twenty universities, with more than a thousand others to act as guards, entered Tiananmen Square to stage a sit-in and a hunger strike. From this day on, the students occupied the square, up until the bloody incident of June Fourth.

The student hunger strike received widespread sympathy and support. Tens of thousands of people from various government departments and other organizations as well as ordinary urban residents staged demonstrations in support. The numbers grew from day to day. The number of hunger strike participants also increased, reaching between two and three thousand people at its peak. Students had become enthralled by the situation, making it even harder to persuade them to leave.

At the time, the students' actions were still mostly spontaneous. Even though they had formed a command center, not one leader among them could make a coolheaded decision. Even when a decision was made, it was not authoritative in any way. Leaders were changed frequently at the command center, and things proceeded according to the ideas of whoever's voice was loudest and most rousing. We tried to persuade the student leaders by mobilizing university leaders and professors to talk to them, but these efforts fell on deaf ears. Because of Li Peng and his associates, the principal guidelines of reducing tension, opening dialogue, and persuasion had not been implemented.

On the fourth day of the hunger strike, some of the students began fainting. I was extremely worried that if this continued, some students might die. We would have a hard time answering to our people.

On the night of May 16, after meeting with Gorbachev, I called a Politburo Standing Committee meeting to discuss issuing a public statement in the name of its five members to urge the students to stop their hunger strike. The draft contained the sentence "The passionate patriotism of the students is admirable, and the Central Committee and the State Council approve of their deeds."

Li Peng opposed it, saying, "Mentioning 'admirable' is quite enough. Do we have to also add that we 'approve'?"

Yang Shangkun replied, "The students propose action against corruption. We can say we approve of this."

I was quite repelled by Li Peng's attitude, and said, "If we don't mention 'approval,' it's as if we'd said nothing at all. Then what's the purpose of issuing a statement? Our current task is to issue a statement that will calm the students' emotions. We must not now quibble over the wording."

A majority of the Standing Committee members agreed to include this line, so it was narrowly passed.

However, by this time I believed that the situation had progressed to a stage where even this statement would not end the hunger strike, since the strongest demand was a reversal of the April 26 editorial's characterization of the demonstrations. I felt that this was a problem that we could no longer bypass. If this key issue was not resolved, there would be no way to end the hunger strike and proceed with dialogue. If the hunger strike continued, then unpredictable but extremely grave consequences would follow.

So for the first time, I formally proposed revising the judgment of the April 26 editorial in a Politburo Standing Committee meeting. Li Peng immediately opposed this.

He said the designation contained in the April 26 editorial was drafted strictly according to Deng Xiaoping's own words and therefore could not be changed. My rebuttal was that the editorial had been drafted according to the minutes of the April 24 Politburo Standing Committee meeting and that Deng had merely voiced support of the discussion that came out of that meeting.

Yang Shangkun warned that revising the April 26 editorial would damage Deng Xiaoping's image. I replied that we could arrange matters in such a way as to avoid causing any damage to Deng's reputation by having the Politburo Standing Committee take collective responsibility. I also said that since I had sent the telegram from North Korea agreeing with Deng's decision, I should take responsibility for the April 26 editorial. If necessary, it could be added that I had approved it.

Li Peng said abruptly, "This is not the proper attitude of a politician!" The result was that a revision of the April 26 editorial was unable to proceed.

I had no other choice but to express my views to Deng personally, in a face-to-face meeting. On the 17th, I phoned to request to see Deng. Later, a member of Deng's staff asked me to go to Deng Xiaoping's home in the afternoon for a meeting.

All the members of the Politburo Standing Committee plus [Yang] Shangkun were already there. At the time, Wan Li, who would have attended, was still abroad. Since I had asked for a personal meeting with Deng, only to have Deng call for a full Standing Committee meeting at his home, I realized that things had already taken a bad turn.

First, I expressed my views, roughly as follows:

> The situation with the student demonstrations has worsened, and has grown extremely grave. Students, teachers, journalists, scholars, and even some government staff have taken to the streets in protest. Today,

there were approximately 300,000 to 400,000 people. Quite a large number of workers and peasants are also sympathetic. Besides the hot issues of corruption and government transparency, the main impetus for all these different social groups is that they want an explanation for how the Party and the government can be so coldhearted in the face of hunger-striking students, doing nothing to try to save them. The key issue blocking dialogue with the students is the judgment passed by the April 26 editorial. The editorial, which caused so much misunderstanding, must have been unclear or incorrectly expressed in some way. The only way to bring about some kind of resolution would be to somewhat relax the judgment from this editorial. This is the key and, if adopted, will gain wide social support. If we remove the labeling of the student movement, we will regain control over the situation. If the hunger strike continues and some people die, it will be like gasoline poured over a flame. If we take a confrontational stance with the masses, a dangerous situation could ensue in which we lose complete control.

While I was expressing my views, Deng appeared very impatient and displeased. As soon as I had finished speaking, Li Peng and Yao Yilin immediately stood up to criticize me.

They placed blame for the escalation of the demonstrations entirely on the May Fourth speech I presented to the Asian Development Bank. That was the first time I heard them voice criticisms of my ADB speech. Though they had opposed it in actuality, they had never said so openly before. The intensity of their accusations caught me completely by surprise. From the unrestrained way in which these two attacked me, I could see that they had already gained Deng Xiaoping's tacit approval.

Hu Qili expressed his view that the editorial should be revised. Qiao Shi equivocated. [Yang] Shangkun opposed revising the editorial, thereby having a very bad impact on the situation. He said, "Liao Hansheng believes that martial law should be imposed. Perhaps we should consider imposing martial law . . ." Previously, Shangkun had always opposed martial law, but this time he quoted [veteran military leader] Liao Hansheng, when in fact he himself had changed his position.

In the end, Deng Xiaoping made the final decision. He said, "The development of the situation has only confirmed that the judgment of the April 26 editorial was correct. The reason that the student demonstrations have not subsided is something within the Party, and that is Zhao's May Fourth speech at the ADB meeting. Since there is no way to back down now without the situation spiraling completely out of control, the decision is to move troops into Beijing to impose martial law."

He also appointed Li Peng, Yang Shangkun, and Qiao Shi as a three-person team to implement the imposition of martial law.

When Deng was finished, I said that having a decision was always better than not having one, but I was extremely worried about the grave consequences this would have. As General Secretary, it would be difficult for me to manage and effectively carry out this decision. Deng said, "If this turns out to be a wrong decision, we will all be responsible."

During this meeting, Li Peng also claimed that contents of Politburo Standing Committee meetings had been leaked to the public, and that there were some bad elements on the inside, [Political Secretary of the PSC] Bao Tong being one of them. I replied, "You must be responsible when making such claims! What evidence do you have?" He said, "I do have evidence that I will reveal to you later."

I walked out as soon as the meeting adjourned. If Deng asked the others to remain or discussed other matters, I never knew.

At that moment, I was extremely upset. I told myself that no matter what, I refused to become the General Secretary who mobilized the military to crack down on students. Upon returning home, under heightened emotions, I called on Bao Tong to draft a letter of resignation for me to send to the Standing Committee.

At that evening's meeting to brief the Standing Committee, I refused to accept the assignment to chair the meeting of cadres to announce martial law. I said, "It seems my mission in history has already ended." Yang Shangkun replied to me, "This kind of issue cannot be raised now. No changes in leadership should be made." He meant that my position as General Secretary should not be changed.

As soon as my letter of resignation reached the Service Bureau of the Central Committee General Office, Shangkun found out about it. He phoned me and repeatedly beseeched me to revoke my decision. Shangkun said, "If this information leaks out, then the situation will be even worse. We should not pour gasoline on a flame."

I conceded his argument and on May 18 notified the General Office to halt the distribution of the letter. My secretary [Li Shuqiao] later retrieved it.

Here I would like to clarify something about this meeting called by Deng that resolved to impose martial law and crack down on the students. There has been public hearsay that the Politburo Standing Committee meeting resulted in a vote of three against two, but in fact there was no "three versus two" vote. There were only a few people in attendance. Among the members of the Standing Committee, it was two against two: Hu Qili and I were for revising the editorial, Yao Yilin and Li Peng were ardently opposed, and Qiao Shi remained neutral by not expressing any clear view.

There was no such thing as a "three versus two" vote. Of course, if the opinions of Deng and Yang, who were not members of the Standing Committee, were added, in the overall count of all the people who attended that meeting, they were certainly a majority. However, in fact, the Standing Committee held no formal vote.

During those few days, many prominent people and senior Party comrades phoned or wrote letters to me and to the Central Committee, appealing to us to treat the students properly, to acknowledge that the students' actions had been patriotic, and to change the wrongful stance assumed toward the students. Among them were those whom Deng Xiaoping had always held in high regard, such as senior comrades like Li Yimang.

On May 18, I forwarded a selection of these letters to Deng and wrote to him to reiterate my position, hoping he would reconsider. Though I knew there was very little hope of this, I had to make one last attempt. The original text of my letter is as follows:

Comrade Xiaoping,

I have forwarded several appeals from influential senior comrades. I hope you will read them.

The current situation is extremely grave, the most urgent matter of which is to stop the student hunger strike (for which people feel great sympathy) so as to avoid any deaths. The crucial request that must be granted in order to stop the hunger strike is the reversal of the labeling and judgment made of them in the April 26 editorial, and acknowledgment of their actions as patriotic.

I have considered this carefully, and feel we must, however painful, resolve to make this concession. So long as our key leaders personally go out among the masses and admit this, the intensity of emotions will be greatly reduced, and then other matters can be resolved. Even if you must eventually take some resolute measures to maintain order, we must take this step first. Otherwise, imposing harsh measures while a majority of people are adamantly opposed may result in serious repercussions that threaten the fate of the Party and the state.

With profound concern, I again appeal to you to consider this suggestion.

Zhao Ziyang
May 18

This was the first letter that I sent to him after the May 17 meeting at his house that decided upon the imposition of martial law. As I'd expected, there was no reply.

On the evening of May 17, the Central Committee General Office made arrangements for leaders of the Central Committee to visit the hunger-striking students who were in the hospital. Li Peng initially said he would not go, but just as the van started up to leave, he showed up. It turns out that he had changed his mind after hearing that I was going.

The same thing happened on the early morning of May 19 when I went to visit the students in Tiananmen Square. He opposed my going and urged the General Office to stop me. I felt that with so many students on hunger strike for as many as seven days, it had become indefensible that none of the leaders of the Central Committee had paid a visit. I insisted on going, saying that if no others went, I would go alone. Once he saw that I was intent upon going and could not be deterred, he changed his mind. But he was terrified and fled very soon after we arrived at the square.

Besides greeting the students, I improvised a speech that ended up being printed in all the major newspapers in the capital. When I spoke, I was merely trying to persuade them to end the hunger strike, telling them they were still young and must treasure their lives. I knew all too well that though their actions had won widespread sympathy both across the country and abroad, it was of no use against the group of elders who had taken a hard-line position. It would not matter if the hunger strike continued or if some people died; they [the elders] would not be moved. I felt it was a waste for these young students to end their lives like this.

However, the students did not understand what I meant. Even less could they imagine the treatment in store for them. Of course, I was later the target of harsh criticisms and accusations for this speech to the students.

After the meeting at Deng's home on May 17, Li Peng and his associates acted abnormally in many ways. Whether I was going to the hospital or to the square to visit students, he repeatedly attempted to block me. When I arrived and I exited the van, he rushed out in front of me, which was contrary to custom. Someone later told me that he instructed people to hint to the cameramen not to include images of me, because it would become "inconvenient" in the case of future leadership changes.

From the evening of May 17 to May 19, none of the issues regarding martial law were imparted to me. I only learned about Li Peng's dialogue with the students on the 19th from seeing it on television.

On the afternoon of the 19th, however, I was suddenly delivered a notice for the meeting that would announce the imposing of martial law and given the text of his [Li Peng's] speech, and was asked to chair and speak at the meeting. Yet I was not notified about how this meeting was to proceed, where it would be held, who would attend, or what other items were to be on the agenda.

His speech even included the statement, "The student demonstrations escalated after May Fourth." Later, they must have felt that the statement too blatantly placed the blame on my May Fourth speech, so when it was published in the newspapers, it was changed to "The student demonstrations escalated in early May." This was an open implication that my May Fourth speech had caused the escalation of demonstrations. Li Peng also announced to members of the State Council that I had made a big mistake. They also held an exclusive meeting prior to the larger meeting to announce martial law.

All of this added to my realization that I had been excluded from decision making. To this day, I still don't know when that decision was made. On the 17th at Deng's place, when deciding to impose martial law, even though Li Peng, Yang Shangkun, and Qiao Shi were appointed to conduct the affair, Deng also noted that "Zhao is still the General Secretary." But in fact, in the several days that followed, I was entirely pushed aside.

On the 19th, I applied for a three-day leave from the Politburo. I suggested that Li Peng chair the Politburo Standing Committee and refused to attend the mobilization meeting to announce martial law.

At the time, the number of demonstrators supporting the hunger strike in Tiananmen Square had become much smaller. The hunger strike was abandoned and turned into a sit-in. Many of the Beijing university students had already returned to their schools. Those who remained in the square were mostly students from other cities.

The announcement of martial law on May 19 [actually May 20] was another stimulant, once again mobilizing the masses. Participants of the sit-in increased and supporters from other social groups crowded the streets. Beijing residents were particularly aggrieved by the decision to call troops to Beijing to execute martial law. Troops that received their orders were blocked along their way, everywhere. Groups of old ladies and children slept on the roads. Troops were stopped in the suburbs of Beijing, unable to enter the city. The standoff lasted more than ten days.

On May 21, Qiao Shi came to my house to discuss the situation. He said, "Quite a number of people are feeling like they are 'riding a tiger, unable to get off.' If it were not for Deng's insistence and his decision to call more troops to Beijing, a great tragedy might be avoided. But now the troops have been blocked from entering, martial law is ineffective, and millions of students, residents, workers, and cadres from government organizations are out on the streets or gathered on Tiananmen Square. If this continues, the capital is in danger of becoming paralyzed."

At that moment, I thought that perhaps if we held the National People's Congress Standing Committee meeting ahead of schedule we could allow the NPC, the organization with proper authority, to use the means of democracy and law to turn the situation around. On May 21, I spoke to [Central Committee Secretariat member] Yan Mingfu about this idea, and asked him to speak with [Yang] Shangkun to see if it was feasible.

Before this, [NPC vice chairman] Peng Chong had come over to talk. He said that since Wan Li was abroad, he [Peng Chong] had held a meeting with the heads of the NPC committee. They all felt that an NPC Standing Committee meeting should be held. He also went to Yuquanshan [Jade Spring Mountain, west of Beijing] to visit [influential Party elder] Peng Zhen, who also agreed that this should be done. They had already written a report to the Central Committee requesting that Wan Li return from abroad ahead of schedule.

In the afternoon of the 21st, [PSC member] Hu Qili came to my house to report that no one had responded to the request to have Wan Li return. It was in limbo. I asked Hu Qili to tell Peng Chong to telegram Wan Li directly in the name of the Party Group of the NPC to request his return. Hu Qili asked if he could say that I had agreed to this, and I said, "Yes."

I then phoned [Vice Premier] Wu Xueqian and asked him to find a way to send the telegram. I later learned that Li Peng sent another telegram to Wan Li to tell him *not* to return. It is possible that he had Deng's prior approval, so Wan Li was unable to make an early return.

On the night of June 3rd, while sitting in the courtyard with my family, I heard intense gunfire. A tragedy to shock the world had not been averted, and was happening after all.

I prepared the above written material three years after the June Fourth tragedy. Many years have now passed since this tragedy. Of the activists involved in this incident, except for the few who escaped abroad, most were arrested, sentenced, and repeatedly interrogated. The truth must have been determined by now. Certainly the following three questions should have been answered by now.

First, it was determined then that the student movement was "a planned conspiracy" of anti-Party, anti-socialist elements with leadership. So now we must ask, who were these leaders? What was the plan? What was the conspiracy? What evidence exists to support this? It was also said that there were "black hands" within the Party. Then who were they?

Second, it was said that this event was aimed at overthrowing the People's Republic and the Communist Party. Where is the evidence? I had said at the time that most people were only asking us to correct our flaws, not attempting to overthrow our political system.

After so many years, what evidence has been obtained through the interrogations? Have I been proven right, or have they?

Many of the democracy activists in exile say that before June Fourth, they had still believed that the Party could improve itself. After June Fourth, however, they saw the Party as hopeless and only then did they take a stand to oppose the Party. During the demonstrations, students raised many slogans and demands, but the problem of inflation was conspicuously missing, though inflation was a hot topic that could easily have resonated with and ignited all of society. If the students had intended on opposing the Communist Party back then, why hadn't they utilized this sensitive topic? If intent on mobilizing the masses, wouldn't it have been easier to raise questions like this one? In hindsight, it's obvious that the reason the students did not raise the issue of inflation was that they knew that this issue was related to the reform program, and if pointedly raised to mobilize the masses, it could have turned out to obstruct the reform process.

Third, can it be proven that the June Fourth movement was "counter-revolutionary turmoil," as it was designated? The students were orderly. Many reports indicate that on the occasions when the People's Liberation Army came under attack, in many incidents it was the students who had come to its defense. Large numbers of city residents blocked the PLA from entering the city. Why? Were they intent on overthrowing the republic?

Of course, whenever there are large numbers of people involved, there will always be some tiny minority within the crowd who might want to attack the PLA. It was a chaotic situation. It is perfectly possible that some hooligans took advantage of the situation to make trouble, but how can these actions be attributed to the majority of the citizens and students? By now, the answer to this question should be clear.

5

The Accusations Fly

Zhao is purged from his leadership role as Party elders close ranks to oppose him. Zhao argues that their tactics violate Party regulations, but he is powerless to fight back. Yet just as he refuses to sign off on the decision to bring the army into Beijing, he declines the Party's demand to make a "self-criticism"—an important tool in the Party's efforts to maintain one official version of the truth. Zhao does express concern about how a comment he made to Mikhail Gorbachev was misconstrued as a veiled attack on Deng.

I want to raise another issue here, that is, the unfair treatment that I received because of the political unrest in Beijing.

I had refused to attend the meeting of May 19 that announced martial law. This made Deng and the other elders extremely angry. On the 20th, Deng called Chen Yun, Li Xiannian, Wang Zhen, Peng Zhen, Yang Shangkun, Li Peng, Qiao Shi, and Yao Yilin for a meeting at his house. Of course, I was not informed. They did not notify Hu Qili, either, so he did not attend.

I hear that in the meeting, Wang Zhen furiously vilified me as being counterrevolutionary. Li Xiannian accused me of setting up "second headquarters." In the end, Deng decided to remove me from the post of General Secretary, but added that the announcement to the public should be delayed until after the completion of some necessary procedures. I was brushed aside just like that.

This was not a Politburo Standing Committee meeting, since only three of its five members were in attendance. Neither Hu Qili nor I had been removed from our posts before the meeting began, so we were still members of the PSC. In my opinion, it cannot be considered legal to have made such a decision when two members of the PSC had not even been notified.

I took a three-day leave, from the 19th to the 21st. Nobody actually told me that I had been removed from my position. Of course, nobody contacted me on any work-related issues, either. Essential communication channels had been cut off, and I had been isolated. I heard through other channels that Li Peng, Yang Shangkun, Yao Yilin, and [Director of Organization Department] Song Ping each held meetings with various departments announcing my "crime." They also organized working groups and drafted documents to prepare for an upcoming Central Committee meeting at which they planned to announce my case. Meanwhile, they assembled in Beijing the first- and second-rank leaders of all the provinces and municipalities to brief them.

Through all these important arrangements, the Politburo did not hold a single meeting; nor did the Politiburo Standing Committee make any decisions. The Standing Committee was made up of five members; with Hu Qili and me excluded, there could be no legitimate PSC meeting. All these arrangements were lacking in legal authority.

The Party Charter lays out these rules: "When the Central Committee is not in session, the Politburo assumes power on its behalf. . . . Meetings of the Politburo are to be chaired by the General Secretary." It is obvious that none of these arrangements were made through Politburo meetings, and of course they were not chaired by me. Therefore, no matter what organization held meetings, or who chaired them, they were all in violation of the Party Charter.

Under these circumstances, in which no one had announced that I had been removed from my post, yet I was unable to use my authority, I worried that I would ultimately be accused of having abandoned my post. Therefore, I talked to [director of the Party's General Office] Wen Jiabao to suggest a Politburo meeting. Wen Jiabao replied that, in fact, the Central Committee General Office had been brushed aside as well. All arrangements had been made by Li Peng and Yang Shangkun, bypassing the General Office. He said that if I really wanted to call a meeting, the General Office would send out the notice, but he believed that the consequences would not be good and hoped I would carefully reconsider.

Since I could not call for a meeting, I asked my secretary to phone Yang Shangkun to ask him over for a talk. My intention was to ask him to clarify whether I had already been removed from my position. I also wanted to explain to him why I had talked to Gorbachev about Deng Xiaoping's position within the Party [Zhao expounds on this in Chapter 7].

On June 2, [Vice Chairman of the Chinese People's Political Consultative Conference] Wang Renzhong and [Vice Minister of State Planning] Ding Guan'gen came to my house and said that in response to my request to speak to Yang Shangkun, the two of them had been sent by the Central Committee and entrusted with this discussion. They said that the Central Committee was soon to hold Politburo and Central Committee meetings to deal with my case and that I should carefully consider preparing a self-criticism.

I started off by explaining to them my discussion with Gorbachev. Then I raised the issue of how the Central Committee's organizations could be functioning when two of the five members of the Standing Committee had been pushed aside. Who was participating in the meetings? Wang Renzhong said there had been no Standing Committee reelections, nor had there been any meetings held of late.

I said that having taken three days' sick leave, I could understand if I was not permitted to resume work. I had no problems with being asked to stand aside, but I should not later be accused of having neglected my work and abandoning my post. That was the reason I had asked to talk with Yang Shangkun. With regards to preparing a self-criticism, I said that I had not been told anything. Criticisms of me were being made everywhere without attempts to check with me about the facts. Documents of criticisms were circulating all over the place, but none had been shown to me. How could I write a self-criticism under such conditions? If I were to be given a chance to speak in the future on issues that I admitted had been in error, I would make a self-criticism.

It was a long talk, lasting more than two hours. I did most of the talking. I spoke about the conditions and my views on the April 26 editorial, the speech on May 3 to the youth delegates, the May Fourth speech at the ADB meeting, and my refusal to attend the May 19 meeting to announce martial law.

And lastly, I strongly protested the way in which they had detained Bao Tong. On May 28, Bao Tong had been called in by the Department of Organization for a talk, from which he never returned. Meanwhile, they searched his office. I had immediately asked my secretary to call [Director of Organization Department] Song Ping to voice my protest. To Wang Renzhong and Ding Guan'gen I said, "If they believe Bao Tong has done anything wrong, the appropriate Party organization should conduct an investigation, but they must proceed according to the Party Charter and the law. Party organizations, much less the Department of Organization, have no authority to deprive him of his personal freedom. We are now in the 1980s; we cannot use these old methods of past political campaigns." I demanded that they relay my message to the Central Committee.

In their assessment of this talk, they deemed my attitude to have been very bad indeed. Wang Renzhong and Ding Guan'gen returned to my home on June 17. They said that on June 19 the Central Committee would hold a Politburo meeting to deal with my case, and they requested that I appear modest, show restraint, and keep calm even if some of the elders used harsh words. I could choose to speak or remain silent, but I was not to argue excessively.

I replied, "If this is a meeting to deal with my case, I must be given the chance to speak freely."

Ding Guan'gen also asked me to reflect seriously on my faults and adopt a proper attitude for the meeting. Wang Renzhong revealed that internally they had decided to maintain my Central Committee membership and Hu Qili's Politburo membership.* He also said that they had already relayed my opinion of Bao Tong's "isolation and investigation" to the Central Committee; Bao Tong was now under "surveillance and house arrest," which [they said] conforms with proper legal procedures.

It seems the purpose of their visit was: one, to notify me about the upcoming meeting, and two, to persuade me not to stage a challenge, or to keep my arguments to a minimum. When Wang Renzhong and Ding Guan'gen first came to my house on June 2 to inform me of the meeting arranged to deal with my case, they said that Deng Xiaoping had mentioned that the handling of Hu Yaobang's case had resulted in criticisms both at home and abroad, so this time with Zhao's case, we must follow proper procedures. He directed them to prepare proper documentation; as soon as these documents were ready, a meeting would be held.

It was all a terrific irony. In fact, I had already been detained and isolated by them without justification or legality. First they illegally deposed me from my position as General Secretary, then they claimed to be in accordance with procedures. This shows that they were apprehensive; afraid of criticism from others.

They would have held the meeting earlier, but it was delayed by the events of June Fourth.

---

*   Hu Qili, who had sided with Zhao in taking a soft line toward the student demonstrations, was also purged from the top ranks of the Party, losing his slot on the elite Politburo Standing Committee.

6

The Campaign Against Zhao

The military "victory" over peaceful demonstrators in Tiananmen Square fails to deliver a sense of political victory. Party leaders, vilified around the world, move quickly to punish Zhao, convening an enlarged Politburo meeting before the end of June to make their accusations. Having been criticized for their handling of Hu Yaobang's dismissal two years earlier, Party leaders make a show of going through the proper steps this time. But Zhao points out the widespread violations of Party procedure and how he is the victim of Cultural Revolution–style tactics. He also reflects on the calculated risks he takes in sticking to his beliefs even as his colleagues turn against him.

The Politburo held an enlarged meeting from June 19 to 21. First, Li Peng, representing the four members of the Standing Committee, set the tone of the proceedings by giving a report that accused me of having committed the serious errors of "splitting the Party" and "supporting turmoil." He proposed that I be removed from my positions as General Secretary, Politburo member, and Politburo Standing Committee member. He also said that further investigations of me would be conducted.

Afterward, the participants took turns speaking, each expounding on those criticisms. The most vicious and slanderous personal attacks came from Li Xiannian. At the beginning of the criticism meeting, Deng Xiaoping was absent. Chen Yun also did not appear, but provided a written statement containing two lines. It said that I had failed to meet the Party's expectations and that he supported the Party's decision to punish me. Wang Zhen's remarks were mainly about how Deng had been too lenient in punishing [Hu] Yaobang, allowing him to keep his membership on the

Politburo and giving him a state funeral, thereby encouraging bourgeois liberalism.

In the latter half of the last day of criticism speeches, Yao Yilin acted as chairman of the meeting. It seemed that they had no intention of letting me speak.

The first time Wang Renzhong and Ding Guan'gen had come to my home, they had requested that I prepare a self-criticism. The second time they came, they had realized I was not going to write one, so they had tried to persuade me to remain silent. When the meeting was drawing to a close, I requested a chance to speak.

He [Yao Yilin] looked at his watch and said, "We've run out of time. If you must speak, keep it under ten minutes."

I was very upset. I said, "After all this time in session to deal with my case, after two whole days of criticisms, how can you now allow me so little time to respond?!"

Without waiting for his go-ahead, I began reading aloud a speech that I had prepared. I checked my watch afterward: it had taken me twenty minutes. In my speech I laid out the truth and the actual context of the debates and rebutted the accusations that had been made against me in the meeting. It came as a surprise to the meeting's participants. Some of them had intense expressions on their faces, appearing irritable and restless while I was talking.

As soon as I finished speaking, Yao Yilin abruptly adjourned the meeting. I immediately left the scene. No one else moved. It was obvious that they had been instructed beforehand that they would be expected to express agreement with the displeasure with my speech and my attitude.

The meeting resumed the next day. A vote was held to decide my case. They took out a statement that contained a resolution to strip me of all my official positions. Li Peng's original report and other people's speeches had all proposed dismissing me from my position as General Secretary and terminating my membership on the Politburo and Standing Committee, but preserving my membership on the Central Committee. But in this statement, my Central Committee membership was removed as well.

It is obvious that after I'd delivered my speech the day before, they had all remained for a discussion and then determined that because of my bad attitude, a more severe punishment was appropriate. Since Deng Xiaoping and Chen Yun were not present during my speech, they must have reported to Deng and Chen afterward.

In fact, I did not really care whether or not I was to keep my membership in the Central Committee, since it really made no difference. However, the Party Charter defines clearly that any member refusing to accept administrative punishment has a right to file for an appeal. The document, titled "Several Rules Governing Political Life in the Party," also states clearly that with regard to the Party's administrative punishments, Party members have the right to make a statement, to request an appeal, to file a complaint, and to make a defense. Retaliation by the prosecutor against the defendant or those who filed the complaint is prohibited. However, I had been given additional punishment for having spoken in self-defense. This was in total violation of the Party Charter and the rules of the Party. Li Peng's initial report and the other speeches all recommended the retention of my Central Committee membership, but when it was later terminated, there was no indication or explanation as to what had changed. This was highly irregular.

Before the voting began, I almost made a statement: "Because I spoke out in self-defense, my punishment has been augmented, setting a bad precedent by blatantly violating the Party Charter, the first such incident since the Third Plenum of the Eleventh Central Committee [1978]." However, I reconsidered: if I were to make a statement with all the elders present, Deng Xiaoping and Marshal Nie [Rongzhen] and others, they would be even more offended. So, just as the words reached my lips, I refrained myself.

When the voting took place on the resolution, however, I not only refused to vote in favor, I raised my hand to vote to oppose the measure and at the same time proclaimed, "I do not take issue with being dismissed from my positions, but I do not agree with nor accept the two accusations!" After I said this, no one, not even Deng or Li Peng, who was chairing the meeting, made a sound. Perhaps they had already anticipated it.

This Politburo meeting that voted to impose administrative punishment on me violated the Party Charter and rules in more ways than what I have just mentioned. First of all, what procedure was being followed in the decision to hold the enlarged Politburo meeting? No Politburo meeting had been held to discuss the matter beforehand. The exclusion of Hu Qili and me from the Standing Committee meeting was also illegal. When Wang Renzhong had come to my house, he had said that no Politburo meetings had been held. Therefore, how these enlarged Politburo meetings had been decided upon, and who had made the decision—all of this was problematic.

The Party Charter clearly states that Politburo meetings should be chaired by the General Secretary. However, before my title was legally removed, I had already been deprived of my right to chair Politburo meetings, which was passed to Li Peng. This was also illegal.

What was especially ironic was that when voting was to begin, Deng Xiaoping actually said, "All participants, whether a member of the Politburo or not, have the right to vote." At enlarged Politburo meetings, non-member attendants are permitted to listen and to speak, but how can they be allowed to participate in the voting? Apparently, they wanted to rally more support. Li Xiannian explained that this right to vote was being granted by Li Peng, the chairman of the meeting. This was completely rule by force! What Party Charter or rules were they following?! The elders, long accustomed to the Party's custom of "acknowledging neither laws nor heavenly constraints," of course, were not concerned.

Now I have spoken of this matter; I don't know how this will be recorded in the Party's history.

A Central Committee meeting was held from June 23 to 24 to pass the political and administrative judgment made against me at the enlarged Politburo meeting. I was notified about the meeting and attended the group to which I'd been assigned, the North China Group. I listened as a few comrades criticized me, then I spoke briefly.

I said, "Thank you all for your advice. I have a written statement that is a revised version of the statement I prepared for the enlarged Politburo meeting. I have already submitted it to the Service Division. I hope copies of my written statement will be distributed to all comrades in attendance."

[Director of the Propaganda Department] Wang Renzhi was also in this group, and said that the Central Committee had agreed to distribute copies of the statement to all the participants. But, in fact, the statement was passed out to participants only as the meeting was about to end, and then quickly retrieved. However, [Beijing mayor] Chen Xitong and [State Education Commission director] Li Tieying's rebuttal of my statement had been distributed earlier. So, in the meeting, it was a bizarre situation in which participants were reading the criticism of my statement without having seen my statement, then were finally shown my statement toward the end of the meeting only to have it immediately retracted again. As a result, I'm afraid many people had to rush through my statement, or did not get a chance to read it at all.

So-called "background information" about June Fourth was also distributed, in the name of the General Office. It amassed a large quantity of material from around the country and overseas, implying that I was a conspirator representing counterrevolutionary forces in the country and overseas aimed at overthrowing the Chinese Communist Party and Deng

Xiaoping. It also included material making false accusations that my staff cooperated with the students, sent information to them, and revealed the military secret of the plan to impose martial law. It was obvious that the point of printing such "background material" was to create a general impression that I was indeed guilty of the most heinous crimes and was unpardonably wicked.

They sought to completely destroy my political and moral standing. Some of the speeches delivered at the meeting were entirely in the style of the Cultural Revolution: reversing black and white, exaggerating personal offenses, taking quotes out of context, issuing slanders and lies—all in Cultural Revolution language. At the time, I thought to myself, if records of this meeting were not clearly marked "CCP Fourth Plenum of the Thirteenth Party Congress," one could easily have mistaken them for documents from the Cultural Revolution.

According to the Party Charter, the dismissal of a member of the Central Committee requires a two-thirds majority in the plenum to pass. It was obvious that the top leaders were not confident they could achieve that. If secret voting were to take place, it was possible that they would not obtain the necessary two-thirds majority. Instead they abandoned secret voting and called for voting by a show of hands. Obviously, in that kind of atmosphere and under that kind of pressure, by having to publicly raise one's hand, a lot of people felt unable to vote according to their real opinions. With everyone watching and cameras rolling, some people were forced to raise their hands even if they were opposed. Therefore, the resolution was unanimously passed.

I must point out that in the past, whether for General Secretary or for Politburo or Politburo Standing Committee memberships, all elections were carried out through secret voting. Voting in this way, with a show of hands, was quite abnormal. In that kind of atmosphere, under that kind of pressure, and with investigations of events and people connected to me already under way, how could people feel free to express their opinions while raising their hands?

By insisting on my view of the student demonstrations and refusing to accept the decision to crack down with force, I knew what the consequences would be and what treatment I would receive. Mentally, I was fully prepared. I knew that if I persistently upheld my view, I would ultimately be compelled to step down. I had already considered this. If I wanted to keep my position, or give up my post in some face-saving way, I would have to give up my viewpoint and conform. If I persisted, then I had to be prepared to step down.

After repeated and careful consideration, I had decided I would rather step down than conform to their view. I had spoken with my wife and children at home about what I was thinking, and had asked them to be prepared.

I was also mentally prepared for the consequences of my speech at the enlarged Politburo meeting. I thought I might be expelled from the Party, since it was necessary for a person who had committed an error to hang his head in guilt in order to be judged as having the correct attitude. I thought that probably I would not be put in prison, since I had done nothing wrong. For people like me who had had some amount of influence at home and abroad, they could not possibly manage to conduct an absolutely secret trial. Hence I determined that stepping down was a certainty, expulsion from the Party was the worst that might happen, and imprisonment was unlikely.

Under a political system such as ours, it made very little difference whether I remained in the Party or was expelled from it. People in my situation who have retained Party membership don't have the normal rights of membership anyway. Furthermore, expulsion from the Party would not affect my beliefs and ideals.

After the Fourth Plenum of the 13th Central Committee, Cultural Revolution–style tactics that had been condemned and abandoned long ago were taken up to be used against me. These tactics included inundating the newspapers with critical articles making me out to be an enemy, and casual disregard of my personal freedoms. Immediately after the Cultural Revolution, having learned from its painful experiences, the Party had passed a new Party Charter at the 12th Party Congress [1982], "Several Rules Governing Political Life in the Party." The rules were aimed at preventing the Cultural Revolution from ever happening again.

After June Fourth, they entirely disregarded these rules in their treatment of me, instead openly violating them and reassuming the ultraleft tactics of the Cultural Revolution. This was something I had not anticipated.

7 | Zhao's Talk with Gorbachev

One of the mysteries about the events leading up to the Tiananmen Massacre is when precisely Deng Xiaoping decided to part ways with his reform ally, Zhao Ziyang. When Zhao met with Gorbachev, he stressed that Deng, despite a lack of official titles, was still in charge. While Zhao says he meant only to highlight the importance of Gorbachev's meeting with Deng, his detractors accused him of trying to subtly place blame for the political turmoil on Deng's shoulders. It's unclear whether Zhao's comment really cost him Deng's trust. But if it did, the losses of hundreds of lives could ultimately be traced to the paranoia and lack of judgment of one man, Deng, in a time of crisis. Zhao's intimate account sheds no light on the mystery, though it reveals his deep sense of regret for any misunderstanding, and his continued gratitude for his relationship with Deng.

Here I'd like to comment on the issue of my talk with Gorbachev on May 16.

Deng was quite displeased with my May Fourth speech at the Asian Development Bank conference. However, I'm afraid my talk with Gorbachev didn't just make him angry, but really hurt him. After June Fourth, he told [Nobel Prize–winning Chinese American physicist] Professor Tsung-Dao Lee that I had pushed him to the forefront during the student turmoil. What he actually meant was that I had abandoned him to confront the public alone. Notions of this kind circulated among the populace as well.

When I talked with Gorbachev, I spoke of Deng Xiaoping's role in our country and in the Party. These comments were entirely intended to uphold Deng's prestige, but resulted in a great misunderstanding. People thought I was shirking responsibilities, pushing Deng to the forefront [and forcing him to] confront the public at a critical moment. I absolutely did not foresee this.

Ever since the 13th Party Congress [in 1987], whenever I met with foreign leaders, especially fellow Party leaders, I always informed them that even though Deng was no longer on the Politburo Standing Committee, his role as the major decision maker in our Party had not changed. This had almost become a convention. In April, I had informed Kim Il Sung in North Korea of the same. What was different with this talk was that the message gained prominence through TV and newspaper coverage.

Why did I do this?

The publication of Deng's April 25 remarks by Li Peng and his associates had resulted in a public outcry. Students and youths were particularly unhappy with Deng. Because of the dissatisfaction with his remarks, they focused on and assailed his special position. I heard many remarks such as "Why does the Politburo Standing Committee have to report to Deng Xiaoping, who is not even a member? This does not conform with the principles of the Party's organization!" The phrase "hanging a curtain to administer the affairs of state" was spreading. Amid all of this, I thought I should come out with a clarification and an explanation.

On May 13, two days before Gorbachev's arrival, I held a dialogue with delegates of workers and cadres from official workers' unions. A worker raised a question along these lines. I replied by explaining that this was in accordance with a resolution passed at the First Plenum of the 13th Central Committee. This plenum had decided that we must consult with Deng Xiaoping on any matters of great importance. This was for the benefit of the whole Party because Deng's political wisdom and experience was richer than that of any member of the Politburo Standing Committee. The answer seemed to go over well, as that worker did not pursue the question any further. Hence, I thought that if we gave the same explanation through the press, it would have a positive effect on Deng's public image. At least it would clarify that this wasn't a case of Deng grabbing power, but rather a collective decision made at the Central Committee's First Plenum.

Therefore, when I met with Gorbachev, I told him that our Party's First Plenum of the 13th Central Committee had formally decided that on major issues, we still needed Deng to be at the helm. Ever since the 13th Party Congress, we had always kept him informed and sought his opinion on major issues. Deng had always been fully supportive of our work and our collective decisions. In fact, the original resolution was not only that we should seek his opinion and keep him informed, but also that he could call for a meeting and make the final decision on major issues. Taking into consideration what the public would be able to accept, I intentionally did not mention this last point. I believed the public explanation that I did make would benefit Deng, and at the very least clarify that it was not an illegal situation, but in fact a legitimate one.

There was another reason for me to make these remarks: Gorbachev's visit was a summit between China and the Soviet Union. Which person actually met with Gorbachev was of symbolic importance in defining such a summit. Of course, both domestically and abroad, everyone knew that the so-called "Sino-Soviet Summit" was between Gorbachev and Deng Xiaoping. But Gorbachev was the President of the U.S.S.R. and the General Secretary of the Communist Party, while Deng was neither President of the state nor General Secretary of the Party, but only the chairman of the Central Military Commission. My sincere intention was to prominently declare that the summit was defined by the meeting between Gorbachev and Deng, not between Gorbachev and anyone else.

Originally, the Foreign Ministry planned to dilute the message, neither avoiding the issue altogether nor being too formal about it; it was not to be included in the declaration or in any formal discussions between the two parties. They asked me to say to Gorbachev, "Our meeting as the General Secretaries of our respective parties naturally signifies the restoration of the relationship between our two parties." But on May 13, two days before I was to meet with Gorbachev, while I was talking to Deng at his home regarding Gorbachev's visit, Deng stated that the relationship between the two parties would be restored after *he* met with Gorbachev. This departed from the original plan of the Foreign Ministry. I paid specific attention to this remark from Deng.

Because of all these considerations, after Gorbachev had already met with Deng, I started my meeting with him by saying that the relationship between our two parties had been restored by his meeting with Deng, that his meeting with Deng was the culmination of his visit. Naturally, I then followed up with discussion of Deng's position and the decision made by the First Plenum of the 13th Central Committee.

My comment was meant to explain two issues simultaneously: why Gorbachev's meeting with Deng defined the summit and the fact that Deng's continued position as the paramount decision maker for the Chinese Communist Party was a ruling of the Central Committee, consequently legitimate. At the time, I felt that my remark was extremely appropriate, resolving problems in a natural way.

After the talk, I initially received positive responses. Later I learned that, on the contrary, Deng and his family were not only displeased with my remarks, but extremely angered by them. This was beyond what I could have foreseen. Exactly why did Deng get the idea that I had intentionally pushed him into confronting the public, while I was evading my own responsibilities? I have yet to learn who it was or how that person managed to provoke Deng.

My intentions were good: to maintain and to protect his prestige, and to do my part in bearing the responsibility. However, it unexpectedly resulted in a great misunderstanding and caused him to feel that I had intentionally hurt him. I indeed feel deeply aggrieved by this affair. I could have chosen to do nothing at all. In fact, it had been unnecessary. I truly, deeply regret it.

Why have I placed such special attention to this matter? Because other issues were caused by a difference of ideas and viewpoints. Since I had persisted with my position, even my dismissal from the position of General Secretary was understandable. I started with only good intentions. No matter what kinds of differences I had with Deng over the June Fourth issue, it was a difference of political opinions.

Before the June Fourth incident, I had always felt that, overall, Deng had treated me very well and shown a lot of trust in me. It is a Chinese tradition to value integrity of character and faithfulness in our relationships. If I had given Deng the impression that I had diverted blame in the midst of a crisis, then not only was this a profoundly false impression of me, but it might cause him deep unhappiness or even emotional pain. The thought of a man of his years, perhaps soon to leave this world, suffering from such an impression was truly unbearable to me.

Therefore, I wrote to Deng on May 28 specifically to explain my remarks to Gorbachev. However, I told him of only one of my considerations, which I mentioned before, that I was asserting that the summit was officially between Deng and Gorbachev, and because of this, I had naturally commented that Deng was still the main decision maker. I did not mention my second consideration, that is, to refute the popular view that he was power hungry, continuing to control the Politburo Standing Committee even though not a member of it. Amid this public criticism, some kind of explanation had been necessary. There was no reply to the letter I sent.

I still hope that before he leaves this world (this is what I wrote down seven years ago [in 1992]), he comes to understand the true intentions of my remarks to Gorbachev. Not because after knowing this he might relax anything related to my case: I have no such wish. I know that even if he knew the truth, he would not relax a thing. I only want Deng to know that, having received his longtime trust and vigorous support, even though I refused to accept his decision of cracking down on the student demonstrations, I am not a man who would sacrifice others to protect myself in a crisis.

I believe that with such an understanding of the situation, he would feel better. I am truly unwilling to see him leave this world with this misconception. Yet I know the chances of his understanding this are very, very slim.

Deng died in February 1997. Zhao never saw him again after 1989.

HOUSE ARREST

I

Zhao Becomes a Prisoner

Within days of the June Fourth massacre, Zhao is under house arrest, hidden away behind the high walls of his courtyard dwelling, where he will spend most of the remaining sixteen years of his life. Even mundane things, such as attempts to go golfing, set off tragicomic clashes with authorities who want him out of the public eye.

The time it takes for the official investigation of Zhao to run its course—more than three years—reflects how difficult it is for the leadership, especially Deng, to decide on Zhao's fate. The subsequent collapse of the Soviet Union and the Eastern Bloc apparently hardens attitudes among Beijing's leaders, who conclude that hanging tightly to power is the key to the Communist Party's survival. The violent response to Tiananmen, they will argue, has been right all along.

But Zhao's investigation ends without a proper conclusion: Party leaders clearly feel that any public verdict would only stir up more arguments about the Tiananmen Massacre itself. A careful study of the list of charges made against Zhao, which he details in this chapter, reveals that while it appears on its face to be a multipart condemnation of Zhao, it reads in part almost like praise for his actions, and certainly offers nothing that could have assisted a criminal inquiry. The document is never made public.

The Fourth Plenum of the 13th Central Committee [June 1989] stripped me of all my positions and resolved to continue the investigation. This was, in itself, historically unprecedented. Since harsh administrative punishment had already been imposed, there should have been no need to continue the investigation. If the matter had not been clarified and required further investigation, then the political and administrative judgments should not have already been made. I guess this was what you might call my "special treatment."

The investigation lasted a total of three years and four months, from June 1989 to October 1992. During this time, I was denied freedom of movement. On the one hand, they said the investigation was intraparty in nature. On the other hand, however, they disregarded the laws of the state and placed me under house arrest. "Several Rules Governing Political Life in the Party" clearly states that even against Party members who have made an error, no actions should be taken that violate the law. I don't know how they hope, in the future, to explain this crude trampling and violation of Party regulations and the laws of the state.

On September 3, 1989, [Vice Chairman of the Chinese People's Political Consulative Conference] Wang Renzhong and [Vice Minister of State Planning] Ding Guan'gen called me to Huairen Tang [Hall of Compassion] in Zhongnanhai [the Party's headquarters] for a talk. They officially notified me of the decision of the Fourth Plenum of the 13th Central Committee to establish a Special Investigative Group to take charge of an investigation of me. Wang Renzhong was to take the lead, with participation by [Director of the Department of Organization] Chen Yeping and [Deputy Secretary of the Central Discipline Inspection Commission] Li Zhengting.

On September 29, these three people, Wang, Chen, and Li, called me to the Security Bureau's meeting hall for a talk. It was my first talk with the Special Investigative Group. I never saw Chen Yeping or Li Zhengting ever again. I heard that the group was reorganized, with Chen and Li no longer involved, but I had no way of finding out why.

Afterward, Wang Renzhong spoke with me alone three times: on December 8, 1989, February 14, 1990, and March 2, 1990. He also sent me three letters, one on July 6, 1989, and the others on August 8, 1989, and November 14, 1989. I also replied to him three times: July 25, 1989, September 1, 1989, and October 7, 1989. By means of these conversations and letters, they asked me a number of questions. I provided explanations and clarifications in response.

Besides investigating whether I had manipulated the turmoil in direct or indirect ways, or had leaked any information to the outside world, the investigation mainly focused on why I had taken a stand and developed a policy that was contrary to Deng's. What was my motivation? They demanded that I admit wrongdoing. They also wanted to settle issues from my years in office, of my having been too tolerant of certain things and having promoted certain people who were deemed bourgeois liberals.

They displayed avid interest in my "unspeakable motive" and "personal ambition." They quoted unrelated materials from overseas publications, to which they added their own speculations, and concluded that since 1988 there had been a movement both within the country and abroad "to overthrow Deng and support Zhao," aimed at forcing Deng to step down and hand over power to me. Purportedly, I was the ideal candidate to lead counterrevolutionary forces at home and abroad to restore capitalism, so "hopes had been placed in me."

They also attacked me for so-called "neo-authoritarianism"* and claimed that the bourgeois liberals regarded me as their "neo-authority" and that the TV series *River Elegy*† had been made to glorify me. They believed that my ardent refusal to agree with Deng Xiaoping had not been a singular occurrence, but that I had been corresponding and collaborating with people from these movements all along. They also thought that because I had been feeling insecure in my position due to economic and political difficulties, I had attempted to shirk responsibilities and fish for political capital by using the student demonstrations to protect myself.

The so-called "background material" distributed at the Fourth Plenum of the 13th Central Committee, together with [Beijing mayor] Chen Xitong's "June Fourth Report" on behalf of the State Council to the National People's Congress, speeches by [influential Party elder] Li Xiannian and others, and the letters that Wang Renzhong wrote to me, all pointedly raised these same questions and accusations.

In the conversations and letters with Wang Renzhong, I emphatically rebutted these accusations and made clarifications.

First, there was no such thing as a movement since 1988 "to overthrow Deng and support Zhao." Someone had fabricated this for some purpose. There had indeed been many rumors circulating during that period; they referred, however, not to "overthrowing Deng" but instead to "overthrowing Zhao." There had been lots of discussion at home and abroad about my position being unstable, that my powers had been reduced, and that the conservatives had been putting pressure on Deng and demanding a change of leadership. I wrote to them that public opin-

---

*   Neo-authoritarianism was a theory put forward by liberal intellectuals who thought that the best way to modernize China's economic and political systems was to have a strong leader, an "enlightened despot." Many believed, incorrectly, that the theory's proponents supported Zhao as the authority figure.

†   *River Elegy* was a controversial multipart TV documentary in China, first broadcast in 1988. It criticized traditional Chinese isolation and embraced Western openness. The Party later denounced the broadcast and blamed it for helping to inspire the 1989 demonstrations.

ion both at home and abroad had always connected my fate and my political future together with Deng's. "Overthrow Deng" and "support Zhao" could not be linked in one saying. If one were to "overthrow Deng," one could not "support Zhao" at the same time, and vice versa.

Second, at the same time that rumors were spreading everywhere that "Zhao's position is unstable," "his power has been reduced," "he is unable to take direct command of economic affairs," Deng revealed his [support of] me many times. He confirmed not only that he had no intention of changing the structure of the leadership, but that he wanted me to continue as General Secretary for an additional two terms.

Just after New Year's Day in 1989, Deng had spoken to Li Peng and had asked him to relay this message to the other members of the Politburo Standing Committee. This was in response to the Standing Committee's administrative meeting in early 1989 at which Li Peng and Yao Yilin had criticized me and made accusations against me on economic issues. When Li Peng explained the incident to Deng Xiaoping, Deng had revealed his intentions, which was to stand by me. He had asked them to support me as well.

At the close of January 1989, just before Deng was to leave for Shanghai for the Spring Festival holiday, he talked with me personally and with sincerity, to tell me he had recently been considering whether or not he should resign as chairman of the Central Military Commission and hand over the position to me. He said, "If I did that, you could do your job better."

He expressed his determination and his faith in me. He also said that without his retirement, other elders would not retire, either, making things more difficult to manage. By retiring himself, it would be easier to persuade others to do so. During the conversation, I also told him very sincerely that I felt that, no matter what, he should not do that: "Your staying on is helpful to me." We were facing difficulties with fluctuating market prices, so it wasn't the right time to raise such an issue. The arrangement with the elders at that time was advantageous to my work. This was the content of our conversation at the end of January 1989.

Even in April 1989, when I visited him at his house prior to my trip to North Korea, he told me that after my return from North Korea, he would call for a meeting especially to talk about my two subsequent terms; not only was the leadership structure not to be changed then, but I would continue into the next term. He also talked with [Party elders] Chen Yun and Li Xiannian, who expressed their agreement.

When I wrote my letter to Wang Renzhong, Deng was still living, so he could confirm the truth of this. Under these circumstances, it's clear that I could not have been feeling insecure about my position.

Third, I did not think that the economic situation was so poor. It must be acknowledged that great achievements had been made in ten years of reform. The nation's economic power had greatly expanded. Living standards had also risen significantly. Though inflation hit in 1988, I believed that the condition was neither all that grave, nor so difficult to resolve. There was no truth to the notion that my image had been tarnished from my failure to manage the economy, so much so that I had had to regain political capital by manipulating the student demonstrations to improve my image. (There were indeed many problems with the economy that year. However, to this day, I still believe that they were not that serious, as proven in the reality of the market slowdown in the spring of 1990. I will talk about this later.)

Fourth, I reminded Wang Renzhong in my letters that I had been in the Party for several decades. It was impossible for me *not* to understand the workings of high-level politics within the Party. Manipulating the student demonstrations for my own personal agenda? There was no way that I could have been that ignorant or juvenile!

Fifth, the reason that I refused to accept Deng's response to the student demonstrations was, as I have explained above, a difference of opinion about both the nature of the demonstrations and the consequences of a crackdown. I felt I had to be responsible to history. I refused to become the General Secretary who cracked down on students.

Wang Renzhong's harshest accusations came in his letter of November 14, 1989, which was followed by a talk on December 8. After that, the situation seemed to become less intense. Perhaps after investigating my case for half a year, they had come to discover that their original analysis and assessments were not supported by the facts.

On February 14 [1990], Wang Renzhong also asked me to expound on my view of the drastic changes that had taken place in the Soviet Union and Eastern Europe. Before the arranged talk, a batch of documents related to those events written by research organizations of the Central Committee had been delivered to me. Wang attempted to persuade me to write a good self-criticism, while revealing to me that some people had suggested expelling me from the Party. Having my self-criticism in hand would make it easier for him to change these people's minds.

I told Wang that I hoped the long investigation would be brought to an end soon. Any wrongdoings to which I'd conceded, I had already acknowledged in my speech at the Fourth Plenum. If I were to write another self-criticism, it would be exactly the same as before.

I also suggested that the investigation pay more attention to researching and checking the facts, and not get caught up with my so-called "attitude problem." The enlarged Politburo meeting had been displeased with the attitude of my speech and had already passed down harsher punishment as a result. What more could they possibly do now in response to my attitude?

The last time Wang Renzhong asked me for a talk was on May 2 [1990]. On February 20, before this talk, I had written to Deng again, for the third time. Of my letters to Deng, the first was to forward letters from senior cadres pleading with him to reconsider his response to the student demonstrations; the second letter explained my comments to Gorbachev. In this third letter, I wrote to ask that my investigation be brought to an end as soon as possible.

Wang acknowledged when we met that he knew about the letter I'd written to Deng. The Sixth Plenum of the 13th Central Committee [held March 9–12, 1990] was to be held soon, but he said that my problem could not be resolved by the plenum. He even mentioned that it might not be necessary to resolve my problem at a Party plenum. I don't know what he meant by this. In any case, he meant to convey that the problem would not be resolved at that time. Talks proceeded very calmly.

On June 21, Wang Renzhong forwarded the investigation report, "Issues Relevant to Comrade Zhao Ziyang and the Political Turmoil of 1989." He asked for my feedback. The document contained thirty items.

Even if one were to overlook the many incidences of quoting out of context, twisting the original meanings of statements, and outright contradictions of fact, even if all of the thirty statements had been accurate, it would still have been insufficient to support the judgment made against me of "supporting turmoil" and "splitting the Party."

On June 27, I replied to Wang Renzhong with a letter containing my suggestions for revisions to the aforementioned document. I refuted twelve items among the thirty. But after that, Wang never communicated with me again, nor did anyone else come by to check over any material with me. In fact, the investigation was aborted without a conclusion.

I was to learn later that after the Special Investigative Group had submitted its report, Central Committee leaders had considered announcing an end to the investigation after the 1990 Asian Games [a regional multisport event held that year in Beijing], but then had started worrying about the possible response, both domestic and international. They also worried about my moving about freely and attending activities. Plus there was the vehement opposition of several elders. They decided instead to drag the issue on without coming to a conclusion; to leave it hanging for an extended time, meanwhile continuing my house arrest in the name of the investigation.

I wrote three letters—on August 28, 1990, December 7, 1990, and May 9, 1991—to Jiang Zemin [who had been brought in from Shanghai to replace Zhao as Party General Secretary], Li Peng, and the Politburo Standing Committee, respectively. The point of these letters was to request an end to the investigation and house arrest and the restoration of my personal freedoms as early as possible.

I also mentioned in those letters that since so much time had already passed since the Fourth Plenum of the 13th Central Committee launched its investigation, I didn't believe there could still be anything left to clarify. I truly had no idea what could cause my investigation to go on for so long. Since June 1990, no one had come to talk to me about issues related to the investigation, nor had anyone come to check on any related material. If anything remained unclear, why didn't they just ask me? I could help to clarify things. This tactic of dragging things out without a resolution, of a perpetual suspension in the name of an ongoing investigation, was beneficial neither to me nor to the Party.

I also pointed out that since the Fourth Plenum, Central Committee leaders had repeatedly announced to domestic and foreign reporters that I was free to move about, that I was neither under house arrest nor even partial house arrest. However, what is the truth? The fact is, since the Fourth Plenum, I have been continuously detained in my house.

In the past, it was common practice to curtail the personal freedoms of senior cadres who had held opposing views or made mistakes, especially during the Cultural Revolution. However, the Third Plenum of the 11th Central Committee had acknowledged the lessons from this past, and now, after more than ten years of implementing reform and with the current emphasis on establishing the rule of law, we must not repeat this behavior.

I therefore demanded my immediate release from house arrest and the restoration of my personal freedoms, regardless of whether or not the investigations were over.

All these letters of mine fell like stones dropped into the sea, disappearing without a trace. Their tactic was simply never to respond.

In fact, limitations on my freedom of movement began as early as June 1989. However, I was never officially notified, and there was no written documentation of it. In order to prove that these limits really did exist, and also because I was feeling gloomy from the protracted house arrest, in October 1990, just before the Asian Games, I made a decision to go out golfing.

When the Security Bureau of the General Office discovered my plan to go out to play golf, they informed the secretary working in my home to advise me against it. They said, "It has never been said that going out was permitted." I replied that no one had ever told me I was *not* permitted to go out. If there was such a rule, then they should show it to me. They neither showed me any such document containing the rules of prohibition, nor allowed me to go out.

They ordered the chauffeur not to drive when the time came. I indicated that if the chauffeur refused to drive, I would take the bus. Of course, they were afraid this would cause a public stir.

At the time, neither Jiang Zemin nor Li Peng was in Beijing. They asked Qiao Shi [the Politburo member in charge of security] for instructions, but Qiao Shi couldn't make the decision, either. He asked the Security Bureau to improvise a decision appropriate to the situation.

Finally, the Security Bureau allowed the chauffeur to drive and sent a police car to escort us. After I played at Chang Ping Golf Course, a Sino-Japanese joint venture, the Japanese staff at the golf course reported the news to the Japanese embassy. This spread soon after to Japanese reporters and other foreign correspondents. The news was released that very day and was followed up with coverage by major international news agencies as well as newspapers in Hong Kong and Taiwan. A Hong Kong television channel even played an old video clip of me playing golf as they reported the story.

Both Jiang Zemin and Li Peng became extremely anxious. They condemned the decision and began an investigation to find out who had allowed me to go out to play golf. After this disturbance, they notified me verbally in the name of the Central Committee that I was prohibited from going out during the investigation. With that, the fact that they restricted my freedom and subjected me to house arrest had finally left an official trail.

In front of domestic and foreign reporters, however, they continued to claim that I was free. It is obvious that they were reluctant to let the public know the truth because they were conscious of being in the wrong.

On October 8, 1992, [Politburo Standing Committee members] Qiao Shi and Song Ping asked me to Huairen Tang in Zhongnanhai for a talk. Ding Guan'gen and Li Tieying were also present. Qiao Shi, representing the Central Committee, announced that the CC had decided to end my investigation while upholding the political and administrative judgment against me declared by the Fourth Plenum of the 13th Central Committee. The announcement was to be included in the public statement of the CC meeting that was about to come to a close. They had come to inform me the day before it was to happen.

After listening to this, I replied by making three points:

First, with regard to the judgment made against me at the Fourth Plenum of "supporting turmoil" and "splitting the Party," I did not agree with it and have declared my reservations. I have not changed my mind and continue to have my reservations.

Second, I demanded that the Central Committee announce its decision to appropriate levels within the Party in a formal document. And when announcing the upholding of the original judgment, the facts on which the judgment was based must be laid out as well. What are the facts that support the original judgment? Are they the thirty items raised? If so, I demanded that all the items be put into the formal document.

Third, since the investigation had drawn to a close, my personal freedoms must be immediately restored. As for what I should be aware of in my activities, the Central Committee can make suggestions and I will respect them, but I absolutely will not accept unreasonable and coercive rules to limit my freedom.

Qiao Shi and the others said they would relay my response to the Central Committee and report back to me with the results.

While I was making my second point—the demand for a public announcement of the judgment—Qiao Shi interjected, "You should think about how to avoid any impact on stability." As I was making my third point demanding the restoration of my freedoms, they said that the 14th Party Congress [October 1992] would attract many foreign reporters. "Your case is very sensitive, and after the public statement is made, there could be a lot of foreign reporters probing around your house." They hoped I would observe Party discipline and take into account the big picture.

In reply, I offered to refrain from going out during the 14th Party Congress. Upon hearing this, they seemed to relax. Song Ping said that after the Party Congress, my outside activities could be increased gradually, in order to downplay the issue slowly over a long period of time. That was how the conversation ended.

I heard later that when they announced the conclusion of my investigation and the upholding of the original judgment, they said nothing more, not even in the Politburo meeting. They did not distribute reports of the Investigative Group. That means that after more than three years of investigation, specifically what was discovered and what the facts were that supported the two-point judgment against me—these all were circumvented with only the announcement of an end to the investigation. Of course, there were no objections. The public statement of the plenum mentioned only the one sentence about "ending the investigation and upholding the judgment." There were no other materials released. The plenum of the Central Committee had made the initial decision to launch the investigation, so when the plenum announced the closing of the investigation, it should have supplied a concluding report to the plenum. But it did not. On the contrary, they said at the convening meeting that it would be sufficient just to mention the issue within each group with no further discussions about the matter.

Judging from how these events were handled, I could see how nervous they were about dealing with my case. They had many concerns and spoke only with great caution.

When Qiao Shi announced the Politburo's decision to me, he read aloud from a written statement. I had originally intended to take notes while he was reading it, but he spoke too quickly. Afraid I'd be unable to catch everything in writing, I asked Qiao Shi for a copy of the statement. Qiao Shi said, "Yes," and told the comrade taking notes, "Give a copy of the notice to Comrade Ziyang." Afterward, however, when I told my secretary to call them to request a copy of the notice, they refused. They did not offer any explanation, either. I don't know what they were afraid of.

Given the situation, I was afraid they would not report my three-point statement in its entirety, as I'd expressed it, especially as the three points were not pleasant to hear. So when I returned from the meeting, I sent them my three points in the form of a memorandum. Of course, as usual, there was no reply.

In any case, they ended the investigation without releasing any documentation to the Politburo or to the plenum of the Central Committee. After three years of investigation and upon the investigation's conclusion, why not release the facts obtained to the public? In fact, they were simply afraid.

What problems had they actually uncovered in the three years of their investigation? On June 21, 1990, Wang Renzhong had provided me with the draft of the thirty-item Investigative Report with a letter attached, saying that if I had any disagreements, I could raise them by writing my comments on the document and returning it to him.

The Investigative Report

The draft was titled "Issues Relevant to Comrade Zhao Ziyang and the Political Turmoil of 1989." The thirty items contained in the document were as follows:

1. On the evening of April 15, Comrades Hu Qili and [Shanghai Party secretary] Rui Xingwen reported to Comrade Ziyang on the situation following the death of Comrade Hu Yaobang: that there was a potential for street demonstrations and gatherings and that someone could take advantage of the situation to stir up trouble. They suggested that the Central Committee issue a notice to warn regional governments to be alert. Ziyang did not take the warning of turmoil seriously, and thought issuing a warning notice was unnecessary. On April 16, the Ministry of Public Security believed the situation could become more serious and issued a warning to the regions within the system of the Ministry of Public Security.

2. During the period of commemoration for Comrade Hu Yaobang, signs of turmoil became more obvious daily. Many comrades in the Central Committee and in the Beijing municipal government believed that the nature of the events had already changed. On numerous occasions, they brought to Zhao Ziyang's attention the need for the Central Committee to have an explicit strategy and plan of action to stop the situation from further development. However, he always avoided any serious discussion about the nature of the matter. On April 23, just before he was to visit North Korea, comrades from the Central Committee again suggested he call for a meeting, but he declined.

3. On April 19, the Shanghai *World Economic Herald* and the magazine *New Observation* jointly held a symposium about the commemoration of Comrade Hu Yaobang, openly condemning the [1987] Anti–Bourgeois Liberalization Campaign. They said the Campaign was unpopular, attacked senior comrades in the Central Committee, and demanded that the Central Committee admit its mistakes, and were the first to propose comprehensive guiding principles for the political turmoil. On April 24, the *World Economic Herald* wrote a detailed report of this meeting and rushed to publish it, echoing the turmoil taking place in Beijing. On April 26, the Shanghai Party Committee handed down administrative punishment, ordered the newspaper to stop distribution, and reorganized the newspaper's staff. This was entirely correct. However,

after Zhao Ziyang returned from his visit to North Korea, he not only refused to provide support for this decision, but also accused the Shanghai Party Committee of aggravating the situation and turning things in a less favorable direction. On May 2, when he talked about the issue with [Chairman of the China Democratic League] Fei Xiaotong and leaders of other political parties, he said, "It would be better if both sides were to back down with dignity to mitigate the situation. Send a message to the Shanghai Party Committee to back down appropriately." On May 11, when he talked with [then Shanghai Party chief] Comrade Jiang Zemin about the *World Economic Herald*, he said, "I will not put pressure on you, nor will I involve myself in this matter. The matter is for you to deal with. If anyone asks me about it in the future, I will reply that I don't know anything."

4. On May 3, before Comrade Zhao Ziyang made his speech at the Seventieth Commemoration Anniversary of the May Fourth Movement, several comrades, Yang Shangkun, Li Peng, Yao Yilin, and Li Ximing, stated their belief that the anti-Party, anti-socialism turmoil that was then developing was the direct evil consequence of the long-term spreading of bourgeois liberalism. Therefore, they repeatedly suggested to Zhao that he use his speech to target the political agenda proposed by the architects of the turmoil by adding content unequivocally condemning bourgeois liberalism. These suggestions were, however, rejected by Zhao.

5. On April 23, before visiting North Korea, Zhao called [his aide] Bao Tong for a talk, asking him to keep an eye on the development of the student demonstrations. On April 30, immediately upon Zhao's return to Beijing, Bao Tong met with Zhao to report that the April 26 editorial had been written with too harsh of a tone, had not reasoned things out fully, and had precipitated the confrontational emotions of previously neutral students. Several days later, Zhao told Bao that he also felt that the April 26 editorial had flaws.

6. On May 1, Zhao asked his secretary Li Yong about the situation with the student demonstrations. When discussing the student street demonstrations of April 27, Zhao said that they were an indication that the students had been displeased by the editorial, but since the Central Committee had made its decision, it would be difficult to reverse the position expressed in the editorial.

7. On the afternoon of May 2, Zhao Ziyang held a symposium to discuss the student demonstrations with leaders of other political parties: Fei Xiaotong, Lei Jieqiong, and Sun Qimeng. By then the Central

Committee had already explicitly proposed the strategy of unequivocally taking a public stand opposing the turmoil. Zhao Ziyang should have implemented the strategy of the Central Committee, but when some people challenged the appropriateness of designating the problem of the student movement as "turmoil" without first analyzing it, not only did Zhao fail to persuade them ideologically, he even said, "Your suggestions today help us to better understand the issue," and agreed with their views. After the symposium, Zhao said to Comrade Yan Mingfu [head of the United Front Work Department] that the designation of the nature of the event made by the April 26 editorial in the *People's Daily* was wrong, that it appeared that comrades on the Politburo Standing Committee had only presented the one-sided view of the Beijing Party Committee when reporting to [Deng] Xiaoping. Now it was very difficult to turn things around. The key was how to persuade Comrade Xiaoping. If he could just say once that the situation had been overestimated, it would unify the thoughts of the members of the Standing Committee, and the Party could make the turnaround. Zhao asked Yan to share his views with Yang Shangkun and expressed the hope that Comrade Shangkun would accompany him to visit Comrade Deng Xiaoping. That evening, after Comrade Yan Mingfu met with Comrade Shangkun, he reported back to Zhao that Comrade Shangkun's response was that Comrade Xiaoping's view regarding the turmoil had already been carefully considered, and could not be changed.

8. On the morning of May 3, Zhao Ziyang talked to Yang Shangkun about the April 26 editorial, after which Zhao told his secretary Li Yong that it seemed it would be difficult to change the stand taken by the editorial. Instead, the effects must be mitigated gradually by turning things around slowly.

9. On the morning of May 4, Zhao Ziyang verbally outlined and Bao Tong put together Zhao's speech to be delivered at the Annual Meeting of the Asian Development Bank Board of Governors. Without consulting with any other comrades on the Standing Committee, he delivered the speech that afternoon in total contradiction to the Central Committee's strategy to stop the turmoil. At that time, serious turmoil was already taking place, but he said the opposite: "There will be no major turmoil in China. I have full confidence in this." The Central Committee had indicated clearly that the turmoil was aimed at undermining the leadership of the Communist Party, rejecting the socialist system, but he said, "They absolutely do not oppose our fundamental system, but rather are asking us to correct the flaws in our work." When all sorts of

facts already demonstrated that a tiny minority of people were manipulating the student demonstrations to wage turmoil, he still said, "It is unavoidable that some people might attempt to manipulate the actions of the students." After his speech, Zhao personally instructed the reporter of the Xinhua News Agency to publish the original speech in its entirety. This constituted an exposure of his divergence of opinion from the Central Committee. After the speech was published, cadres, Party members, and the populace broadly responded with confused thought because there appeared to be two different voices within the Central Committee. Some universities announced a boycott of classes and the street demonstrations reemerged. The whole situation took a turn for the worse.

10. On the morning of May 5, Zhao Ziyang met with Peking University president Ding Shisun and the vice president of Beijing Normal University, Xu Jialu. Zhao said, "I intentionally tried to reduce tensions with my speech at the Annual Meeting of the Asian Development Bank. We shouldn't discuss the nature of the movement now. Frankly, we don't even know who the tiny minority of people are."

11. In the afternoon of May 5, Comrade Zhao Ziyang invited himself to the member symposium of young staff from several Beijing universities held by the Central Committee of the China Democratic League. Some people expressed disapproval of the April 26 editorial and support for Zhao's ADB speech. When the meeting ended, Zhao said, "Everybody spoke well. Thanks!" He thereby voiced his agreement with the opinions expressed in the meeting.

12. Even as the situation with the turmoil was taking a turn for the worse, and with propaganda reports in some publications starting to head in an obviously wrong direction, on the morning of May 6, Zhao Ziyang called Hu Qili and Rui Xingwen for a talk, and told them, "Currently, freedom of the press is a hot issue. We could learn some lessons from the recent press coverage. In the beginning, control was tighter, but then it became more relaxed. The street demonstrations have been reported on, and the press seems to have become more open. There is no big risk in this." He even said, "In the face of the popular wishes of the people, and the progressive trend worldwide, the only thing we can do is manage the situation by responding to the circumstances. The student demonstrations have highlighted an issue: the people strongly demand reform and worry about the overall halting of reform." On May 9, Hu Qili organized Zhao's remarks into a brief that was disseminated to press organizations after Zhao had inspected and approved it. On May 12, Com-

rade Hu Qili and [a secretary of the Party's Central Committee Secretariat] Rui Xingwen briefed leaders of Beijing press organizations at a dialogue meeting. By that time, more than a thousand people from Beijing press organizations had signed a petition and taken to the streets to protest. Some newspapers published articles attacking the Party and the government, causing propaganda and public opinion to veer even more out of control. *People's Daily* and many other news organizations covered the street protests, sit-in demonstrations, and hunger strikes extensively, showing support for the demonstrations and prompting more and more people to participate. The social order of Beijing had fallen into utter chaos.

13. On April 21 and again on May 21, Comrade Zhao Ziyang met with Comrade Du Runsheng [who headed efforts to reform rural policies] to discuss the student demonstrations. After these meetings, Comrade Du Runsheng twice called for meetings at the Hall of Science, each time with more than ten participants, to talk about Zhao's ideas. They discussed their assessments and made suggestions for handling the student demonstrations. Zhao very much approved of everyone's suggestions and hoped to make the student demonstrations a turning point for resolving several important issues then under heightened public attention.

14. The Politburo Standing Committee held a meeting on May 8 to hear a report prepared by the Group to Stop the Turmoil. What they should have done was discuss how to adopt resolute measures to stop the turmoil, but Zhao Ziyang instead spoke emphatically on so-called "anti-corruption" efforts. On May 10, the Politburo held a meeting in which Zhao reported on the May 8 Standing Committee meeting and proposed six concrete measures for fighting corruption and promoting political reform. These measures were not discussed and agreed upon at the Standing Committee meeting.

15. In these two meetings, the question of how to respond to illegal student organizations was brought up many times. Comrade Zhao Ziyang said, "In many places where local official student associations cannot win majority support, reelections can be held. They should not be afraid of stepping down and letting others take over as a result of elections."

16. On May 9 and 10, a symposium on Contemporary Socialism Studies was held in Beijing. It was proposed in the meeting that socialist reform must overcome barriers on the way to a market economy and democracy; that issues of socialist democracy, freedom, and human

rights were all of importance and significance. Zhao Ziyang met with comrades participating in the symposium and said, "The main lesson we must learn from this student protest is that we must speed up the process of political reform." The May 12 issue of the *People's Daily* published a headline story that covered the meeting, titled "Reform Must Overcome Barriers on the Way to Market Economy and Democracy." In actuality, it provided theoretical grounds for the turmoil, and assisted in the escalation of the turmoil.

17. On the afternoon of May 16, Comrade Zhao Ziyang met with Gorbachev. As soon as the conversation began, he said. "On issues of importance, the Party still needs Deng Xiaoping to be at the helm. Since the 13th Party Congress, whenever we deal with major issues, we always inform Comrade Deng Xiaoping and seek his guidance." He also said that this was the first time he had ever revealed this Chinese Communist Party decision. The day after the talks, the slogans used in the street protests converged on attacks on Comrade Deng Xiaoping. Slogans such as "Overthrow Deng Xiaoping!" and "Support Zhao Ziyang!" flooded the street protests and Tiananmen Square.

18. On the evening of May 16, the Politburo Standing Committee held an emergency meeting. Comrade Zhao Ziyang suggested telling students that the April 26 editorial was in error. He suggested that it be said that the draft of the editorial had been sent to North Korea for his approval, and that he bore full responsibility. He repeatedly said that the April 26 editorial had problems for which an explanation was essential, and that without taking this step, no progress could be made. If the situation were not turned around, there would be no way out.

19. On the afternoon of May 17, the Politburo Standing Committee held another meeting. Comrade Zhao Ziyang continued to uphold his incorrect position while the majority of comrades on the Standing Committee ardently opposed him. They believed that continuing to back down would result in major nationwide upheaval and inconceivable consequences. Comrade Deng Xiaoping ardently supported the position of the majority of the comrades on the Standing Committee. To bring an end to the turmoil, the meeting resolved to call in a part of the military to station itself in Beijing and martial law was imposed on certain districts of the city. Zhao believed, on the contrary, that imposing martial law would lead to grave consequences. He stated that he was unable to carry this out.

20. After the Politburo Standing Committee meeting of May 17, Comrade Zhao Ziyang ignored the resolution of the Standing Committee and dared to immediately propose to resign. He asked Bao Tong to draft

a letter of resignation, which he then signed and sent out immediately. The next day, after being criticized by Comrade Yang Shangkun, Zhao retrieved the letter.

21. The Politburo Standing Committee meeting of May 17 set the major strategy of the Central Committee. Comrade Deng Xiaoping had specifically emphasized the need for every comrade at the meeting to seriously maintain strict secrecy. However, Comrade Zhao Ziyang told Bao Tong and his secretary Zhang Yueqi, "The Standing Committee meeting this afternoon has made a resolution. I was sharply criticized in the meeting. I originally proposed a relaxation of the stand taken in the April 26 editorial, to make matters more manageable, but my proposal was turned down. The Standing Committee criticized me, saying that my May Fourth speech had aggravated the situation. I voiced my reservations over the issue." He also told Bao Tong that Li Peng had accused Bao Tong of revealing secrets. After Bao Tong returned to [his job at] the Research Office of Political Reform, he immediately called together some of his staff for a meeting. He said that somebody had accused him of revealing secrets and that he might be relieved of his position soon and placed under investigation by the Central Committee. He bid them farewell. He revealed to a few people that there had been a difference of opinion between members of the Standing Committee and that Zhao's proposal had been rejected.

22. On May 18, Zhao Ziyang wrote a letter to Deng Xiaoping, continuing to appeal to change the designation of the nature of the events made in the April 26 editorial. In the letter, he stated that of the students' demands, the critical issues that needed to be addressed in order to end the hunger strike were the removal of the labels and the changing of the designation made in the April 26 editorial, and the acknowledgment that their actions were patriotic: "I have considered this carefully, and feel that we must, however painful it is, resolve to make this concession."

23. In the early morning hours of May 19, Comrade Zhao Ziyang visited the students holding the hunger strike in Tiananmen Square. He told the students that the issue over the nature and responsibility of the demonstrations would be resolved eventually. He also said, "You are still young, and have long futures ahead of you, unlike us; we are already old and do not matter anymore." He thereby revealed that there were differences among the Party's highest level of leadership and that he might be stepping down.

24. On the evening of May 19, the Party's Central Committee and the State Council held a meeting of cadres in Party and political organi-

zations to announce the decision made by the Central Committee to take resolute measures to stop the turmoil. Before the meeting, the Politburo Standing Committee had attempted repeatedly to persuade Comrade Zhao Ziyang to participate in this meeting, but Zhao refused. This, therefore, revealed his intention to openly split with the Party.

25. On May 19, the Party Group of the Standing Committee of the National People's Congress wrote a request for instruction to the Politburo Standing Committee, in which it was suggested that Comrade Wan Li, in view of the crisis situation, terminate his state visits overseas and return home. On May 21, Hu Qili asked Comrade Zhao Ziyang how to reply to the request. At the time, Zhao had already applied for a leave. Without consulting with Comrade Li Peng, who was in charge of the affairs of the Central Committee and had been assigned foreign affairs duties, he took it upon himself to agree to send a telegram to Wan Li requesting that he return ahead of schedule.

26. On the morning of May 21, Zhao Ziyang told Yan Mingfu that if the student demonstrations dragged on, and continued for a long time, there was no way to predict the consequences. The only way to ease the situation was to hold a National People's Congress Standing Committee meeting.

27. On May 21, Zhao Ziyang also told his secretary Li Yong, "I think we should hold another Politburo meeting" and asked Bao Tong to draft a speech for him.

[Item 28 is not mentioned in the recording.]

29. Comrade Zhao Ziyang has emphasized that there should be less control over and less intervention into literature and works of art.

30. A few people who have stubbornly maintained bourgeois liberalism through the years have been praised, entrusted with heavy responsibilities, and protected by Zhao Ziyang. Among these were [liberal scholar] Yan Jiaqi and [head of Zhao's economic reform think tank] Chen Yizi, who became important figures in plotting the turmoil and organizing conspiratorial activities during this turmoil. After the suppression of the counterrevolutionary riot, these people fled overseas, and continue to carry on ferocious activities opposing the Chinese Communist Party and China's socialism. Bao Tong, who had always been trusted and given important responsibilities by Zhao, attacked Li Peng and other leaders of the Party and the state after the announcement of martial law, together with Chen Yizi and others.

The above are the so-called "facts and evidence" to support the judgment against me of "supporting turmoil" and "splitting the Party" found as a result of the lengthy investigation. Even if one were to overlook how many of the thirty items contradict the facts, even if they had all been factual, in my view, they were still not enough to support the judgment made against me.

2
Zhao's Lonely Struggle

The Communist Party launches a long-term campaign to essentially erase the Tiananmen incident from history. A first step involves restricting the liberties of the former General Secretary who had opposed the crackdown—neutralizing him as a political force. After Deng dies, in 1997, Zhao writes a letter to the Communist Party making one final appeal to his former colleagues—many of whom had once supported his position—to reverse the harsh official verdict on the Tiananmen incident. But China's politics have moved in a new direction. Zhao's replacement, Jiang Zemin, who owes his position to the events of 1989, presumably sees the letter as a challenge to his power and retaliates by putting further limits on Zhao's freedom.

After the investigation ended, they continued to subject me to house arrest, limiting my personal freedoms.

While the investigation was being conducted, they detained me at home for a whole three years. With the investigation over, my personal freedoms should have been basically restored. I had already raised the issue of restoring my personal freedoms when Qiao Shi and Song Ping came to announce the end to my investigation. They did not say anything at the time except to suggest that expanding my freedoms should be gradual so that the impact would be mitigated.

In fact, as soon as they announced an end to the investigation, they immediately set down six rules to limit my activities. However, while they imposed the six rules, they never showed them to me nor spoke to me about them face-to-face—possibly because they felt guilty and feared being caught with evidence that could be exposed to the outside world and get international and domestic media attention.

Instead, they instructed the Security Bureau of the General Office and my household staff to carry them out. Of course, the comrades working in my house were forced to obey orders from above. But because they were not supposed to say that these were rules imposed by their superiors, they often nagged me with made-up excuses. Because they were acting so unreasonably, for a period of time there was often friction and confrontation between me and them. Later, I discovered that they were not to blame, because they were only carrying out instructions from above.

I felt that they should have told me specifically what the rules were—what was allowed and what was not—so I could understand. For example, after the investigation was over, I asked to take a trip to Guangdong for the winter because of my trachea problem, which causes me to cough severely in the dry northern winter but is much improved in the southern climate. They responded by saying that [Hong Kong's last colonial governor] Chris Patten was attempting to extend democratic elections [across the border from Guangdong] in Hong Kong, so the situation was very delicate; therefore, it was not convenient for me to go to Guangdong.

I thought that was ludicrous! Whatever Chris Patten was doing in Hong Kong was a matter of diplomatic affairs; what did that have to do with my being in Guangdong? But they insisted by saying, "You shouldn't go to Guangdong, but it is okay for you to go to Guangxi, Yunnan, or Guizhou."

I decided to go to Guangxi, but just as I was preparing to leave, they added another stipulation: that I was limited to the city of Nanning in Guangxi. In fact, after I arrived in Nanning, they used every means possible to block me from going anywhere else.

After I returned to Beijing, I wanted to play golf at Chang Ping Golf Course but was told it was not permitted. I asked where such a rule had come from. They would not tell me, but continued to say that I could not go. I called security staff officer Wang Tonghai and told him I wished to make a statement. The contents of the statement were as follows:

Today the Security Bureau prevented me from going to Chang Ping to play golf. I was not even allowed to go to Shun Yi County Golf Course (also Japanese managed), where I had gone last December. I believe this is a case of the Security Bureau taking actions beyond its authority, violating the Central Committee's intentions. They even admonished me to consider the bigger picture. I don't know how you can explain this! Last year, during the 14th Party Congress, when Qiao Shi and four other senior comrades came to talk with me, I clearly made a request to have my freedoms restored upon the end of the investigation. As for my activities, I was willing to consider the ramifications. If there were suggestions from the central leadership, I would respect them, but I absolutely would not accept any arbitrary coercive rules to limit my freedom. At the time, the four senior comrades made no objections to my statement. I do not understand what authority the Security Bureau has to prevent me from going to play golf today. I will not accept any similar restrictions in the future.

I asked Wang Tonghai to relay this message in its entirety to his superiors.

Another time, I asked to go to Yang Feng Jia Dao Club to play pool. At first they refused, but I insisted. They said the chauffeur would not drive me. I said I could take a bus. They finally acquiesced, but they restricted it to two morning sessions a week. I went two or three times, during which I did not see anybody in the club. I learned later that they had emptied the club, preventing other comrades from being there to create a kind of "private function" just for me. Why? Because Yang Feng Jia Dao Club was a club for old senior cadres, and they were afraid that I would meet old friends and acquaintances. Of course they certainly couldn't be so naive as to believe that upon running into these people, I would launch into provocative speeches and start organizing a network.

Concern over the alleged "impact" [of any outings] was the excuse they made to cover their plan that I never again appear in public—so people would gradually forget me, consigning me to oblivion through silence. The so-called "fear of impact" implied that the very sound of my name would cause social instability.

Perhaps they finally realized that continuing with this arrangement was not practical, and that it might be better to clarify the matter. Meng Xianzhong from the Party branch of the Central Committee General Office was sent to announce the General Office's position, that is, the six rules for limiting my activities.

Four of the items specifically defined my limitations:

1. Guests may be received at home, but no reporters or foreigners are allowed.
2. Outdoor activities require an escort of guards from the Security

Bureau. Walks in suburban parks are allowed. However, the guards must prevent visits to places that are crowded with people.

3. Considering that golf courses in the Beijing area are all managed by foreign investment companies or are joint ventures, and players on the courts are all foreigners or people from Hong Kong or Macau, it is therefore recommended that in the near future, these golf courses be avoided. As an alternative, the golf course of Shun Yi [County], operated by local Chinese peasants, can be used.

4. Traveling outside of Beijing can be arranged, but at the present time, only to inland provinces. Coastal or sensitive areas should be avoided. A detailed travel itinerary must be approved by the Central Committee.

Because these were the formal rules set by the Central Committee to limit my freedom, I responded with a letter to Jiang Zemin and the Politburo Standing Committee. My letter read as follows:

1. On June 25, the Party branch deputy secretary of the General Office, Comrade Meng Xianzhong, read several restrictions for limiting my activities that had the approval of the Central Committee. Only then did I learn that after the end of my investigation, many limits on my personal freedom continued to exist, and were being executed according to rules that had been approved by the Central Committee. I believe, however, that these rules are incompatible with the principle that the Party must operate within the bounds of the constitution and the law. They also violate the principle that "no treatment shall be used against a Party member that violates Party discipline and the law." (See Article No. 10, "Several Rules Governing Political Life in the Party" issued by the Central Committee.) Therefore, I demand that the Central Committee reconsider and retract these rules.

2. The rules bar me from foreign-invested or joint-venture golf courses "in the near future." I am also not allowed to go to coastal provinces "at the present time." I have no idea what the terms "near future" and "present time" mean. These rules were made in October of last year; since then eight months have passed. What meaning could these terms "near future" or "present time" now have?

3. The actual restrictions to my freedom in the past half year have exceeded the boundaries of these rules. For example, if the rules bar me from coastal provinces, why was I confined to Nanning when I went to Guangxi early this year? Again, if the rules bar me from crowded areas in

Beijing, why place restrictions on the times when I may go to the Yang Feng Jia Dao Club? Is the senior cadres' club considered a crowded area? Surely, this is impossible for anyone to understand.

Naturally, after the letter was sent out, there was no reply.

They have always been very nervous when dealing with such matters. When Meng Xianzhong was sent to announce the six rules, I asked to see the document. He said he could read it aloud to me but could not give me the document. I asked the secretary to write down what he was reading aloud, which was difficult for him to forbid. When I invited him to confirm what had been written down, he refused: "Whatever you have written down is your responsibility. I will not read it."

There was a fear of being exposed, of having it leaked to the outside world. In this way, they could deny responsibility in hopes of preventing unpredictable consequences. This was truly abnormal.

They said that I could receive guests at home, as long as they were not reporters or foreigners. But in reality, no one has been allowed in without an appointment. Without letting me know, they have turned everyone away. I don't even know who has come by. I informed them in advance of some visitors I was expecting, but they were still subjected to approval. Upon arrival, they are subjected to ID checking and registration, and all efforts are made to block visits. My place has always been a highly sensitive location; with the addition of so many rules and procedures, it has become too troublesome for many people. As a result, the entrance to my home is a cold, desolate place.

I receive even fewer visitors when I travel outside of Beijing. Besides service personnel and top provincial leaders, no one is allowed to know about my arrivals. They are kept secret.

For example, an old acquaintance, Comrade He Yiran, called and asked to meet with me. It was not allowed. Another example was my old friend Liu Zhengwen in Anhui, who has since passed away. When I arrived in Hefei, he tried to visit me. He phoned but was told I was outside the area. The second time he called, he was told that I had already left. They were afraid of my meeting people.

Once I was in Sichuan and some of the city and county level leaders found out and wanted to come to see me. When the matter was later reported to the Central Committee, the Central Committee criticized Sichuan provincial leaders and demanded an explanation for why the secret had not been strictly kept, resulting in so many people attempting to visit Zhao.

I went out of town every winter, except in 1997 and 1998. I wrote seven letters to Jiang Zemin and the Politburo about my going to Guangdong, but received no replies. I received a response only through the General Office, telling me that I could not go to Guangdong, but could go to other areas. In January 1993, I went to Nanning in Guangxi, passing through Changsha on the way back; in 1994, I went to Guizhou, and spent a week in Chengdu; in 1993, I spent time in Heilongjiang; in 1994, I went to Changchun and Harbin; in 1995, to Jiangxi and Anhui; in 1996, to Wuxi in Jiangsu and Zhenjiang; in 1997, to Hangzhou and then Sichuan; from the winter of 1997 to the spring of 1998, I did not leave Beijing; in 1999, I went first to Hangzhou and then to Yantai. In January of this year, that is, 2000, I went to Guilin and then Sichuan. The range of movement has been gradually enlarged.

In addition to the annual denials of my requests to go to Guangdong and Hainan, requests to go to Wuxi and Suzhou were turned down in 1995, as were requests to go to Guangdong, Hainan, and Fujian during the winter of 1999 and spring of 2000. Instead I went to Guangxi and passed by Sichuan on my way back.

As a result, I concluded that they had said "no coastal areas allowed" as a way to hide their intention of preventing me from going to Guangdong. If they had mentioned only Guangdong, it would have been too blatantly singled out. But aren't Yantai and Hangzhou both in coastal regions? I was allowed to go to those places, but not Guangdong. As for why Guangdong was excluded, I have no idea.

In autumn of 1995, Comrade Chen Yun died. I was in Beijing at the time. I was very sad when I heard the news. Even though I hadn't always agreed with his ideas about reform, I felt nevertheless that in many ways he was deserving of respect. I wanted very much to go to Chen's family to offer my condolences and express my sentiments. I made a request to the General Office and they quickly replied, saying that it was inconvenient. In the end I was not permitted to go. I was later to learn that after I had made my request, the General Office had contacted Comrade Chen Yun's family, hoping they would express a desire to have me stopped from going. Instead, the family expressed a willingness to receive me, so the General Office had no other choice but to tell me it was "inconvenient." They have always denied me the right to go to similar events, yet at the same time they do not want the outside world to know that they impose such restrictions.

When Comrade Deng Xiaoping passed away [in February 1997], I was resting in Hangzhou. I was very sorrowful when I heard the news. I immediately phoned the General Office asking that it relay a message to leaders of the Central Committee: first, to express my condolences and second, to request an immediate return to Beijing to take part in memorial services. The Central Committee quickly replied to say that there would not be a ceremony to bid farewell to the deceased, and asked me not to return to Beijing.

In May 1997, on my way back to Beijing from Chengdu, I heard that Comrade Peng Zhen had died. As soon as I arrived in Beijing, I called Peng Zhen's family and told them I would go to their home to pay my respects. I then called the Security Bureau to inform them that I was going to Peng Zhen's house. As soon as the General Office learned of this, they sent Meng Xianzhong to my house to dissuade me from going. Meng said, "Peng Zhen's family has not yet set up the mourning hall," and he told me I must "consider the big picture" and "consider the ramifications."

I was very angry with Meng for telling me a barefaced lie, and we quarreled. Why should I not be permitted to commemorate an old comrade's death? What was there to fear?

On September 12, 1997, I sent a letter to the 15th Party Congress and to nine other people through the General Office Service Bureau and asked them to forward it to the Congress. In addition to the seven members of the Politburo Standing Committee, one was addressed to Yang Shangkun, and another to Wan Li, because they had been involved. The letters were sent through the General Office Service Bureau. I learned afterward that at least two of the nine people never received my letter: Yang Shangkun and Comrade Wan Li. As for the members of the Standing Committeee, I speculate that they might have received it. I had asked them to forward copies to the entire Congress, but this was blocked.

Now I will relate the contents of the letter, since there has been hearsay in public about the content, some of which has been inaccurate. The original letter is as follows:

To the Presidium of the 15th Party Congress and All Representative Comrades:

The 15th Party Congress is our Party's last Congress of the twentieth century. In just over two years, time will march into the twenty-first century. At the critical moment of reflecting on the past and marching toward the future, I sincerely wish the Congress full success. Please allow me to propose the issue of reevaluating the June Fourth incident, which I hope will be discussed.

The events of June Fourth, which shocked the world, are now eight years past. In hindsight, there are two questions that should be answered with an attitude of honoring the facts.

First, no matter what extreme, wrong, or disagreeable things occurred in the midst of the student demonstrations, there was never any evidence to support the designation of "counterrevolutionary rebellion." If it was not a "counterrevolutionary rebellion," then the means of a military suppression should never have been used to resolve it.

Even though the military suppression quickly quelled the situation, we have no alternative but to admit that the people, the army, the Party, and the government, indeed our entire country, have paid dearly for that decision and action. The negative impact continues to exist in the relationship between our Party and the masses, the relationship between the two sides of the Taiwan strait, and our country's foreign relations.

Because of the impact of the incident, the political reform initiated by the 13th Party Congress died young and in midstream, leaving the reform of the political system lagging seriously behind. As a result of this serious situation, while our country's economic reform has made substantial progress, all sorts of social defects have emerged and developed and are rapidly spreading. Social conflicts have worsened, and corruption within and outside of the Party is proliferating and has become unstoppable.

Second, could a better method have been found to respond to the student demonstrations so that bloodshed could have been avoided while still making the situation subside? Back then I proposed "resolving the issue according to democracy and law" and indeed strived for such an outcome. Today, I still believe that by adopting such measures, the situation could have ended peacefully without bloodshed. At least the serious and bloody confrontation could have been avoided.

As everyone knows, most of the students were demanding the punishment of corruption and the promotion of political reform, and were not advocating the overthrow of the Communist Party or the subversion of the republic. The situation would have subsided if we had not interpreted the students' actions as being anti-Party and anti-socialist, but had accepted their reasonable demands and had adopted measures of patient negotiation, dialogue, and reducing tensions.

If so, not only would all the negative impacts of the bloody confrontation have been avoided, but a new kind of communication and interactive pattern would have been established among political parties, the government, and the people; and there would have been a boost to the reform of the political system, so we could have not only made substantial progress on economic reform, but brought about new prospects to reforming the political system of our country.

Sooner or later, the issue of reevaluating June Fourth must be resolved. Even if it's delayed for a long time, people will not forget. It is better to resolve it earlier rather than later, proactively rather than passively, and in stable rather than in troubled times.

With the national situation now stable, the consensus of many people is a desire for stability and an aversion to chaos. The heightened emotions of the past have subsided. If our Party could take it upon itself to initiate a proposal to reevaluate the June Fourth incident in these conditions, and take the lead in the process, it is fully possible not to be affected by extreme emotions from various sources, and to move the process of resolving a difficult historical issue along the correct tracks of reason and tolerance. The principles of resolving historical problems could be followed, such as "not nitpicking over details" and "focusing on the lessons to be learned rather than individual blame."

If this was done, not only could a difficult historical situation be resolved, the stability of the situation could be maintained while simultaneously creating a better international environment for our country's reform and openness.

I hope that we can examine the situation and make a decision soon. The above suggestions are offered for the consideration of the Congress.

Zhao Ziyang
September 12, 1997

I did not disseminate this letter, nor did I go through anyone to make it public. However, overseas media quickly learned about this letter, and commotion ensued.

Meng Xianzhong soon came to see me. He pointed out that conditions nationwide were excellent at the time and asked me not to undermine the great situation and to obey Party discipline. He implied that I had not observed this discipline. I replied immediately that I was a member of the Communist Party, and that the Party Charter clearly gave Party members the right to offer suggestions to the Party Congress. He said that there had already been a conclusion made about June Fourth. I said that the Party Congress, being the highest authority of the Party, had the right to decide whether or not to reevaluate June Fourth. Even if there had already been a resolution, it could still be reevaluated. Certainly, it could choose to reaffirm its past decision, but this was within the authority of the Congress. Any decision of the Party could be discussed by the Congress.

He also said that I shouldn't have disseminated the letter. I replied that I had only sent it to nine people, all via the Service Bureau. In fact, I wanted to know, to whom did they forward my letter? Naturally, the conversation was very unpleasant.

Around the same time, Comrade Yong Wentao passed away. We were old colleagues and had worked together in Guangdong. I asked to attend his funeral. Previously, I had been permitted to attend funerals for people at the minister level, though not those for members of the central leadership. However, this time they told me that because I had disobeyed Party discipline, I was not allowed to go out.

What followed was the prohibition of all visitors from my house. The severity of the prohibition was even harsher than it had been during the investigation. An old lady from Guangdong who had once been a helper in my house, and was now quite elderly, traveled thousands of kilometers to see me, but was kept waiting outside my house for several hours. Even when my wife returned home from shopping, her purse would be searched by the guards at the gate. Obviously the stationed soldiers were not responsible for this; the order had to have come from at least as high as the General Office of the Central Committee. Hence, I wrote a letter to the General Office as follows:

Leaders of the General Office of the Central Committee:

Greetings!
Recently, the Security Bureau of the General Office has instructed the guards at my home to prohibit me from receiving visitors, going out, and playing golf.
Attending a comrade's funeral was also prohibited. Even relatives visiting from afar have been stopped at the gate. However, all of these things were allowed even under the six rules limiting my freedom imposed after the 14th Party Congress. This would mean that after five

and a half years of semi–house arrest, I am now to be subjected to full house arrest. This is in serious violation of the law. Obviously, the Security Bureau or the troops standing guard could not have taken it upon themselves to make such a decision. What is the real reason for this? Have the original rules been abolished and are there new rules in place? In any case, I have not been informed.

There is no alternative but to regard this kind of undeclared house arrest as a crude trampling of the socialist legal system. As a member of the Party, if I have violated Party discipline (which in fact is not the case), the Party's administration is within its rights to take disciplinary action, including expelling me from the Party; but it has no right to limit my personal freedoms or deprive me of my rights as a citizen. The Party Charter strictly prohibits the use of tactics that violate the Party Charter or the laws of the state in its treatment of members. Those organizations or individuals who violate these rules must be punished through Party disciplinary action and the laws of the state.

As a citizen, even if I had violated the law (which is absolutely not the case), limits on my freedom of movement must follow legal procedures and only law enforcement agencies of the state have the power to administer them. These are stated clearly in the laws of the state. Though the General Office is an extremely important organization of the Central Committee, it is not a law enforcement agency of the state and has no right to carry out the authority belonging to the law enforcement agency of the state.

In the past, during those years when we "acknowledged neither laws nor heavenly constraints," similar incidents to those described above often occurred, which formed a certain mentality and pattern of behavior among some people. Nevertheless, that era has long since passed.

Since the Reform and Open-Door Policy, our Party and the state have always emphasized the establishment of the rule of law. Especially after the recent 15th Party Congress, incidents such as these should not be allowed to happen.

Comrade Jiang Zemin, in his 15th Party Congress Political Report, solemnly pledged to the world to perfect the socialist legal system, including upholding the principle of rule of law, guaranteeing that all matters of state would be conducted according to the law, declaring that all laws would be observed, that violators would be punished, and that no individual or organization would have special authority outside the boundaries of the law; that all government organizations would conduct their affairs in accordance with the law, and that the rights of citizens would be safeguarded in concrete terms. I trust General Secretary Jiang Zemin was serious about this and was intent on carrying it out and was not just paying lip service.

Allow me to ask, as a citizen who is being prevented from going out and receiving visitors and deprived of other rights: Does this accord with the principle of doing things according to the law? Is it true that you have placed yourself in the position of having special authority outside the boundaries of law? The General Office is an organization of the Party that is right under the noses of the central leadership. How is it that you have not checked your own behavior with all the principles of establishing the rule of law that were announced at the 15th Party Congress?

Of course, this letter yielded no results.

Since I did not receive any replies, after a while I wrote again to the Politburo Standing Committee, that is, to each of the seven members of the Standing Committee newly elected at the 15th Party Congress. In the past, whenever I had sent letters to the Standing Committee, only one or two people received them. Therefore, this time I sent each one of them a copy. The letter was as follows:

Comrade Jiang Zemin:

Greetings!

On September 12, I wrote a letter to the 15th Party Congress, suggesting a reevaluation of the June Fourth incident. I trust that you have all seen it. Since I sent the letter, I have been prohibited from receiving visitors or going outside my house. My personal freedoms have been completely restricted. The former conditions of my semi–house arrest have turned into full house arrest.

With regard to this serious violation of the law, I have written to the General Office of the Central Committee demanding to have this matter resolved. However, my house arrest continues to this day. For this reason, I have no choice but to bring this issue to your attention.

As a Party member, making a suggestion to the Party's congress is a normal exercise of Party membership rights. This is clearly stated in the Party Charter. Regardless of whether my suggestion was correct or wrong, and regardless of whether the Party Congress discusses it or not, I could not have violated the Party Charter or the laws of the state. However, house arrest and the deprivation of my personal freedoms as a citizen suggest that I am receiving the treatment of a criminal. I do not even know what specific laws I have violated, nor do I know which state law enforcement agency and what procedure of law have been used to authorize my house arrest. How can subjecting a person to this kind of undeclared house arrest and depriving his rights as a citizen not constitute a crude trampling of the socialist legal system?

In our Party's history, besides during the years of the Cultural Revolution, deprivation of personal freedoms and subjection to house arrest for holding divergent views have been rare. Even at the height of Chairman Mao's waging of class struggle in 1962, as angry as he was by Marshal Peng [Dehuai]'s long statement of criticism, he did not deprive Peng of his personal freedoms and even sent him to work at the development command center. However, after our Party has learned the harsh lessons of being too "leftist," and after we have repeatedly emphasized over the past ten years establishing a socialist rule of law, especially after General Secretary Jiang Zemin has just solemnly declared that our Party will administer the nation according to the law and establish the rule of law, it is indeed inconceivable that such a crude violation of the socialist legal system is happening right under the noses of the Central Committee.

Since June 1989, I have been illegally subjected to either house arrest or semi–house arrest. This has gone on for eight and a half years already. I don't know for how much longer this deprivation of freedoms will continue. This undoubtedly is doing great harm to my physical and mental health, as I am approaching eighty.

Nevertheless, the more serious harm is being done to the image of our Party and the Party's Central Committee. Would people not compare what has happened to me to those principles announced at the 15th Party Congress, and thereby come to their own conclusions regarding the credibility of these newly announced principles? Furthermore, when later generations evaluate this period of Party history, they most certainly will not view this incident of prolonged house arrest and the deprivation of personal freedoms of a Party member for holding a divergent view as a glorious moment.

I hope this letter of mine will gain the attention of the General Secretary and comrades on the Standing Committee. I hope this blatant behavior of violating laws and regulations under the very noses of the Central Committee will be terminated soon. I hope my house arrest

will be lifted and my personal freedoms restored, so that I will
not spend the rest of my years in these lonely and despondent
conditions.

I herewith offer a salute!

Zhao Ziyang

This letter was sent, but as before, there was no reply. Later, the General Office called my secretary to confirm that they had received the letter.
They said that first of all, this was not house arrest (they were very afraid
of calling it "house arrest"); and second, that I had brought it upon myself. Perhaps they were implying that I was to blame for the letter addressed to the 15th Party Congress [being leaked] overseas. That was the
only reply I received to my two letters. The reality was that I continued to
be detained at home.

Some time passed until it was just before Jiang Zemin's visit to the
United States, with still no indication of any intention to relax my conditions. Then oddly enough, one day the family doctor assigned to me from
the Health Division of Zhongnanhai [site of the Party's headquarters]
came to my house and suddenly mentioned that it was not good for me to
stay at home all day.

I laughed and replied, "What choice do I have?"

He said, "Why don't we write a letter to the General Office to raise
this issue, so you can go out and play golf?"

I said, "I am not permitted even to receive visitors now, let alone go
out to play golf."

He said, "We will file a report."

This was unprecedented behavior for a member of the Health Division of Zhongnanhai and not at all in line with customs and rules. [Members of the Health Division] were never allowed to intervene in matters of
this kind, nor had this doctor ever suggested this before.

It occurred to me that perhaps Jiang Zemin was hoping that during
his visit to the United States, if someone were to ask him about Zhao, he
could reply that Zhao was not under house arrest but had recently even
gone out to play golf. With this in mind, I replied to him, "You should not
get involved in this. Anyway, I have no interest in playing golf these
days."

I gave him the cold shoulder. Why would a doctor intervene in such
matters? Only by orders of the General Office. Then the Party branch of
the General Office called my secretary to say that playing golf was now
allowed. Though I had previously been denied the right to attend the fu-

neral of Yong Wentao, going to similar funerals in the future would now be permitted. No mention was made about receiving visitors.

It was therefore made clear that there had been a relaxation of the rules. No visitors or other outings were permitted. However, for the sake of some good publicity, I was allowed to go play golf and attend funerals. I didn't know whether to laugh or cry at such tactics. I simply refused to play golf and absolutely refused to go out; nor did I attend any funerals.

As a result, in 1997, I did not go anywhere for the winter. I spent the entire winter in Beijing. Even though Beijing was dry and dusty, and worsened my respiratory problem and made me cough a great deal, I still refused to leave.

Speaking of these trivial matters is meaningless. However, this illustrates the kind of mentality they had. On the one hand, they disregarded the law and unreasonably limited my activities; on the other hand, they were fearful of exposure and the foreign media.

From October 1997 to December 1999, not only were the original six rules not relaxed, but stricter limits had been added, denying me visitors and the right to leave my home. These conditions lasted for more than two years.

With the passing of time, there was a little relaxation. Relatives were allowed to visit, as were some of the comrades holding lower-level positions, or retired elderly comrades. Yet many retired senior leaders, for example those who held minister or vice minister level positions, were still not allowed to visit me. Of course, they never spelled these terms out clearly.

In the latter half of last year [1999], I asked Comrade Zhao Jianmin [the governor of Shandong Province] to visit, but the General Office immediately told me that he was not allowed to come. Another time, I asked Comrade Xiao Hongda [director of the General Office of the Central Military Commission] to visit, but this was also turned down by the [Central Committee] General Office.

In December 1999, as my former secretary, Comrade Yang Wenchao, reached the age of retirement, a new secretary was assigned. In order to announce the assignment of the new secretary, two comrades from the Party committee of the General Office were sent to talk with me.

I used the opportunity to raise two issues: first was a request to leave Beijing during the winter season, hopefully to Guangdong or Hainan; second, I demanded an end to the ten years of house arrest, especially the full house arrest conditions imposed after the 15th Party Congress.

After a while, they relayed to me through the secretary that I was not to go to Fujian, Guangdong, or Hainan, but that other places were permitted, so their position had slightly relaxed. Visitors were generally permitted, as before. Some were allowed, some were not.

I immediately asked for Comrade Zhao Jianmin to come over. His visit was approved, and he came and visited for a while. Later, Comrades Xiao Hongda, Du Daozheng [director of the General Administration of Press and Publications], and Yao Xihua [chief editor of *Guangming Daily*] also came over for visits. In general, it appeared that the conditions had returned to those of the original six rules.

THE ROOTS OF CHINA'S ECONOMIC BOOM

PART 3

THE ROOTS OF CHINA'S ECONOMIC BOOM

I

Conflicting Views at the Top

How did Zhao first rise to prominence? His national political career took off after he earned widespread praise for launching innovative rural reforms in Sichuan as the province's Party secretary in the mid-1970s. He was made an alternate member of the Politburo in 1977 and within three years was China's Premier, in charge of the nation's economic affairs.

Zhao talks about the effort to restore China's economy after the damage that Mao's policies had inflicted. He also discusses his role in mediating occasional conflicts between paramount leader Deng Xiaoping, the leading proponent of China's economic reforms, and Chen Yun, a respected elder who wanted to proceed more cautiously.

After the Third Plenum of the 11th Central Committee [which in 1978 launched the reform era], there were two viewpoints held by those in the central leadership. Even before that, it's fair to say there had been two: one represented by Deng Xiaoping and the other by Chen Yun.

Deng believed in expanding the economy with an emphasis on speed and opening up to the outside world, adopting reforms that moved toward a market economy. Chen Yun upheld the approach of the first Five-Year Plan in the 1950s; that group insisted on a planned economy and had reservations about the reform program.

After more than ten years of back-and-forth between the two, Deng's idea triumphed and was accepted by more and more people. Reality has proven that it was correct.

[Hu] Yaobang and I were basically on the same side as Deng Xiaoping. [Influential elder] Li Xiannian was fully on Chen Yun's side, and even more extreme and stubborn. The major distinction between him and Chen Yun is that Chen Yun genuinely believed in his viewpoint, whereas Li Xiannian was thinking more about which approach might benefit or hurt him personally. During the Cultural Revolution, he basically had been in charge of economics. Together with Yu Qiuli, who headed the State Planning Commission for a long time, the two were in charge of the economy.

This includes the two years immediately following the fall of the Gang of Four [in 1976], when they carried out an "all-out fast-paced campaign" that caused economic imbalances and set unattainable goals of importing major projects with the so-called "Import Great Leap Forward." All this was done under his and Yu Qiuli's leadership.

As reforms progressed, Li Xiannian, feeling that his work had been rejected, often expressed displeasure with notions such as "If whatever is being done now is all correct, then was the past work all wrong?" He always opposed reform and often complained about it.

Others who supported Chen Yun's viewpoint included Yao Yilin, who later succeeded Yu Qiuli as the director of the State Planning Commission. He was the Vice Premier in charge of general economic policies in the State Council.

I had always fully supported Deng's reform. Indeed, I was enormously enthusiastic about it and worked hard to bring it about. I did, however, have reservations over Deng's emphasis on speed. Of course, if everything else is going well and the economy is running smoothly, faster is better; nobody could object to that. However, our past mistaken tendency to focus on pursuing output values taught us that an overemphasis on pace can result in a blind pursuit of high targets and speed, at the expense of efficiency.

My production targets were relatively modest and I emphasized economic efficiency. Deng understood my view on this matter. There was no conflict.

On the issue of reform, [Hu] Yaobang and I had the same basic view. We were both enthusiastic. However, we had differences on specific steps, approaches, and methods—especially on the question of speed, Yaobang was even more aggressive than Deng. Deng merely wished things could go faster. Yaobang actively promoted the concept everywhere and demanded that people do such things as "quadruple it, ahead of schedule." Since I was in charge of overall economic work, the difference between our approaches was evident.

As for Comrade Chen Yun, I had enormous respect for him in the years when I first started working in the central leadership. I felt that of the elder generation of leaders, Comrade Chen Yun was the one with the most profound knowledge in economics; he had unique and penetrating insights.

His first Five-Year Plan had been very successful; of course, it was based on the Soviet economic model. After 1957, he insisted on thinking independently, and he disagreed with Chairman Mao's Great Leap Forward.* At a time when the entire Party was delusional, it wasn't easy holding to his own views. Furthermore, after the Three Transformations† during the 1950s, he [Chen] first proposed that within the predominantly planned economy, a small amount of freedom should be allowed. He believed in allowing for as lively a market as possible within the structure of a planned economy.

This was not easy, since at that time the Party was committed to expanding the role of planning until it accounted for the entire economy. Also, in 1962 when the economy was in crisis, he saved the situation. He carried out very effective measures, including raising the price of sugar, importing soybeans, and combating a water retention epidemic caused by starvation. He had turned things around quickly. Of course, efforts also were made by Comrade Liu Shaoqi [China's President from 1959 to 1968] and Premier Zhou [Enlai, China's Premier from 1949 to 1976], but Comrade Chen Yun proposed many of the measures.

After I moved to Beijing, I agreed with his opposition to the overemphasis on speed, so as to avoid major economic fluctuations. And he expressed support for my urban economic reform aimed at easing the reliance on the state for jobs and expanding autonomy for enterprises. In the initial few years, the two of us had a good relationship. I was even able to mediate and ease communication between Deng and Chen. Since I was in charge of the economy, I asked for both men's opinions and then proposed ideas of my own. They were mainly based on Deng's opinions, while also taking Chen Yun's into consideration. The result was that the two of them could reach agreement.

Problems developed as reform deepened. New issues emerged as we pushed forward, but Chen Yun's ideas remained unchanged. Within the Party, Comrade Chen Yun's views on the economy would have been

---

*   The Great Leap Forward was Mao's catastrophic plan, launched in 1958, to engage the masses in fast-paced economic development. It led to economic collapse, and to the starvation of millions.

†   Three Transformations was Mao's social program to nationalize agriculture, handicrafts, and the mercantile sector in the 1950s.

PRISONER OF THE STATE

considered open-minded in the 1950s and 1960s. But as he persisted in his belief in "small amounts of freedom under a predominantly planned economy" or "planned economy as primary, market adjustments as auxiliary," he became more and more out of tune with the overall goals of reform and the reality of the time. The distance between us grew greater.

An Early Setback

Zhao's first big challenge as Premier is a measure, introduced by two Party elders, to slow the economy to ward off inflation. Although Zhao generally approves of the measure, he gets a firsthand taste of just how rigid the administrative tools of central planning can be.

In 1979 and 1980, a readjustment was made under the leadership of Comrade Chen Yun to correct imbalances in the economy. The Central Committee had established a Finance and Economic Commission, and Comrade Xiaoping had pushed for Chen Yun to head it. This occurred before I had come to Beijing. Later, under my leadership, the name of the group was changed to the Central Economic and Financial Leading Group.

The goal of the two-year economic readjustment was to correct problems that had emerged during the leadership of [Vice Premier in charge of economic affairs] Li Xiannian and [Vice Premier] Yu Qiuli. Yu Qiuli and [another Vice Premier] Kang Shien were critical of and basically opposed the readjustment. That helps explain why Yu Qiuli was later reshuffled out of the State Planning Commission and replaced by Yao Yilin.

After the two-year readjustment of 1979 and 1980, a further readjustment was proposed for 1981. This was the first major issue I encountered upon taking the leadership of the State Council.

When the sixth Five-Year Plan was being discussed in May and June of 1980, I had hoped to double the size of the economy within ten years. The goal was to shoot for 5 percent to 6 percent growth from 1980 to 1985, and then relatively faster growth in the next five years.

However, when the Planning Commission was drafting the plan for 1981, it discovered that the financial deficit had exceeded 10 billion yuan for 1979 and 1980, and it forecast that the 1981 deficit would also be high. At the same time, prices were going up, causing widespread complaints.

When Chen Yun learned of the situation, he suggested that we achieve both a financial balance and a credit balance in 1981. He believed that it would be better to sacrifice rapid growth in order to establish a financial balance. He was worried that year after year of deficits would result in worsening inflation. Li Xiannian went further, suggesting that not only should the budget be balanced, but there should be a surplus. Since the two had long-standing experience in making economic policy, further readjustment to the economy in 1981 became a certainty. This meant scaling back plans for construction projects, and slowing the pace of development.

The Planning Commission's revised economic plan was submitted to a Politburo Standing Committee meeting for discussion on November 28. After Xiaoping, Chen Yun, and Li Xiannian approved it, it was communicated nationwide via a Central Committee Work Meeting on December 26 attended by provincial and municipal leaders.

With reforms producing consecutive years of good harvests and a vibrant market, living standards had risen. Under such good conditions, many comrades around the country saw the adjustment as unnecessary. The adjustment meant some contracts with foreign companies would have to be revised; equipment that had been delivered for certain projects would have to be put into storage.

As a result, there was some talk abroad about the Chinese economy being in trouble. Elsewhere there was praise. From the material that I read, only Japan believed that the readjustment was necessary to put the economy on the right track.

Chen Yun and Li Xiannian proposed the readjustment. Even though Deng Xiaoping agreed to it at the Politburo Standing Committee meeting and gave a speech to that effect at the Central Committee Work Meeting, it was not what he really wanted. He was not happy to have to pull the plug on major import projects and put equipment into storage. He agreed with Chen Yun and Li Xiannian's views only to show his support for Chen Yun.

Until that moment, Deng Xiaoping still considered Chen Yun the primary decision maker on economic issues. In his mind, decades of experience had shown that Chen Yun had the deepest understanding of economic issues and was wiser than he. Even though the situation was not to his liking, he expressed support for Chen Yun.

[Communist Party General Secretary Hu] Yaobang did not say anything at the meeting. In my opinion, he did not entirely concur but found it difficult to express opposition, since two elders had proposed the measure and another had agreed to it. However, after a year had passed, in spring of 1982, when Yaobang visited the provinces for inspection, he said "the 1981 readjustment has caused the economy to take a dip." Naturally, when this reached Chen Yun's ears, he was not pleased.

Even though I was the leader of the Central Economic and Financial Leading Group, I had just joined the central leadership and was not yet familiar with the national economic situation. I genuinely trusted Chen Yun. Even though his opinion differed from my idea of "doubling in ten years," I had agreed with Comrade Chen Yun's idea. In hindsight, the further readjustment had been necessary, and the end results were good.

For a time after the Third Plenum of the 11th Central Committee [1978], our economy was still in a hole. For many years—before and during the Cultural Revolution—we had been lagging in many respects, including urban construction, agriculture, and people's living standards. To shift to a healthier economic state, we had to go through a process of "relearning." In this situation, it was impossible to attain rapid economic development. Nor was it possible to engage in large-scale infrastructure construction.

For example, in order to revive the rural economy and enhance incentives for farmers, the prices of agricultural goods were raised. The aim was to reduce the urban-rural income gap. I was still in Sichuan when the policy was put forward, and I participated in the discussion. There were two key points. First, prices for agricultural and other rural products had to be raised, or else farmers would not have incentive to produce. Second, even though it was impossible at the time to remove the state monopoly on agricultural and other rural products, the quotas for mandatory procurement had to be reduced, especially in major grain-producing areas. For years, those quotas had been too high. Farmers had to work too hard to meet them.

After the Third Plenum of the 11th Central Committee, there were good harvests several years in a row: 1979, 1980, 1981, 1982, 1983, and 1984. The rural areas experienced a new prosperity, in large part because we resolved the issue of "those who farm will have land" by implementing a "rural land contract" policy. The old situation, where farmers were employees of a production team, had changed; farmers began to plant for themselves.

The rural energy that was unleashed in those years was magical, beyond what anyone could have imagined. A problem thought to be unsolvable had worked itself out in just a few years' time. The food situation that was once so grave had turned into a situation where, by 1984, farmers actually had more grain than they could sell. The state grain store-houses were stacked full from the annual procurement program.

Two other factors contributed to the change. One was the elevated price of agricultural products. Farmers could make a profit from farming. The other was the reduction in the quotas for mandatory state procure-ment, which meant taking less food out of the mouths of farmers.

For more than two decades, farmers had not had enough to eat after handing over the grains they had produced to the state after every har-vest. Of course, the reason that we were able to introduce this new policy was because the Third Plenum of the 11th Central Committee had de-cided that China could import grains. Comrade Chen Yun said the im-ports were allowed so that industrial crops could be preserved, but in fact, the imports fulfilled urban consumption demands, thereby reducing the rural mandatory procurement quota [purchased in part for urban markets]. The quantity of grain imports was huge in those years, between 10 million and 20 million tons. Major grain-producing regions could sell their surplus at a higher price and make a profit. Together, all of this gave rural areas instant prosperity.

These policy implementations came at a cost. While the prices of agricultural products had gone up, urban food prices could not be imme-diately raised, since urban workers had limited purchasing power. There-fore we had to finance additional subsidies for agricultural and other rural products. At the same time, foreign currency was needed to import grains, which affected the import of machinery. Plus, urban housing needed to be expanded. And since factories now had more autonomy, the wages and bonuses of the workers were raised. All of this involved additional expenditure. But these things all were part of the recovery process, which paved the way for the good situation of later years.

After the Third Plenum of the 11th Central Committee, our country's financial revenue gradually declined in proportion to the gross national product, while expenditures steadily increased, thus resulting in a deficit. This was the price we had to pay; it was normal and solvable. In 1984, I began proposing a gradual raising of the revenue-to-GNP ratio. To re-duce the deficit, we temporarily scaled back infrastructure construction and reduced the pace of economic development. There was no other choice.

If we had ignored the situation and launched an "all-out fast-paced campaign," we would have faced seriously high inflation and put greater strains on farmers and workers. The readjustments in 1979 and 1980 and again in 1981 had been necessary. As a result of the 1981 readjust-ments, the agricultural sector continued to enjoy big harvests, the market continued to prosper, and the nation's economy showed no negative growth. On the contrary, the economy grew by an annual rate of 4 percent. And as the readjustment deepened in 1981, growth increased. The growth rate in the first quarter was relatively low, the second quarter was better, the third quarter was higher, and the fourth quarter was significantly higher. This proves the readjustment was good and the economy had recovered.

Here's how we kept the economy growing: by scaling back infrastructure projects and reducing heavy industry, iron and steel production, and machinery production; by expanding light industries such as consumer products and textiles while allowing and encouraging private businesses; by developing service industries. The cities continued to prosper and living standards continued to rise. Employment rates rose. In the end we achieved a balanced budget and the people were generally more satisfied.

That said, the policy had its shortcomings. We still hadn't entirely corrected the traditional way in which the Planning Commission cut back on infrastructure projects, which was to "cut straight across the board." With the old system still in place, it was hard not to do so, and so we set quotas for each region.

In order to save projects that really should not be cut, however, I asked the Planning Commission to be flexible with a part of the budget so that we could revive some of these projects. After the general spending reduction, we reviewed which cuts would incur too great a loss, or which projects were so beneficial they should continue. Of course, there could not be a large number of exceptions, but we were able to reduce the negative impact of "cutting straight across the board."

Still, in retrospect, the readjustment was too severe. We should have made exceptions for all projects where equipment had already been received or was urgently needed and could be installed and put into production quickly. This would have been more cost effective, particularly if you consider the cost of storage. Even though some of these projects resumed a year later, time and money was wasted. Some of the projects took years to recover.

The reason we didn't take more flexible measures was mainly because we lacked sufficient domestic funds to pay for these projects; the deficit needed to be reduced so that a financial balance could be achieved. It was all too mechanical.

For example, if the deficit had not been eliminated immediately and some of the budget had been spent on worthwhile projects, the investment could have been returned in a year or so. And under the open-door policy, we could have resolved the problem by taking out more foreign loans.

But Chen Yun was concerned and firmly insistent. He was afraid of excessive and overly large projects and insisted on the reductions. At the time, there were things we didn't clearly understand, since we did not have enough experience.

3
Opening Painfully
to the World

*Along the coast, China's leaders set up several Special Economic
Zones for free-market experimentation. By limiting such reforms to
these few areas, China's liberals avoid the kind of costly political
debates that could have stymied any nationwide effort to adopt
these liberal policies.*

*When it becomes clear that the SEZs really are becoming
capitalist enclaves, however, Chen Yun fights back, launching the
"Strike Hard Campaign Against Economic Crimes." Zhao and Hu
Yaobang feel powerless to stop the influential Party elder.*

*There are other clashes in the early days of China's opening up
to the outside world. A plan to lease property on Hainan Island to
a foreign investor, for example, triggers a major controversy. Many
argue that such a deal would compromise China's sovereignty. In
the end Zhao convinces Deng Xiaoping that there is nothing to
fear.*

Comrade Chen Yun was deeply concerned about the open-door policy,
and his differences with Deng Xiaoping were quite pronounced.

The Special Economic Zones (SEZs) were proposed by Deng Xiaoping. He gave approvals for Shenzhen and Zhuhai in Guangdong Province and Xiamen in Fujian Province, and would later add others. Chen
Yun had always objected to the idea of SEZs. He never set foot in any of
them. I've heard that he sent envoys to the SEZs who at first returned
with negative reports, but later were more positive. But he always had
doubts and objections.

At the December 1981 meeting of provincial and municipal secretaries of Party committees, and in his talk with leaders of the Planning Commission who visited with him during the Spring Festival, Chen Yun emphasized that the primary purpose of the SEZs was experimentation and learning. He added that SEZs could not be expanded any further and that we must make note of their negative aspects.

Originally, there were to be more SEZs along the coastal regions, including around Shanghai and in Zhejiang Province. But Chen Yun said that those areas were not to establish SEZs. This region, as Chen Yun put it, was famous for its concentration of opportunists who would, with their consummate skills, emerge from their cages if given the slightest chance. The Research Office of the Secretariat directed by Deng Liqun also collected material that attempted to prove that the SEZs would degenerate into "foreign concession zones." At one point, these criticisms were widespread, a result of the influence of Chen Yun and Deng Liqun.

On the issue of foreign investments, Chen Yun was completely at odds with [Deng] Xiaoping. Xiaoping believed in bringing in large-scale foreign investments. He believed it was difficult for a developing economy like China's to take off without foreign investment. Of course, he only dealt with major issues and didn't intervene much as to how this might be brought about. But he supported all of it: preferential loans, non-preferential loans, joint ventures. Chen Yun was very cautious about foreign investments. The case file for the Shanghai-Volkswagen joint venture remained in his office for a long time before he finally gave his consent.

Chen Yun believed that foreign direct investments [FDI] were not the solution for China's development. He often said that foreign capitalists were not just looking for normal profits, but "surplus profits." In other words, it would be impossible to gain any benefits from FDI. He often warned Gu Mu, who was in charge of foreign trade and economic affairs, to raise the level of vigilance. He said that preferential loans extended to China by foreign entities were for buying equipment. Though these appeared to be preferential, the purpose was [for foreign companies] to export products and the discount in loans was made up for in the profits made selling the products. When taking such loans, we had no freedom to choose, but were forced to buy designated products. FDI without spending limitations came with very high interest rates, which we could not afford.

He was also critical of joint ventures. I felt that Chen Yun's thoughts were stuck in the theoretical expressions of "finance-capital" found in Lenin's *On Imperialism*. After reforms had been launched, he read Lenin's

On Imperialism again. He once told me that Lenin's characterization remained valid, and that we were still in the era of imperialism.

The "Strike Hard Campaign Against Economic Crimes" began in the coastal regions in January 1982. It started with an urgent notice sent in the name of the Central Committee, and it would have enormous repercussions. At the time I was in Zhejiang. I learned later that the campaign was begun in response to a report about smuggling activities in Guangdong that had been sent to the Central Discipline Inspection Commission.

On the document Chen Yun wrote a note, calling for "a hard and resolute strike, like a thunderbolt." Afterward, [Party General Secretary Hu] Yaobang chaired a Secretariat meeting and issued the urgent notice. In March, after my return to Beijing, the Central Committee held a special symposium on Guangdong and Fujian provinces and disseminated a summary nationwide, directing other regions to act in line with the spirit of the document. In April, the Central Committee and the State Council again issued a "Resolution to Strike Hard Against Serious Economic Crimes."

In 1981, the reforms were still new. This nationwide campaign, conducted in the coastal regions, brought enormous harm to them. The reforms had revitalized the economy but also led to activities such as smuggling, speculation, bribery, and the theft of state property. But they should have been dealt with on a case-by-case basis.

Instead, the extent of the problem was overestimated and an inappropriate determination was made. The unavoidable circumstances that accompanied efforts to relax rules in the name of stimulating the economy were characterized as "the important manifestations of class struggle in the new environment" and "the result of sabotage and erosion of our system by class enemies using decayed capitalist thought."

It was also stated that "bourgeois lifestyles have been on the rise." And it was proposed that "from now on, the struggle against the corruption from decayed bourgeois thoughts shall be strengthened. Emphasis is placed on preserving the purity of communism in the process of reform."

This kind of labeling and the way in which the campaign was conducted inevitably affected issues that were emerging with reform. The overreaction toward smuggling in Guangdong and other coastal regions had much to do with Comrade Chen Yun's objections and suspicions of reform and economic stimulation. He believed that these were dangerous policies.

When the strike against economic crimes was proposed, it was announced that the SEZs must also uphold "planned economy as primary, market adjustments as auxiliary." This would have rendered the SEZs meaningless. He [Chen Yun] also announced the strengthening of central control over foreign trade: there was to be no trade or economic activities with foreigners except involving companies designated by the state and these had to follow official rules and procedures. As a result, some powers that had already been handed down to the SEZs were taken away. He also set guidelines for increased quotas for mandatory state procurement of agricultural and rural products and a reduction in high-priced procurements. He then proposed limiting workers' bonuses in the coastal region to a level only slightly higher than those in the inner provinces.

The strike against economic crimes had turned into a campaign against economic liberalization. It took back some of the power that had been handed down. Permission for Guangdong and Fujian provinces to proceed with special and flexible policies had been stripped down to almost nothing.

Chen Yun played a major role in causing this situation. The trigger was the report of the Central Discipline Inspection Commission, but without Chen Yun's directive in response, there would have been no such campaign. Hu Qiaomu [a conservative Politburo member who had once been Mao's secretary] also played a very harmful role.

Deng Xiaoping perhaps did not realize the seriousness of the matter, because he had always tried to manage reform with one hand while curbing economic crimes with the other. He did not seem aware of how seriously this campaign could impact the overall implementation of reform. Both Yaobang and I were caught in a passive position. Even though the urgent notice was issued by a Secretariat meeting chaired by Yaobang, he was merely executing an order.

Even though the Guangdong and Fujian provinces symposium was held by the two of us and we both spoke at the meeting, we were in a bind. At the meeting, comrades from both provinces expressed deep concerns. They believed that such a campaign would make it difficult to deploy any special policies or flexible measures. On the one hand, both of us had to persuade them to accept the notice passed down by the Central Committee, but on the other hand, we needed to persuade Comrade Chen Yun to protect reform programs as much as possible, to minimize harm to the excellent situation that reforms had brought to the coastal region.

During the proceedings of the meeting, Comrade Chen Yun proposed removing Ren Zhongyi, the Guangdong Provincial Party Committee secretary. He believed that places such as Guangdong and Fujian should not have leaders like Ren Zhongyi, who were "so clever," but should be led instead by people who were very principled, or in Chen Yun's words, "as firm as an unmovable nail."

Yaobang and I repeatedly appealed to him, until Chen Yun finally gave up. One reason was that he could not come up with a suitable replacement on short notice. The one person he proposed for the position was suffering from health problems, so he was forced to give up.

The campaign, which lasted over a year, caused a lot of problems. Some mistakes or shortcomings in people's work were taken as crimes. There were many instances of convictions without a crime and severe punishments for minor infractions. Situations originally viewed as a benefit of reform were treated as profiteering and embezzlement.

For example, these activities were all treated as crimes: technicians working for collectives who had a private business or paid jobs in their spare time; organizations using the extra foreign currency that they had been allowed to keep after exporting goods or trading other currencies; public relations expenses between procurement people and their trading partners. Many people were wrongly convicted. Later, these cases had to be reevaluated and reputations restored.

This led people to start having doubts about the reform. They didn't know what was allowed and what was not. They were confused. Some comrades working in the economic arena had to wait and watch before taking any action. Some procurement personnel and sales staff refused to go out for several months.

As a result of the notice from the Central Committee, people in the disciplinary and organizational agencies around the country who maintained their traditional views and were uncomfortable with reform took it upon themselves to go to factories and enterprises to conduct repeated inspections and investigations, causing tremendous headaches for the businesses. Many reform programs came to a standstill.

In the autumn of 1988, there was concern about a project in Yangpu on Hainan Island.

The Yangpu region was a stretch of barren land. It would have been difficult for us to develop it, but if we rented it to foreign businesses, they would be able to develop it quickly. [Hainan's Party secretary] Xu Shijie and [Hainan's governor] Liang Xiang got in touch with [the Hong Kong subsidiary of Japanese construction company] Kumagai Gumi with such a proposal, and the company agreed to invest several billions.

I reported the Yangpu project to Chen Yun, but he did not express his view. I then reported it to [Deng] Xiaoping, who was very supportive and said that it should be done quickly.

At the time, many people across the country had not yet had a chance to think this thing through. In the past, China had been colonized or half colonized, so people were very sensitive to the issue of sovereignty. Zhang

Wei [vice president of Tsinghua University] had done some research and written a report saying that large areas of land rented out to foreigners were like independent territories within a country, implying a selling out of sovereignty. This became a major issue at the National People's Congress in 1989 and caused quite a disturbance. Xu Shijie gave an explanation at the Congress, but many people did not want to listen to it; their opposition was fierce. I don't know whether the opposition had ulterior motives, but they were determined to cancel the project and wanted to hold the Hainan officials responsible.

When [Party elder] Li Xiannian learned that the Yangpu project was being led by [Vice Premier] Tian Jiyun and had my approval, he wrote a document accusing the project of being "a loss of dignity, an insult to our nation, and a betrayal of our nation's sovereignty." It was another example of Li Xiannian's resistance to reform, and his vigilance in finding opportunities to attack and incite others to oppose me. Prior to this, I had never had any conflicts with Comrade [Party elder] Wang Zhen, and I had always been able to discuss issues with him and win his support. However, the situation changed in 1988 when he began actively opposing me. After June Fourth, he accused me of being a "counterrevolutionary" and the "behind-the-scenes boss for a small gang of conspirators." His change of heart was probably the work of Li Xiannian and Deng Liqun.

Li Xiannian also sent a letter to Comrade Deng Xiaoping condemning the project. Deng was not aware of the details, but after seeing that so many people opposed the matter, he said, "For the time being, this project should not proceed." Just prior to this, Comrade Chen Yun had also forwarded a document to me and had asked me to be "cautious on this matter."

The center of the controversy was the issue of sovereignty, so I had people prepare a detailed document explaining how the development of Yangpu had nothing to do with sovereignty. I sent a letter, along with some information, to Deng. I wrote, "Whether the lease is a good deal or not is something that can be studied. However, this has absolutely nothing to do with sovereignty."

Later, when Deng asked me for details, I said, "Yangpu is a stretch of barren land. If we don't lease it out to foreign businesses, in ten or twenty years, it will still be a stretch of barren land. If we do lease it out, and they are not afraid of investing several billions of Hong Kong dollars, what do we have to fear? It is totally counter to common sense to say that this affects our sovereignty."

Deng replied, "This is a good idea. I wasn't clear about this before."

Later, [the Hainan officials] Liang Xiang and Xu Shijie wrote directly to Deng Xiaoping to explain details of the Yangpu development plan. After Deng read their letter, he forwarded it to me with his comments: "The original accusation was not accurate. I'd said not to proceed for the time being, but if the situation is different, as explained here, then we should proceed with enthusiasm." Even though [Party elder] Wang Zhen had never been enthusiastic about economic reform, after I told him about Deng Xiaoping's comments, he also expressed approval.

In hindsight, it was not easy for China to carry out the Reform and Open-Door Policy. Whenever there were issues involving relationships with foreigners, people were fearful, and there were many accusations made against reformers: people were afraid of being exploited, having our sovereignty undermined, or suffering an insult to our nation.

I pointed out that when foreigners invest money in China, they fear that China's policies might change. But what do we have to fear? For example, there were allegations made that the SEZs would turn into colonies. Macau, they pointed out, had originally been leased to the Portuguese for drying their fishing nets but had eventually turned into their colony. However, the Qing dynasty was corrupt and impotent, and that was not the case with the People's Republic of China. There is only the fear among foreigners that China might change and one day renounce previous agreements and even confiscate their investments. On what grounds do the Chinese fear the foreigners? If they have invested their money in China, what does China have to fear?

Another example of this involved test drilling for offshore petroleum. Foreign capital was needed, but there were too many demands put into the contracts out of fear of being exploited. The approach was too conservative and nitpicked over trivial matters while losing sight of strategic interests.

In general, some people were fearful of being exploited. China had closed its doors for many years in the name of independence and self-reliance, but in fact it was a self-imposed isolation. The purpose of implementing an open-door policy was to conduct foreign trade, to trade for what we needed. Some people felt ashamed about the idea of importing. What was there to feel ashamed about? It wasn't begging! It was a mutual exchange, which was also a form of self-reliance. This issue had caused us to make many costly mistakes. This was a close-minded mentality, a failure to understand how to make use of one's own strengths.

[Premier] Li Peng also was not supportive of the Yangpu project. He issued an order to the Office of SEZs saying that the Yangpu development project should not start without notice from the State Council. As a result the project was shelved. Li Xiannian and Li Peng together damaged the development of Yangpu, and it was very difficult to recover afterward.

I shall talk about another issue related to the real estate market and to attracting foreign businesses for large-scale development: the problem of buying and selling for a quick profit [referred to by skeptics as "profiteering with special license"]. If we could resolve this problem, opening the real estate market would significantly benefit our reform by promoting rapid urban development and an improvement of the investment environment. Treating land as a commodity, making it available for market exchange, and forming a real estate industry—these were major policy issues. For many years, the constitution had restricted land from being transferred or leased, so the issue remained unresolved for a long period of time.

At the beginning of reform, only Shenzhen had land designated for lease, which was leased to Hu Yingxiang [a Hong Kong businessman better known as Gordon Wu] for development. It was the subject of major debate at the time. It was argued that the area designated to foreigners was too large.

During the early days of reform, the first problem in attracting foreigners to open factories and businesses was that our infrastructure was not good enough. In order to build up infrastructure, we needed large investments. Since we did not have this money, things were at an impasse. The development zones began in this way: first, the area was developed, making the land a commodity, then water, electricity, and roads were brought into the area, basic facilities were set up, then factories and office buildings were built. The calculation used at that time was that more than 100 million yuan per square kilometer was required; it's probably more nowadays. Therefore, the pace of creating development zones was very slow.

We also had a similar problem with urban development. We had no funds to build roads for cities or to bring in water and electricity. A lot of land was lying idle.

It was perhaps 1985 or 1986 when I talked to Huo Yingdong [a Hong Kong tycoon better known as Henry Fok] and mentioned that we didn't have funds for urban development. He asked me, "If you have land, how can you not have money?"

I thought this was a strange comment. Having land was one issue; a lack of funds was another. What did the two have to do with one another? He said, "If municipalities have land, they should get permission to lease some of it, bring in some income, and let other people develop the land."

Indeed, I had noticed how in Hong Kong buildings and streets were constructed quickly. A place could be quickly transformed. But for us it was very difficult.

I thought that what he had said was reasonable, so I suggested that he go to Shanghai and talk to the mayor and Party committee secretaries. I don't know whether he went or not. His view did inspire my thinking. We had land but no funds, while the Hong Kong government auctioned off a piece of land every year, not only bringing in income for the government, but also allowing the area to develop quickly.

I thought about this later when visiting Shanghai. The Pudong area was right across the river from Shanghai's city center. In order to develop Shanghai, building up this area would require less investment and be more efficient. It was an extremely good location. However, in order to develop this area, we needed a huge amount of funds to build infrastructure and then attract foreign businesses.

It was around 1987 when Shanghai referred a Chinese American, Lin Tung-Yen [the founder of T. Y. Lin International], to speak with me in Beijing. He asked whether it was possible to rent Pudong. The term of the lease had to be long enough: thirty to fifty years. After leasing the land, he would need to have transfer rights. Investors could then get mortgage loans from the banks. I asked him if he thought foreigners would be willing to invest after such a land transfer and what else was needed. He said it was easy and that the conditions of the SEZs were not needed; the conditions for Shanghai's Minhang economic zone were sufficient. I had thought that the conditions offered could be even more preferential than Minhang's, approaching those of the SEZs, so I was indeed interested. Since this Chinese American had been referred by [Shanghai Party chief] Comrade Wang Daohan, I asked Comrade Wang Daohan to take charge of this matter.

Because it was Shanghai, the move was sure to attract everyone's attention. So in order to persuade all sides, I thought that in addition to Wang Daohan, we would also need to include [director of the Shanghai Advisory Committee] Chen Guodong, because of his relationship with Chen Yun. Comrade Chen Yun would find it easier to accept something coming from him. I knew Chen Guodong was cautious and would possibly even have objections to the idea, but that did not matter. It could be studied further. Therefore, I told Comrades Wang and Chen to keep in touch with Lin Tung-Yen.

This was an important matter, because when we had earlier thought about opening up Shanghai, Chen Yun had expressed concerns. He said that in dealing with regions such as Shanghai and Zhejiang, one must proceed with caution, because people in these areas were especially skilled and familiar with capitalist behavior. [Chen Yun himself was a native of Shanghai.] The reform of Shanghai lagged for two reasons. One was that it was a critical region, and the other was Chen Yun's attitude.

This issue was therefore postponed for a long time. I hear that last year [1992]* when Deng Xiaoping took his tour of the southern regions, he remarked that Shanghai's reform had been overly delayed. I agree. If it had been started earlier, the situation would have been quite different.

As early as 1986 or 1987, plans were made to develop Pudong using the method of granting land leases. I had reported the issue of Pudong to Chen Yun, but he did not comment. I also reported it to Deng. He was extremely supportive, saying, "Do it as soon as possible!" But at the time, I felt that since there was not a consensus among the elders, it should be studied further.

There was another case. Wang Jikuan [a consultant for a State Council think tank] reported that an American automobile manufacturer proposed building a car factory in Huiyang, Guangdong Province, that could produce three hundred thousand cars a year. Some of the parts could also be manufactured in China, enough for thirty to forty Chinese factories to be involved in upstream businesses. It was a sole ownership venture that did not require our investment.

I wrote a letter to [Director of the State Planning Commission] Yao Yilin saying that it was a good deal. At that time, many foreign businesses were afraid of China's policy reversals and were afraid to invest, especially in sole ownership ventures. If this case proceeded and did well, it could set a good example.

Yao Yilin, however, was negative about it. He referred the case to the Ministry of Machine Building Industry, but since it had always wanted to build up an independent domestic auto industry, it was against foreign investments in the industry. Yao Yilin agreed and said it should not be permitted. Li Peng immediately took their side, saying that it should not be approved, and then forwarded their report to me.

A very good deal thus ended up scrapped.*

---

* Although Zhao recorded these journals in 1999–2000, he was usually reading from texts that he had prepared in some cases many years earlier.

4

Finding a New Approach

How did a communist leader arrive at the conclusion that China should abandon its centrally planned economic policies and move toward free markets? It started with Zhao's realization, first achieved when he was a provincial administrator working on rural policies, that China's economy was woefully inefficient and needed to be quickly transformed.

I gave a government work report at the [Fourth Session of the Fifth] National People's Congress in November 1981. It was titled "The Current Economic Situation and the Principles for Economic Development." In the report, I proposed that economic development should proceed at a more realistic, more efficient pace and provide people with more concrete gains.

To support this direction, I proposed a ten-point guideline for economic development. This was my first extensive speech about the economy after becoming Premier of the State Council. Some people at the time called it my "administrative principles."

After the Cultural Revolution, while I was working in Sichuan, I intently studied the economy. Two realizations gradually crystallized in my mind. One was that the old ways of conducting economic affairs appeared superficially to develop at an adequate pace, but the resulting efficiency was extremely low. People received no practical gains. The second was that even though the scale of the economy was extremely large, the old methods could not unleash its full potential. A new direction needed to be found that fundamentally reformed the old ways.

In the 1981 government work report, I stated, "The core issue is to improve efficiency in production, construction, distribution, and other aspects of the economy in every possible way."

I then reviewed the problems of our economic development since the establishment of the People's Republic of China. In 1980, as compared with 1952 [the year at which the economy was considered to have fully recovered from civil war], industrial output had grown 8.1 times, GDP had grown 4.2 times, and industrial fixed assets had grown 26 times. However, average consumption had only doubled. It appears that though industrial fixed assets had grown a great deal, industrial output had not grown as much, nor had GDP; average consumption even less. The GDP growth rate was much lower than the growth rate of agricultural and industrial output; the rise in living standards was also significantly lower than GDP growth, yet industrial fixed assets had grown much more.

This showed that our economic efficiency was very low. The improvement in living standards was not commensurate with what people had contributed with their labor. Therefore, I believed that the key problem with our economy was our efficiency and not the nominal speed of production growth.

Later, at the All China Industrial and Transportation Conference held in Tianjin in 1982, I gave a speech on issues of economic efficiency. I pointed out: "The prolonged neglect of efficiency in industrial production, and the blind pursuit of production output and the pace of growth have resulted in many absurd undertakings. Often we have fallen into the situation of 'good news from industry, bad news from sales; warehouses are full and finances show a deficit.' In the end, our banks have had to print money to patch up the holes, bringing harm to the state and the people." I proposed a concept for approaching the economic efficiency issue: "Produce more products that society truly needs, using the least amount of labor and material resources." That is, cut waste as much as possible while increasing social wealth, the key being that the products we make must actually be in demand. Otherwise, increased production just means more waste. There had been too much pursuing rapid production for its own sake. Factories produced large quantities of things that nobody wanted to buy. These were then stored in warehouses and finally ended up as trash.

How could economic efficiency be improved? How could products be made that were suitable to the needs of society? There were many aspects to this, but fundamentally it was related to the economic system. The solution was to adjust the economic structure and reform the system. There was no other way.

The reason I had such a deep interest in economic reform and devoted myself to finding ways to undertake this reform was that I was determined to eradicate the malady of China's economic system at its roots.

Without an understanding of the deficiencies of China's economic system, I could not possibly have had such a strong urge for reform.

Of course, my earliest understanding of how to proceed with reform was shallow and vague. Many of the approaches that I proposed could only ease the symptoms; they could not tackle the fundamental problems.

The most profound realization I had about eradicating deficiencies in China's economy was that the system had to be transformed into a market economy, and that the problem of property rights had to be resolved. That was arrived at through practical experience, only after a long series of back-and-forths.

But what was the fundamental problem? In the beginning, it wasn't clear to me. My general sense was only that efficiency had to be improved. After I came to Beijing, my guiding principle on economic policy was not the single-minded pursuit of production figures, nor the pace of economic development, but rather finding a way for the Chinese people to receive concrete returns on their labor. That was my starting point. Growth rates of 2 to 3 percent would have been considered fantastic for advanced capitalist nations, but while our economy grew at a rate of 10 percent, our people's living standards had not improved.

As for how to define this new path, I did not have any preconceived model or a systematic idea in mind. I started with only the desire to improve economic efficiency. This conviction was very important. The starting point was higher efficiency, and people seeing practical gains. Having this as a goal, a suitable way was eventually found, after much searching. Gradually, we created the right path.

5

Zhao and Hu Clash

China's economic system in the early 1980s still has all the signatures of a typical socialist economy: production quotas are handed down to every unit. As Premier, Zhao Ziyang tries to move away from this outmoded approach, but in this arena he clashes with his ally, Party General Secretary Hu Yaobang.

The conflict highlights that there is no clear delineation between the Party chief's duties and the Premier's responsibilities as head of government. In theory, Zhao, as head of the State Council, should manage economic affairs. In reality, the Party still interferes. This same issue will emerge later when Zhao is General Secretary and Li Peng is Premier.

It is precisely because I disagreed with the old ways of pursuing production figures and speed, and emphasized instead economic efficiency, that [Hu] Yaobang and I clashed on economic issues after I came to Beijing.

The difference of opinion emerged as early as 1982. When Yaobang was in charge of the drafting of the Political Report for the 12th Party Congress, the question arose as to what to say about the economy. Initially, most of the people on the drafting committee had prepared the report according to the basic tone of my 1981 government work report. However, Yaobang disapproved. He proposed a different approach. The drafting process for the sections on the economy was stymied.

When the problem was reported to Deng Xiaoping, he decided that the economic section should in fact be drafted along the lines of the government work report. Yaobang reluctantly accepted.

Since I had not participated in the drafting process, I did not know how many conflicts of opinions had arisen. The issues weren't raised at Politburo Standing Committee meetings or Secretariat meetings, so I wasn't sure what views Yaobang had or why he disagreed with my government work report.

From his comments and actions, however, it seemed that he mainly disagreed with my idea of emphasizing economic efficiency instead of production figures and speed. Whenever he talked about economic issues, he emphasized growth in terms of volume and speed of output, rarely mentioning efficiency. He often talked of "quadrupling" or "quadrupling ahead of schedule."

My proposal to "guarantee 4 percent and pursue 5 percent growth" in the sixth Five-Year Plan was a moderate goal. Even though Comrade Xiaoping also regarded output values as extremely important, often asking about the annual growth rate, he expressed an understanding of my view of focusing on efficiency. Nevertheless, Yaobang disagreed. Even though the report to the 12th Party Congress was drafted according to Deng's directive and followed the basic tone of the government work report, his [Hu's] mind was not changed.

After the 12th Party Congress, when he went out to the provinces, he was even more determined to emphasize lifting production targets. Wherever he went, he called for "quadrupling ahead of schedule." He praised any situation where production targets were high, and harshly criticized any that was not, without giving attention to economic efficiency or analyzing the specific reasons for the differences in growth.

As a result, local officials acted according to Yaobang's directive, demanding funds, permission for projects and more energy, as well as raw materials and supplies from the Planning Commission and the State Council. For a period of time, the competition was fierce among the different regions for rapid growth and in the demand for raw materials and funds. I found many things difficult to manage.

In 1983, the difference between Yaobang and me on this issue grew more apparent. He even deployed mass campaigns for economic development. For example, wherever he went, he actively promoted a campaign to "increase average annual rural incomes by one hundred yuan," which was initiated in Boding District in Hebei Province. He believed that incomes would grow at a pace of one hundred yuan per year, for as many years as the campaigning was done. In the past, we had suffered because of these kinds of methods, which could so easily turn into empty formalism.

During my visit to Africa in January 1983, Yaobang put out a report in which he proposed borrowing the rural land contract scheme for use in urban reform. In principle, that was fine. However, urban conditions were much more complicated. What form the contracts would take for different industries and enterprises, and how to "contract out"—all of this needed to go through experimentation and proceed gradually. We could not contract out everything, nor move on all fronts at once.

After Yaobang's speech, some of the state-owned department stores in Beijing started to contract out. Immediately there were instances of arbitrary price rises and "bulk sales." What were these bulk sales? They referred to state-owned department stores selling wholesale to individual retailers who would profit from reselling to consumers at a higher price. The state-owned department stores appeared to be selling large volumes of products quickly, completing their task of contracting out. That is not the way commerce should be conducted.

As soon as I returned from Africa, I put a stop to this. I suggested that urban reform must be done through experimentation, and must be gradual. That same year, during the Spring Festival of 1983, I spoke about this at the celebration assembly. At the time, Yaobang was spending his Spring Festival in Hainan. He said to cadres there, "'Doing it all at once'?" he asked, "In fact the situation is more like 'nobody moves even when you push!'"

During this time, when he went to the provinces for inspection tours, he often criticized or made comments that implied criticism of the economic work being conducted by the State Council. These remarks were taken down in notes and spread around, which meant people became aware of the differences between Yaobang and me on economics.

Deng Xiaoping learned of this situation. On March 15, 1983, Deng asked Yaobang and me to his home for a talk. I spoke about my views and reported on the economy while Yaobang listened calmly. He expressed his agreement with some of my points and provided his explanations of others. The talk went relatively well. In the end, Deng Xiaoping said that he supported my views on economic issues. He criticized Yaobang for speaking too carelessly and not being sufficiently prudent and said that it was a serious shortcoming for a General Secretary to pull stunts.

Deng also said, "Mass campaigns should not be used in implementing reform. Reform must go on throughout the process of the Four Modernizations.* It is not an issue that can be resolved in a few short

---

*   The Four Modernizations identified the primary areas where Deng Xiaoping hoped to advance reforms and develop China's economy. The four fields were agriculture, industry, technology, and defense.

years." He also said, "The situation is very good, but we must keep our heads cool."

In order to avoid the occurrence of different voices coming out of the central leadership, a rule was set in this conversation: the State Council and the Central Economic and Financial Leading Group were in charge of economic affairs. Important decisions and orders, as well as judgments about what was right or wrong, were to be discussed by the leading group and issued through its channels. There would be no multiple spokesmen or policies being issued from different places. Certainly the Secretariat would manage some economic affairs, but mainly concerning principles and major policies. It was not to intervene in specific economic tasks.

After this talk, Yaobang's direct interventions in the State Council's economic affairs declined, and his criticisms of the State Council lessened. But deep in his heart, he had not given up his views. He continued to voice his opinions.

After the talk we had with Comrade Xiaoping, I felt that things were easier to manage. From then on, my approach was to accept whatever I could. That is, I would follow his [Hu's] ideas whenever I thought they were correct. If what he said was impractical, he still had the right to express his opinion. But since his views did not represent the collective decision, we were not forced to follow everything he said. Yaobang knew this, because of our talk with Deng. He still had ideas that I didn't agree with, but if we did not act in accordance with them, he didn't insist.

Important economic proposals or opinions from State Council studies were given to the Politburo Standing Committee [PSC] or the Secretariat for discussion. Sometimes, even though Yaobang did not agree, it was not easy for him to voice opposition. He would say, "Fine, so be it." But afterward, he told [PSC member Hu] Qili, "This was a coerced signature. We don't even know what the State Council discussed on this matter, so we have no other choice but to agree." In the 1960s, when Chairman Mao was not satisfied with the State Planning Commission, he had similarly used phrases such as "coerced signature." With Yaobang expressing similar sentiments, I had to pay attention.

In order to improve communication with Yaobang, I suggested that when the State Council and the Central Economic and Financial Leading Group were holding discussions, we invite Hu Qili and [Deputy Director of State Planning] Hao Jianxiu and other comrades from the Secretariat to participate, so they could report on the discussions to Yaobang. I also suggested to Yaobang that he send staff to sit in on meetings of the State

Council and the Central Economic and Financial Leading Group. However, for reasons that I don't know, Yaobang did not do this.

I also proposed that for major economic issues that were about to be put into formal discussion by the Standing Committee and the Secretariat, reports could be made to Yaobang personally beforehand, for the sake of better communications and to give him enough time for careful consideration. Yaobang agreed with the idea of our reporting to him before going to the Politburo Standing Committee. In the beginning, he seemed engaged, but after several occasions he lost interest and asked for it to be stopped. This issue was never resolved.

It seems that the fundamental issue concerned the differing directions in thinking about economic issues, including the difference in working styles. Yaobang could not force his opinions on the State Council and the Central Economic and Financial Leading Group, because Xiaoping had set down the rules. So perhaps the problem could not be resolved through better communications or by having him participate in the State Council's discussions on economic affairs.

Even though this problem persisted, after the talk at Deng Xiaoping's place, we both were careful about how we dealt with one another, and our relationship did not become too tense. At least from the outside, there were no longer two noticeable voices on economic issues.

6

Playing a Trick on a Rival

Deng Xiaoping famously declares that he wants "no squabbling"
among Party leaders. Yet fundamental differences persist over the
pace and direction of reform. Zhao reveals how, since open debate
isn't permitted, indirect means are required to resolve conflicts.

Zhao describes how he used a semantic trick to overcome
opposition from leftist Party elder Chen Yun, thus freeing himself to
ignore Chen's desire to retain a greater role for state planning in the
economy. Zhao has no regrets, believing he has done the right thing
for China's development.

Comrade Deng Xiaoping had long emphasized the power of the market. "Socialism does not exclude a market economy," he said. He
repeated the message many times. He said that, in combining planned
and market economies, we could be flexible as to which was actually
playing the leading role. The Decision on Economic Reform passed at the
Third Plenum of the 12th Central Committee [in 1984] stressed the importance of the natural laws of supply and demand and the power of the
market. It defined the economy of socialism as that of the "commodity
economy."*

Deng thought highly of this decision, and even regarded it as a "new
theory of political economy." In a private conversation I had with Deng in
1988, in referring to the ideas of [Party elders] Chen Yun and Li Xiannian,
Deng said that our economy was modeled after that of the Soviet Union.
But since the Soviets themselves had abandoned the model, why should

---

* "Commodity economy" was a euphemism for "market economy" to avoid ideological conflicts in the early stages of economic reform in China.

we still hold on so tightly? Of course, by 1992, Deng had expressed this opinion more clearly in his talks. Even though he said different things at different times, he was always inclined toward a commodity economy, the laws of supply and demand, and the free market.

Comrade Hu Yaobang was similarly unenthusiastic about the planned economy. According to my observations, he believed it was the highly concentrated top-down planning model that had limited people's motivation and creativity and restricted self-initiative at the enterprise and local levels. He believed that building a socialist society entailed allowing people, enterprises, and local governments to act independently, while the state continued to direct and mobilize them with social campaigns.

Chen Yun and Li Xiannian, however, emphasized the importance of a planned economy, especially Chen Yun, whose views had not changed since the 1950s. He included the phrase "planned economy as primary, market adjustments as auxiliary" in every speech he gave. The tone of his speeches didn't change even after reforms were well under way. His view was that dealing with the economy was like raising birds: you cannot hold the birds too tightly, or else they will suffocate, but nor can you let them free, since they will fly away, so the best way is to raise them in a cage. This is the basic idea behind his well-known "Birdcage Economic Model."

He not only believed that China's first Five-Year Plan was a success, but also, until the end of the 1980s, he believed that a planned economy had transformed the Soviet Union in a few decades from an underdeveloped nation into a powerful one, second only to the United States. He saw this as proof that economic planning could be successful. He believed that the reason China had not done well under a planned economy was mainly the disruption caused by Mao's policies, compounded by the destructive Cultural Revolution. If things had proceeded as they had in the first Five-Year Plan, the results would have been very positive.

In terms of foreign affairs, Chen Yun retained a deep-rooted admiration for the Soviet Union and a distrust of the United States. His outlook was very different from that of Deng Xiaoping, and there was friction between the two.

In the 1980s, [economic adviser] Ivan Arkhipov came to China. The Soviet Union sent him to help China with economic planning, and he had a good relationship with Chen Yun. Deng gave Chen Yun talking points for his meeting with him and ordered him to follow them. Xiaoping was worried about what Chen Yun might say to Arkhipov and feared it might cause confusion on foreign policy. Chen Yun was reluctant but followed the orders. [General chief of staff of the People's Liberation Army]

Xu Xiangqian held similar views. He also believed that, after all, the Soviet Union was a socialist country, while the United States was an imperialist nation.

As we were starting to carry out the rural household land contract plan, Chen Yun gave a speech at the Rural Work Session meeting in December 1981. He said that the rural economy must also be mainly planned, with market adjustments as auxiliary. Grains, cotton, tobacco, and other crops should have quotas set for planting areas. Pig farming should also be assigned target figures.

During the Chinese New Year holiday in January 1981, Chen Yun again gathered leaders in the State Planning Commission to talk about strengthening economic planning, and then released the news to the newspapers. He said that because economic planning was unpopular, it had become difficult to carry out the work of the Planning Commission, but that the planned economy should not be forsaken.

For the Third Plenum of the 12th Central Committee in October 1984, Comrade Chen Yun submitted a written statement. Even though he still insisted we were right to disregard laws of supply and demand in our food production policies in the 1950s, he did agree with the draft of the Decision on Economic Reform that was proposed to the Plenum.

Before the draft was submitted to the Plenum, I wrote a letter to the Politburo Standing Committee about economic reform. Deng Xiaoping, Chen Yun, and Li Xiannian all expressed their approval. Chen Yun even wrote in his statement that because of the expansion of the scale of our economy, many practices of the 1950s were no longer feasible. I think his statement was a good one: he was supporting the idea of reform. Nevertheless, at a national conference in September 1985, he again stated, "The economy must be based on 'planned economy as primary, market adjustments as auxiliary,' a phrase that has not gone out of style."

This statement could have constituted a problem. The expression had been used in the years before the Third Plenum of the 12th Central Committee, but since then the decision to reform had been made, and we had agreed that the socialist economy was a commodity economy and that we must fully realize market potential. We had also discarded the idea that "planning comes first, pricing comes later," which Mao had upheld. How could we still say "planned economy as primary, market adjustments as auxiliary"? It was clear that if the statement were to be circulated, it would conflict with the decision made at the Third Plenum of the 12th Central Committee.

Chen Yun sent me the draft of his speech for review, and I felt uneasy reading it. His speech was an obvious retraction of his statement at the

Party Congress a year earlier. If he proceeded with this speech, it was sure to cause confusion at the conference. Yet I also knew that because he had already written it, even though it hadn't been delivered it would be impossible to persuade him to change his view.

I visited him at his home and suggested that he add a paragraph: "The so-called 'market adjustments as auxiliary' applies to the scope of production in which the level is set in accordance to market demand without planning. It is an adjustment free of planning." He himself had used similar expressions in the 1950s, so he gladly accepted my suggestion and asked his secretary to add it to his speech immediately.

Why did I make such a suggestion? Because by adding this phrase, we could limit the scope of "market adjustments as auxiliary" to small commodities that were free of state planning. We would not include the large bulk of commodities, referred to by the Third Plenum of the 12th Party Congress as "indirectly planned," that followed market demand.

By adding the phrase, commodities were divided into three groups: the first was "planned commodities"; the second "indirectly planned," which included the majority of commodities; the third was the so-called "secondary market-adjusted" small commodities. The latter two groups, which together consisted of at least half of all commodities, were produced according to market demand. By adding the phrase, we could explain all of this, and there would be no apparent contradiction with the Decision on Economic Reform.

Of course, Comrade Chen Yun would not have explained things in this way; he meant something altogether different. But at least we could explain them that way. Without the phrase, he would have simply said "planned economy as primary, market adjustments as auxiliary" and limited the scope of adjustments according to market demand.

It all seems like a game of semantics, but there was nothing else that could have been done. Chen Yun was enormously influential within the Communist Party and in economic policy. If we had distributed his statement without modification, it would have caused major confusion within the Party.

In 1987, I said in the Political Report of the 13th Party Congress that going forward, the economic mechanism should be "the state intervenes in the market, and the market drives the enterprises." Since the overall political climate was very positive toward reform, the drafts of my reports were always sent to Chen Yun for his opinion. Even though he never openly expressed opposition, he never approved, either.

He never again formally expressed his support as he had in the Third

Plenum of the 12th Central Committee. When I was starting to deliver my Political Report at the opening of 13th Party Congress, he got up and left the conference room. This was his way of expressing disapproval of my report. Why do I think so? At the time he was not in bad health, so he should have had no problem staying to listen. By contrast, when I delivered the Ten Strategies for Economic Development after I became the Premier in 1981, at a time when he was not in good health, people tried to persuade him to leave the hall to rest, yet he refused to leave and had said, "I need to listen to the end of Ziyang's report." His action then was a sign of support. In general, Party elders often left a conference during the proceedings, but by contrasting these two incidents, his attitude was clear.

(As an aside: after the June Fourth incident in 1989, Yao Yilin, who regarded Chen Yun as his economic mentor, proposed "breaking out of Zhao Ziyang's policy influence" by publicly condemning the expression "the state intervenes in the market, and the market drives the enterprises.")

I also progressed through stages in my understanding of the planned economy. In the beginning, I was concerned that in a country as big as China, with its divergent conditions and underdeveloped communications and transportation networks, if all commodities from production to distribution were centrally directed and planned, then bureaucratic red tape, breakdowns, and mistakes seemed inevitable.

Later, after I'd come to work at the Central Committee, I realized that economic inefficiencies and the breakdowns between production and consumption had an inherent cause, and that was the planned economy itself. The only way out was to realize market potential by allowing the laws of supply and demand to take effect. I had no idea, though, whether or not we, as a socialist country, could adopt the free-market fundamentals of Western nations.

Because of my uncertainty, in my government work report of 1981 on "Ten Strategies for Economic Development," I divided the planned economic system into four sectors according to the natures of enterprises and commodities. The first sector was defined as production wholly under the control of the state, including key enterprises that formed the backbone of the economy and major commodities essential to people's livelihoods. The second sector was made up of the numerous small commodities produced according to the planning of producers and distributors themselves in response to market forces. I also identified two other sectors: one in which planning played the dominant role while market demands took on a minor, adjusting role; and the other where market forces played the primary role while state planning took on a minor role. At the time these classifications were approved by Chen Yun as well.

When the document drafts for the Third Plenum of the 12th Central Committee were being prepared, I presented the drafting group with several concepts, which later were included in a letter I wrote to the Politburo Standing Committee. These concepts were as follows.

1. The Chinese economy is a planned economy, not the free market economy of the West.
2. The nature of the Chinese economy is a "commodity economy," not a "product economy."*
3. Planning consists of direct planning and indirect planning; direct planning must be reduced as indirect planning is expanded.
4. Indirect planning means mainly responding to market demand with intervention by economic means, while direct planning must also respect the laws of supply and demand.

These concepts were ultimately included in the Decision on Economic Reform passed at the Third Plenum of the 12th Central Committee. After that, the "commodity economy" was clearly defined. Aside from unplanned small commodities, the "indirect planning" sector that was to rely on market adjustments would continue to expand. In this way, the proportion of the Chinese economy that relied on market adjustments would grow.

By the time of my report to the 13th Party Congress, it was clear that the mechanism for the Chinese economy was to be "the state intervenes in the market, and the market drives the enterprises." In other words, we had already realized an economy dependent on free-market principles. It was only because of ideological barriers that the term "free market" wasn't being used.

---

*   This is not consistent with the records as published in "Selection of Important Documents of the Twelfth Party Congress," People's Publishing House (Beijing), 1986, volume 2, p. 535, which says: "Self-initiated production and trade through the free market are limited to small merchandise, three designated categories of agricultural products and services; all of which are auxiliary to the economy."

7

One Step at a Time

There have been two basic approaches to reforming the economies of socialist countries. One involves "shock therapy," changing the rules all at once; the other adopts a far more gradual process. By taking a step-by-step approach, China has largely been able to avoid the economic dislocations experienced in the former Soviet Union and Eastern Europe. Zhao offers insights into how China made that choice.

How did China come to adopt an approach of gradualism? In my ten years running the economy for the Central Committee—until the time that I stepped down—we pursued a gradual transition. There were two major aspects. The first was the emergence of a new, market economy that gradually matured beyond the realm of the planned system. For example, as rural reform got under way, state quotas for mandatory procurement were reduced; as the mandated quantities were reduced, agricultural production increased, so the proportion of the state quotas dropped year after year. There was an increasing quantity of products making it to market.

In 1985, taking things a step further, we eliminated the mandatory procurement program in agriculture, and basically became market oriented, freed from the planned economy, with the exception of a few products like cotton.

The emergence of township and village enterprises, private manufacturing and commercial enterprises, joint ventures and solely owned foreign enterprises—all of these were set up outside the planned economy. Together they formed an economic sector that responded only to market forces. This sector started from nothing, and has experienced vigorous development in recent years, growing at levels far exceeding the state-owned or collectively owned sectors. It has brought prosperity to the Chinese economy and a new economic system: the market economy.

As the market sector grew day by day, China's economic system eventually experienced a qualitative change, even without fundamental reforms of the original economic model of state planning. This is the principal reason that economic reform in China has not only promoted prosperity, but also maintained political stability.

The other important aspect was the reduction of the planned economic sector. The change was not instantaneous. Instead it began with a small number of minor changes, but it gradually involved bigger changes.

Policies and measures were introduced to shift more power to lower levels of administration and expand the autonomy of enterprises. To reform economic planning, there was a gradual reduction of direct planning, an expansion of indirect planning, a reduction in material resources allocated by the state, and an expansion of the types and quantities of products that were traded by state-owned enterprises themselves. Trading was permitted for key material resources beyond the fulfillment of state-allocated quotas, and even within the quota, a portion could be directly traded as well. In addition, we also introduced a contract scheme for enterprises and pricing reform. All of these measures played strong ancillary roles while the market sector continued to grow.

At the time, the major components of the market sector were agriculture, rural products, light industries, textiles, and consumer products. Products involved with the means of production were mostly still controlled by state-owned enterprises.

There have been criticisms of the transitional approach: "no overall strategy," "taking one step and waiting to see what happened," "no foresight," "blind," etc. There are fewer such criticisms these days.

However, there have been shortcomings resulting from the coexistence of the two systems that should not be underestimated. When the negative impacts exceed what society can endure, problems will erupt. Only by achieving further economic and political reforms can such problems be resolved. It was correct to adopt gradualism in the early stages, but that cannot continue over the long term.

8

The Economy Gets Too Hot

In 1984 and again in 1988, China's economy overheats. Zhao justifies his response to the first crisis, contrasting it with the failure of the government's policies four years later. In 1988, following a botched effort to reform the pricing system, the inflation rate shoots up and sparks bank runs and panic buying. Zhao expresses regret for his handling of things.

The economic readjustments made in 1981 reduced the growth rate for agricultural and industrial output to 4 percent. The next year, the economy started to grow faster and eventually got on a healthy track. Economic development in 1983 and 1984 was very good; not only did the economy grow rapidly, but demand and supply were relatively in sync. Various indicators were healthier; economic efficiency had noticeably improved and people's living standards had risen a great deal.

However, starting from the fourth quarter of 1984, the growth rate became excessively high, credit was overextended, and the scale of national infrastructure construction was too great. As a result, prices rose even faster.

In the beginning of 1985, as these signs of overheating emerged, the Central Economic and Financial Leading Group and the State Council tried to cool the economy by strengthening macroeconomic control, reining in credit and lending and reducing infrastructure construction. However, since the banking system had not yet been reformed, control over credit and lending had to be done through administrative means, assigning credit quotas to lower levels.

Reactions from all sides were strong and caused considerable difficulties for the smooth running of the economy. Credit quotas were passed down from the State Council through the Central Bank to provincial and district level branches. As a result, local governments filled their credit quotas with preferred projects, especially special construction projects, and had nothing left for projects that could not afford to be ignored. This forced the central government to raise the credit quota.

For example, as soon as credit controls were imposed, many local governments complained they lacked funds for the annual grain procurement, though they used the assigned credit elsewhere. The credit limits were tightened only to be relaxed soon thereafter.

So in 1985, the growth rate was still exceedingly high, even though macro controls had been implemented in the beginning of the year. The overheating got worse.

How could we handle the situation? Two approaches were considered. We could use the traditional method: repeat the readjustments of 1981 by again putting the brakes on the economy and cutting infrastructure construction.

The other way was to address the problem gradually. The first method would result in great losses all around; and it wasn't practical, since many infrastructure projects had just been resumed after being delayed by the 1981 readjustment. Cutting them again would have caused considerable domestic and international damage. That's why I decided to take measures for a "soft landing," that is, to make gradual adjustments over several years rather than in only one.

A decision was made to continue relatively tight control over credit and financial policies for two more years. Infrastructure construction was to remain at 1985 levels with adjustments made to the priority and timing of specific projects. If the growth rate remained the same for two years, the situation could ease back to normal. With the execution of this plan, overall conditions were good in 1986.

The positive results continued. In 1987, GNP and GDP each expanded by more than 10 percent. Industrial output grew more than 17 percent. Agriculture grew nearly 6 percent. Retail prices rose by 7.3 percent. The situation with fixed-asset investments and infrastructure construction was basically good.

Overall, after two years of the "soft landing" approach, the situation improved. The overall economic environment was no longer tense. When the Central Committee and the State Council reviewed the situation at year's end, they acknowledged that instead of taking abrupt adjustment measures, the "soft landing" method could work.

That was originally the strategy for 1988 as well. When we were discussing plans for 1988 at the national planning work congress in September 1987, I made a speech on behalf of the Central Committee. I pointed out that in order to implement policies for stabilizing the economy—especially the rise in prices—finances and credit needed to be tightened, infrastructure construction needed to be reduced, consumption funds needed to be controlled, and at the same time steady production growth needed to be maintained. The strategy for the economy in 1988 can be summarized in two points: further stabilizing of the economy and deepening of reform.

With the strategy set, why was inflation in 1988 so high, with the retail price index rising 18.5 percent? Since the beginning of reform, this had never happened.

The inflation resulted from a combination of factors. I mentioned then, and I still believe today, that the primary cause was the inappropriate response taken in 1988 to reform the pricing system.

Price reform—the gradual adjustment of the pricing mechanism—is an extremely important issue in economic reform. We had always believed that if pricing were not sorted out, then economic reform could not be accomplished.

After two years of the "soft landing" approach, in 1986 and 1987, the conditions were in place in 1988 for taking a bigger step in reforming the pricing system. However, the proposed reform—"making a breakthrough in the pricing system difficulties"—was all wrong in its guiding principles and in its implementation. The result was a grave error that caused a serious setback for the economy.

How did this occur? As I mentioned before, the "soft landing" policy had originally been expected to continue. But in the spring of 1988, there was a strong reaction to the rise in prices and to the two-track pricing system, which encouraged corruption. Also, Deng Xiaoping had repeatedly urged us to be decisive in price reform, which he believed required a breakthrough, saying, "a quick sharp pain is better than prolonged pain."

With all this in mind, I started to be swayed away from incremental steps and toward the all-at-once idea. Though fixed prices had risen, the situation with incorrect pricing had not changed, so perhaps it was better to make a major adjustment all at once. Over a period of time, say two to three years, we could increase prices at a certain rate, for example 30–50 percent, to bring prices of commodities to reasonable levels and thereby eliminate the twisted and unreasonable pricing system.

After my proposal was passed in principle at the enlarged Politburo Standing Committee meeting in spring of 1988, Yao Yilin was assigned to lead the State Planning Commission in a study of the specifics of implementation. In the summer of 1988, the proposed plan by Yao Yilin and the State Planning Commission was passed, after back-and-forth discussions at an enlarged Politburo Standing Committee meeting in Beidaihe [the beach resort where Party leaders convene each summer]. The implementation was set to begin in the fourth quarter of 1988 or in early 1989, but it was canceled because of high inflation.

Since the Third Plenum of the 12th Central Committee, our strategy for pricing reform had combined readjustments with a relaxation of controls. Some prices were adjusted by the government in a top-down fashion, while others were allowed to adjust according to market forces. The same commodity whose price was set by the government within the planned sector's quota might then be sold in the market at an open price. This was the two-track pricing system.

The intent was to respond to the market and gradually relax price controls, to let the market take over. However, the proposed pricing reform was not in line with the gradual reform strategy but relied on large-scale government-administered price adjustments. This reflected the sentiments of the time: to rush through price reforms, and to eliminate the two-track pricing system in order to unify or at least reduce the gap between set prices and market prices.

This was not the correct way to carry out price reform, because ultimately it was not a shift from price controls to market mechanisms. It was using planning methods to adjust prices. It was still the old way of planned pricing. It is clear now that if high inflation had not occurred, and this price reform plan had been carried out, it would not have resolved the problem and could have set back price reform.

The most direct cause of the high inflation of 1988 was that before plans for price reform had even been drawn up, the media campaign started. All of a sudden, rumors were widespread: "prices will rise by 50 percent, wages will double." The rumors caused a public panic, greatly affecting people's anticipation of rising prices. "Psychological anticipation" was an issue that we did not understand at that time. However, nations with market economies paid a lot of attention to this issue when they needed to control inflation. They tried to find ways to avoid causing an overreaction through "psychological anticipation"; we on the contrary had encouraged and stimulated it.

In the end nothing happened, but people believed that prices were going to rise, and we could not provide reassurances to the contrary by, for example, raising interest rates for bank savings, which would have meant a pledge to people that their bank savings would grow at a rate exceeding inflation; or providing value-guaranteed deposits. While people were anticipating that a big price hike was coming, there were no reassurances given about the interest on their savings, so everyone worried that the rising prices would devalue the years of savings they'd deposited in the bank. Since the Third Plenum of the 11th Central Committee [1978], people who had been living frugally had deposited more than 100 billion yuan into the bank. When they anticipated that their hard-earned savings would be devalued by inflation, they rushed to withdraw their savings from the bank and purchased commodities. This caused bank runs and panic buying in the summer of 1988.

Panic buying for certain supplies had occurred many times in the past, so it was not unfamiliar to us. But this time it was different. In the past, panic buying had been caused by shortages; people were worried about the future availability of soap, table salt, flour. But this time, the purpose of purchasing was not for personal use, but value saving, so the situation was more prevalent and serious than ever before.

Many shops and enterprises raised their prices, and bank savings dropped 40 billion yuan more than anticipated. Banks had to print money to cover withdrawals, resulting in a big increase in currency in circulation.

As soon as the panic buying started, we should have immediately and decisively taken measures to raise deposit interest rates, or announce value-guaranteed deposits. If we had, the situation could have been better and the losses suffered would have been less.

At the time, the Central Economic and Financial Leading Group had proposed the measure to the State Council, but Li Peng and Yao Yilin were worried that raising interest rates on deposits would have resulted in higher interest rates on bank loans to enterprises beyond what enterprises could afford, thereby affecting production. They did not take immediate measures and, as a result, losses that could have been reduced instead continued to grow.

Ultimately, though, they were left with no choice but to take action. After the announcement of value-guaranteed deposits, bank deposits quickly stabilized and gradually bounced back. This proved that when faced with bank runs and panic buying, if we had provided guarantees on savings, we could have greatly reduced the losses.

The high inflation of 1988 saw prices rise by 18.5 percent. The problem was not a loss of control over credits and loans, nor was it overspending on infrastructure. These two factors had not exceeded the limits set under the policy for "soft landing."

The main problem was the drop in savings deposits caused by the mistakes in price reform. In hindsight, if we had continued the policy of mixing readjustments and relaxation of controls, or even if we had moved faster to relax price controls while raising interest rates beyond the level of the price increases to guarantee the value of deposits, then 1988's high inflation might have been avoided.

Facing high inflation and bank runs and panic buying, to quickly stabilize the situation we announced the cancellation of price reform and shifted economic policy to "adjustment and reorganization." These proposals were initiated by me and passed by the Politburo meeting and plenum of the Central Committee. In retrospect, I believe that canceling the price reform package was correct but shifting from the original policy of "stabilizing the economy and deepening reform" to "adjustment and reorganization" was inappropriate.

Even though the proposed "adjustment and reorganization" did help to quickly stabilize the economy, it caused yet another setback to reform.

First of all, in order to slow the rise in prices, almost all of the administrative measures for controlling prices had been restored. Officials at all levels of government were made responsible for the implementation. This meant that years of revitalization had been retracted in favor of the old ways of price controls.

In the name of "adjustment and reorganization," Li Peng and others at the State Council took back power that previously had been handed down to lower levels and put controls back on measures that had been freed. Everything was going in the opposite direction set by reform, setting back what had already been reformed in the economic system. Precisely for this reason, in less than a year there was an economic recession and market slump, and other serious economic problems continued until Comrade Xiaoping's speech during his tour to the south [in 1992].

In summary, we made one mistake after another. I learned a very profound lesson from this.

In the spring of 1989, I sent Comrade An Zhiwen [deputy director of the State Commission for Economic Reform] and other comrades to Hong Kong and invited some economists to discuss China's problems. Six economists participated, all members of the Taiwan Academia Sinica. They included the chief of the Chung-Hwa Institution for Economic Research, Tsiang Sho-Chieh, who had tremendous influence in Taiwan.

During the discussion, they expressed opinions on the inflation of 1988. First, they agreed that the mainland had achieved a great deal during the ten years of reform, and that even though there were problems, from an economic point of view they were not serious, including the 18.5

percent rise in the price index. If appropriate measures were taken, they were resolvable.

Second, on price reform, they believed that economic development needed to obey market rules, regardless of the political system. Since inflation had worsened last year, there was talk of price reform being slowed down and a return to administrative control over some prices. However, though it was understandable for this action to be taken as a temporary measure, it should not be in place for long. If the incorrect pricing system were not reformed, the economy could not continue to run. The way out was the balance between supply and demand, and to bring the currency under control. Under these conditions, most commodity prices could be relaxed, while a small portion of prices, such as for public services, could be determined by the government according to a certain profit ratio. They emphasized that pricing must be decided by the market. Otherwise, there would never be correct pricing.

Another issue they discussed was the policy for tackling inflation. They believed that the reason for the mainland's inflation was mainly the fiscal and financial deficit and that the key to resolving this was raising the interest rate above the growth rate of the price index and letting it float freely according to the market's supply and demand for currency. This would yield benefits in increased savings and controlling the size of loans.

After I read the recommendations of Tsiang Sho-Chieh and the others, I referred the summary to Comrade Xiaoping and ordered the State Economic Reform Commission to organize relevant agencies to discuss the issue.

I had intended to reevaluate our entire approach to the economy and price reform, but because of the student demonstrations, this matter was set aside.

9

The Magic of Free Trade

Restoring foreign trade is one of the crucial steps in transforming the Maoist economy of "self-reliance." Zhao's experiences as a provincial administrator have made him an outspoken advocate of free trade. Still, how is it possible that Zhao, a product of the Maoist era, has such confidence in Western economic principles? Zhao reveals his thinking and argues that reforms have simply made China smarter.

For many years, our economic development efforts yielded poor results. They demanded a great deal of effort while providing few rewards. Besides the economic system, there were other problems, such as the closed-door policy, which made self-reliance an absolute virtue. It became an ideological pursuit and was politicized.

Consider agriculture, for example: if it is to achieve efficiency, the first principle should be to apply the strengths of local land conditions. One should plant whatever is most suitable to the land. However, for a long period of time, we were not allowed to do that.

One incident in particular had a profound impact on my thinking. In 1978 [actually 1979], when I was still working in Sichuan, I led a delegation to visit England and France, and stopped in Greece and Switzerland on my way back.

I arrived first in southern France on the coast of the Mediterranean Sea, a region world-renowned for economic development. The climate there was very dry and no rain falls in the summer. Under such conditions, according to our past way of thinking, in order to plant crops we would "change the conditions defined by heaven and earth" by creating huge irrigation projects. They did no such thing, but instead planted grapes and other crops that were suited to the dry climate. The result was the natural formation of the French wine industry. The farmers there are very wealthy.

I saw another example in England, where wheat was growing very well along the east coast, while the west coast was covered with meadows. It was my first trip abroad and, puzzled by the scene, I asked the reason. I was told that there was enough sunlight on the east coast to make it suitable for wheat, while the west coast had plentiful rainfall but less sunlight and was better for grass. Hence the development there of animal husbandry, cattle raising, and milk production.

On my way back through Greece, comrades in the embassy accompanied me for a tour of the hilly regions where the weather was dry and there was no rainfall in the summer. According to our approach, the conditions would have been considered very tough for agriculture. We would have replicated the Dazhai model,* using terraced fields and irrigation projects. But they did not do that. The hills were covered with olive trees and the olive oil industry flourished. The farmers' living standards were high. Why were they able to do this? Because they were not living in an autarky, but instead relied on trade with the outside world and utilized their strengths to export their goods in exchange for what they needed.

In 1981, after I had come to work in Beijing, I went to Lankao County [in Henan Province] and spoke with farmers there. It was a sandy region, capable of high yields of peanuts. But since the policy was to make grain production a priority while focusing on self-reliant food production, they were not allowed to plant peanuts, but instead planted corn. Their corn yields were low, and the farmers were highly critical of the policy.

Another example was the northwest region of Shandong Province, where the soil had a high alkali salt content. Most of the region was suitable for cotton growing at considerably high yields. But for years, policy had prevented them from growing cotton, allowing only wheat. The result was that the more wheat they planted, the lower yields they got and the more likely the farmers were to be starving.

In 1983, I spoke with comrades in Shandong and asked if they could plant cotton. They said the problem was a lack of grains. Later, we decided that northwest Shandong should switch to planting cotton. They would sell cotton to the state (at the time, the state was importing large

---

* Dazhai was the name of a mountainous village in Shanxi Province that became a model for self-reliant agricultural production during Mao's time. Skeptics later questioned its purported accomplishments.

quantities of cotton) and in return the state would provide them with grain supplies.

The result was that it took only one to two years for them to overturn a difficult economic situation and attain high yields in their cotton production. For a time, cotton flooded the market, resulting in oversupply. The farmers' incomes quickly increased and rural conditions greatly improved. Their cotton production also yielded a by-product: cotton seeds. What was left over after extracting for cottonseed oil became fertilizer. The land that was not high in alkali salt continued to plant wheat and also saw an increase in yields from the supply of fertilizers. Everyone benefited.

Local folklore held that "one *mu* of wheat will feed all, half a *mu* of cotton yields extra."* Before, when they planted one and a half *mu* of wheat, they were hardly able to feed themselves; later, one *mu* of cotton was enough and they were even able to sell the extra back to the state.

Shandong and Lankao were able to plant what was suited to their environment because we were practicing the open-door policy and importing large amounts of wheat from abroad—as much as several tens of millions of tons annually during those years. So long as we allowed farmers to plant whatever was appropriate and had the highest yields, agriculture improved. Without the open-door policy, we would have been forced to produce everything ourselves, and if we remained fixated on self-reliance, nothing could have happened.

One reason that huge efforts yielded measly results in agriculture was public ownership. The other was the self-imposed autarky that prevented us from taking advantage of the land and resulted in "double efforts yielding half the results." For years we forced the planting of wheat in areas that were not suited to wheat production, so we had to make great efforts to build agricultural infrastructure and irrigation projects. Some of the projects were indeed necessary, but if we could have utilized the natural advantages of the land, we wouldn't have needed them all. Also, the irrigation system could have been more efficient, and focused on places where it was most needed.

The same was true in industry. Our industrial development strategy in the past was "Don't start cooking without first having rice." We attempted to start everything from the very beginning, down to the raw materials.

For example, in steel manufacturing, we started first with the search

* A *mu* is a Chinese unit of area equal to 0.167 acres.

and selection of iron mines, then coal, railroad building, iron smelting, steelmaking and processing, and finally the building of machinery. But we have only low-quality iron mines with a low percentage of iron. Many tons had to be mined to yield one ton of iron. Our main iron and coal mines were in the west, so long-distance transportation was required. Imagine how long it took to build a steelmaking firm; the scope of the infrastructure; the length of time for investments to yield a return; how much of the investment could be recovered.

With reform, we are much smarter. We import ore from Canada and Australia, where it is cheap and high in quality; transportation by ship is cheaper than by train. Some coastal cities can handle downstream processes, starting with steel rolling. Where do they get the ingots? From imports. As soon as processing started, there were profits. The investment was quickly recovered from the revenue, which was then invested in upstream steel processes and in the importing of iron from abroad.

The production of synthetic fibers had the same problem. Previously, if we were to produce synthetic fibers, we had to first start with oil production and oil refineries before making synthetic fibers. Later, some of the synthetic fiber factories started with production first, then proceeded with upstream processes afterward. In 1981, during the adjustment period, we had imported a set of synthetic fiber production lines, from raw material processing to wiredrawing. It was put on hold. When it was resumed we were already smarter, so we started with the wiredrawing process for the end product. This was how Yizheng Synthetic Fiber Factory of Jiangsu Province started. It grew quickly and soon had revenue that it reinvested in upstream processes.

All of this illustrates that only under the conditions of an open-door policy could we take advantage of what we had, and trade for what we needed. Each place and each society has its strengths; even poor regions have their advantages, such as cheap labor. That is a great advantage in international competition.

The result of doing everything ourselves was that we were not doing what we did best. We suffered tremendous losses because of this. I now realize more and more that if a nation is closed, is not integrated into the international market, or does not take advantage of international trade, then it will fall behind and modernization will be impossible.

10

Freedom on the Farm

*To lift living standards in some of China's poorest areas, the
government reintroduced the rural household land contract scheme*
in the early years of reform, which brought back economic incentives, a vital step in China's reforms. With all land owned by the
government, the basic premise of the scheme was to contract land
to individual farming families to allow them a degree of freedom
and incentive to work the land.*

*Party veteran Liu Shaoqi had once supported the idea to
counter the effect of Mao's radical policy of creating people's
communes. Since Liu ultimately lost in a political showdown with
Mao, the rural household contract scheme remained a sensitive
policy issue. Many Party cadres knew from experience that it had
lifted agricultural output, but few dared to openly support it.*

*The result of the scheme for the rural economy was the complete
dismantling of Mao's people's communes, which freed more than
800 million farmers. Zhao's early support helps open the door to his
promotion to central positions overseeing reform.*

No one had foreseen how good the results would be or that the
changes would be so dramatic. No one had planned on implementing the rural household land contract (RHLC) scheme nationwide or even
spreading it to most of the rural areas. It was a step-by-step process by
which we continuously deepened our understanding.

In the revised Working Rules of People's Communes passed by the

---

* The "rural household land contract scheme" is also known as the "rural household responsibility system."

Third Plenum of the 11th Central Committee [in 1978], called the "Sixty-Item Regulation," the item about management and operations clearly stated that no household land contracts were permitted, that is, land would not be divided up by households.

In September 1979, the Fourth Plenum's "Decision on Accelerating Rural Development" similarly stated, "Division of land by household or household land contracts are not allowed except when special conditions are required for certain industrial crops, or when an individual household is located in a remote mountain region without convenient transportation." At my suggestion, the original text "are not allowed" was changed to "are not encouraged." In general, we still believed that household land contracts should not be pursued, though the tone was not as rigid.

Contracting land to groups of households and to individual households was first initiated by the farmers themselves, in poor rural regions. It started in Anhui and Sichuan provinces. At the time, allowing such contracts in poor regions did not cause much controversy.

In 1960, when the economy was suffering, [Anhui Party chief] Zeng Xisheng applied the "designated land responsibility system" in Anhui. I applied a "payment proportional to production responsibility system" in Guangdong [where Zhao was then a senior official]. Henan Province had applied a "land borrowing scheme"; Zhangjiakou in Hebei Province had applied a "group land contract scheme," and other places had used various forms of the idea. All of these places were able to increase production and ease the acute food shortages of that time. Therefore, the schemes were recognized by many officials for having increased production and improved a difficult situation. Since the Cultural Revolution was over and our policy had shifted toward economic development and promoted the ideas of "emancipating the mind" and "practice is the sole criterion of truth," people were less fearful and able to think more realistically.

At that time, I envisioned that the nation's rural regions could be divided into three categories: first, the areas where public ownership was relatively stable, production levels and living standards were high, and the scale of public property was big or collective enterprises had been developed; second, the middle group; and third, the areas where productive forces were seriously damaged and people were on the verge of starvation.

I believed that people in the third category most urgently needed the household land contract scheme, which was the fastest and most effective way to change things. In 1980, after I started working in the central government, I suggested in a meeting that the household land contract scheme be started in the poorest rural communes, which altogether included about 100 million people. This was a major policy decision, meant to stabilize rural regions and allow farmers to recuperate. It even gained support from [Director of the State Planning Commission] Yao Yilin. As for the second category, I believed we could wait and see whether or not to proceed with the scheme. As for the first category, I didn't think there would be any demand for it.

The intraparty dispute over the household land contract scheme became public when it was about to be expanded from the third to the second category of rural regions. Those who were opposed took issue with the basic principle.

[Politburo member] Hu Qiaomu asked me to be cautious. He said, "The household land contract scheme of Anhui has already spread from north of the Huai River to the south. Even Wuhu County, a bountiful land, has implemented the household land contract scheme." He was clearly opposed. [Party elder] Li Xiannian came back from a trip to Jiangsu Province complaining about the RHLC scheme of Anhui under the pretext of reporting the opinions of the Jiangsu provincial party committee. [Vice Premier] Wang Renzhong also opposed the RHLC scheme. He was former chief of the State Agricultural Commission, and as early as 1979 had asked the *People's Daily* to publish a letter, purportedly from Luoyang [a city in Henan], criticizing individual household and group household land contracts. Shanxi Province had opposed the relaxation of rural policies and criticized the reforms of Anhui and Sichuan provinces even earlier. In 1978 and 1979, they flooded the newspapers with critical articles.

At that time, [Mao's short-lived successor] Hua Guofeng did not support RHLC schemes, either. He believed that the rural areas, especially in the south, required collective operations in order to carry out everything: from harvesting the crops in the fields to threshing, drying, and transportation.

Chen Yun had not directly expressed whether he supported or opposed it. Once, he sent some people to ask me: there were often rains during the harvest season in the south, so if the drying process was not fast enough, the grain would grow moldy—had this problem occurred since the start of the household land contract scheme? After looking into it, I replied to him that after the introduction of the contracts, the process was running even smoother than before. He did not make any further comments.

The first secretary of Heilongjiang Province also opposed the household land contracts. At a rural administration meeting held by the Central Committee at which many provincial leaders expressed their support for the scheme, he famously said, "You go ahead and walk on your broad highway; I will continue to walk on my single-plank bridge." He meant that even if all the other provinces carried out the household land contract scheme, Heilongjiang Province would not follow suit.

The first secretary of Fujian Province also opposed the scheme, resulting in a major rift with the other standing secretaries in his province. Shaanxi's first secretary prohibited the scheme from being used in the province's Guanzhong area. Both the first secretary and the governor of Hebei Province opposed the scheme. The governor of Hebei was the former standing secretary of Shaanxi Province. When this comrade was working in Shaanxi and other regions were starting to relax rural policies, he, on the contrary, moved accounting management from the production team level up to the division level.

Implementing the household land contract scheme nationwide would not have been possible without Deng Xiaoping's support. The fact that it did not meet much resistance from central leaders had a lot to do with Deng's attitude. Though he did not comment much on this issue, he always showed support for views held by me, [Hu] Yaobang, and Wan Li. He said he was pleased with the changes that had taken place after the implementation of the household land contracts. In 1981, some of the farmers in the disaster area of Dongming County in Shandong Province jointly wrote a letter to Deng Xiaoping to express their gratitude, saying they now had food to eat, thanks to household land contracts. He forwarded this letter to all central leaders.

In early January 1981, I traveled to Lankao in Henan Province, Dongming in Shandong Province, and other poor rural areas. I saw with my own eyes the changes that had taken place as a result of the household land contracts in these regions and experienced the warm support of the local cadres and the people. It made an extremely deep impression on me. When the cadres expressed the people's wishes to renew the household land contracts for another three years, I immediately replied, "Yes." Even though I had not instantly changed my opinion that the household land contract scheme was to be only a temporary solution, I was moved to believe that this issue needed reevaluation.

Upon returning to Beijing, I briefed Deng Xiaoping, Hu Yaobang, and other central leaders on what I had seen. There was no doubt that the household land contract scheme had helped increase production and raised farmers' living standards.

However, it was impossible not to wonder whether family-run small-scale operations could sustain the continued development of agriculture. The key issue was how to integrate the enthusiasm of individual contract holders with the need for developing commercial and large-scale production operations, to avoid having agriculture turn into a small-scale farming economy. I thought the household enterprise contract held promise as a solution to this. This scheme grew out of the practical experience of cadres and citizens and was later called "individual contracts combined with joint operations."

Another issue was the emergence of rural household enterprises. When I visited Western Europe in 1978 [actually 1979], I noticed that many of the agricultural operations there were not very big. Many were small farms. Whatever issues they couldn't tackle by themselves, they did through cooperative associations. The results could be as good as any large-scale operation. Switzerland, especially, left me with a deep impression. My previous belief that high agricultural productivity required large-scale operations had started to change. I no longer saw the implementation of household land contracts in joint productions in the rural regions as implying a return to the past to a small-scale agricultural economy.

As far back as when I was in Sichuan, I had promoted contracting out planting, and the farming of fish, flowers, and herbs to people with special expertise and management skills. I later visited many chicken, pig, and dairy farms as well as agricultural produce processing facilities and rural sewing businesses. In 1981, when I visited Shanxi on an inspection tour, I commented that the emergence of private rural household enterprises marked the beginning of a rural merchandise economy.

The transformation of the nationwide system of a three-tiered ownership of people's communes into the RHLC schemes was a major policy change and a profound revolution. It took less than three years to accomplish this smoothly. I believe it was the healthiest major policy shift in our nation's history. It was conducted even while most of the leaders and cadres remained skeptical. However, not one person was punished, nor any senior leader openly criticized. Of course, two years later, some provinces still sent people out to prevent the implementation of household land contracts, and at that point we issued administrative orders to stop them.

As the implementation of the RHLC scheme expanded, starting from the grassroots and spreading upward, its superiority as a system became increasingly obvious. The vast majority of leaders and cadres gradually came around from their original opposition. This was a significant development, and an experience worth learning from.

During this major policy change, the central government did not apply uniform standards and issue unified directives. Local governments were free to choose whether to implement and how. Both the "broad highway" and the "single-plank bridge" were permitted. Local leaders were told not to intervene when people initiated household land contracts themselves. Meanwhile, the central government made an effort to study the overall situation and learn from its achievements before providing guidance.

The adaptation of this method yielded great benefits and did not slow the speed at which changes were taking place. Since the power to choose was given to local leaders and cadres, and they were given time to make their choice (time enough to shift from unwilling to willing), the shifts occurred voluntarily. This reduced the possibility of conflicts and negative effects. It gave local authorities enough time to make a choice, to realize the superiority of the schemes and to figure out how to adopt them to their own development conditions. As it moved from the poorest regions to average and wealthier ones, the policy was gradually perfected.

I mentioned above that I was enthusiastic about the system of rural household enterprise contracts. My views on this were fully expressed in the documentation of a meeting of provincial and municipal first secretaries on the household land contract scheme, held in September 1980. The summary was distributed nationwide on September 29, 1980, by the Central Committee.

The summary indicated, "The Specialized Household Contracts System is one in which, under the management of the production team, those with expertise in agricultural production will be assigned land contracts; those with expertise in planting, animal husbandry, fishing, and mercantile operations will be assigned specialized contracts for their group or household." The guiding principle was to utilize the incentive of individual contracts while avoiding the paltry returns of the small-scale agricultural economy where one family does everything.

However, this idea [introducing incentives for large-scale and specialized agricultural operations] was not realized because it failed to recognize the fact that the rural merchant economy had not been fully developed. The diversification of operations, industries, and commerce had just begun. There was not much specialization of expertise while people were stuck in their old ways of thinking. So besides a few specialists and a few major wheat production contracts, most rural land was contracted out according to household head count.

What actually happened matched the level of rural economic development and productivity that existed at the time. The results showed that it did not act as an obstacle to the development of rural productivity, but on the contrary, greatly stimulated the rural economy.

Certainly, the scheme of dividing the land up equally and contracting to households could not change the root problem of low rural labor efficiency. As rural commerce grows, so will the development of specialized operations and rural industries. The issues of specialization of expertise, labor migration, and large-scale farming will eventually have to be dealt with again. Of course, it will no longer take the form of the collectivization that existed in the 1950s. It is very possible that a more suitable form is the family farm operation. In order to adapt to this kind of demand, the ability to freely trade, rent, and inherit land should be permitted and the most important rural productive resource, the land, should be made freely available on the market and given legal protection. This is an issue that must be confronted.

Zhao in 1948, just before the Chinese Communist Party won the civil war. Already a county administrator with a successful record in land reform, Zhao was soon to be sent to Guangdong and eventually became the Party Secretary in the coastal province.

Zhao was very public about his love of golf, cultivating an image that would have been unthinkable for a Communist Party leader in Mao's era. That image probably reinforced the impression among conservative Party elders that Zhao had learned "too much foreign stuff."

The reform-minded General Secretary Hu Yaobang and Premier Zhao Ziyang
operated in a political environment where the Party elders dominated. From
left: Hu Yaobang, Deng Xiaoping, Li Xiannian, Zhao Ziyang, Deng Yingchao
(widow of deceased Premier Zhou Enlai), and Peng Zhen.

Deng Xiaoping warned Zhao before the 13th Party Congress not to include
anything resembling the Western-style tripartite division of powers. The final
report should include "not even a trace of it," Deng said.

President Ronald Reagan, right, escorted Chinese Premier Zhao Ziyang following a White House meeting on January 10, 1984. *AFP/Getty Images.*

After thirty years of rupture between the Soviet Union and China, President Mikhail Gorbachev paid an official visit to Beijing, where he was greeted by General Secretary Zhao Ziyang on May 17, 1989. Zhao, who advocated talking with pro-democracy student demonstrators on Tiananmen Square during the visit, was later ousted from his post. © *Jacques Langevin/CORBIS SYGMA.*

This photo was taken by Yang Shaoming, son of Yang Shangkun and a family friend of Zhao's. It shows a meeting at Deng's house in the summer of 1989, after the army crushed the students at Tiananmen Square. It is the only known visual record of the actual setting where the crackdown decision had been made.

General Secretary Zhao Ziyang addressed the pro-democracy hunger strikers through a megaphone at dawn on May 19, 1989, in one of the buses at Tiananmen Square in Beijing where the students were sheltered. Zhao had pleaded in vain against using force on the demonstrators. *STR/AFP/Getty Images.*

(Left) Under house arrest in the summer of 1993, Zhao could exercise his love of golf only by hitting a ball into a net in the courtyard. Some attempts to visit public golf courses during his years of isolation were blocked by officials who did not want Zhao to be seen in public.

(Below) At home on February 7, 1992: dinner has to await the outcome of Zhao's chess game against his wife, Liang Boqi. Grandson Wang Doudou looks on.

In 2004, three generations of family gathered in the courtyard. From left: Wang Doudou (grandson), Zhao Ziyang, Zhao Wujun (son), Li Juanjuan (daughter-in-law), Liang Boqi (wife, sitting), Wang Yenan (daughter), Zhao Dundun (grandson), Wang Zhihua (son-in-law), Zhao Tuotuo (granddaughter), and Wang Jianli (daughter-in-law).

The former Premier's guards turned into his jailers. In this family outing, Zhao relaxed with his grandson while five "guards" hovered in the background.

Zhao in his study, where he somehow managed to create a taped account of his rise and fall without anyone knowing. A set of these tapes was ultimately discovered after his death, hidden in plain sight: among his grandchildren's toys.

The Coastal Regions Take Off

The early success of the reform program inspires Zhao to formulate a bolder strategy for developing the coast. The idea is to develop an entirely export-oriented economy in that area. To an extent this has already begun with the opening of several special economic zones along the coast, but Zhao believes a more comprehensive policy would lead to rapid development and link China to the global economy. It's clear he would have liked to pursue this idea further if he had been given the time.

In the winter of 1987, I went on inspection tours of the coastal regions, after which, in January 1988, I proposed strategies for developing the coast.

During those tours, I came to believe that the international market provides the right conditions for our coastal regions to accelerate their development, because labor-intensive production will always shift to places where labor is abundant and cheap. Some developed countries have moved their own output toward more knowledge-, technology-, or capital-intensive products, which offers developing countries an opportunity. It's kind of a law of nature. Japan went down this road, as did the four Asian Tigers of Taiwan, Singapore, Hong Kong, and South Korea. That's how the four Tigers took off.

Our coastal regions possessed great advantages. They had a rich supply of high-quality labor, better than that in other developing countries. Transportation was convenient, information was available, and people were becoming more aware of the international market and competition and could respond more quickly than the inner provinces. Also, the infrastructure was better and the area had a greater capacity for producing light and textile industries. Our coastal regions had all the conditions necessary to go through what the Asian Tigers had gone through.

This approach would greatly speed the development of the coastal regions. The proposed strategy called for developing an export-oriented economy, which would mean 100 million to 200 million people joining the global market and participating in international exchange and competition. It would foster "two ends extending abroad," meaning finished products would feed into the international market, while raw materials and other resources would be imported from the international market. If the production of all export commodities relied instead on just internal resources, it could lead to domestic shortages. A competition for raw materials between the eastern and the central and western regions could destabilize the nation's economy.

When the strategy was proposed, Comrade Xiaoping was supportive and praised it highly. He said we should seize the opportunity by taking bold and decisive actions so as not to lose any opportunities. Some of the coastal regions were also supportive and enthusiastic. They saw how bright their futures could be.

But there were also opposing points of view. [State Planning director] Yao Yilin and Li Peng had concerns. There was still the issue of resolving the nation's overheated economy and reaching a "soft landing." If the coastal regions were to speed up their development, wouldn't the economy become overheated again? In fact, this concern was needless. The so-called "overheating" was not a simple issue of the pace of development being too slow or too fast, but about whether the pace was more than what could be absorbed. The issue was mainly about overinvestment, belated returns on investment, or investments that yielded low returns. In addition, consumption funds were huge, causing an overabundance of currency in circulation.

These problems would not exist if the coastal regions proceeded with the strategy. First of all, there was no need for large amounts of investment; second, their products could be sold quickly; and third, raw materials could be imported from abroad.

The economies of the four Asian Tigers had proven this. It was at a time of relatively high inflation that they had developed their export-oriented economies, exporting labor-intensive products while importing raw materials. The result was the sped-up development of their economies with consecutive years of sustained growth. At the same time, their inflation rates dropped and their economies grew more stable.

China is a big country with diverse regional conditions. We often tried to apply a single approach suitable for the entire nation, but that tended to ignore regional strengths and characteristics. For example, the coastal regions could have developed faster without the problem of economic overheating, but since we were trying to reduce the nationwide problem, we limited the development of the coastal regions as well, which cost us opportunities. We proceeded in that way for many years. If we were to do anything, we would do it all across the nation; when we made adjustments to slow things down, we slowed down every region. The coastal areas had missed development opportunities many times.

A few Party elders had another concern. For example, Chen Yun worried that, while "two ends extending abroad" was a good concept, it would not prove easy. I understood his fears: If we agreed to import raw materials but then our products could not be exported abroad, how would we balance our foreign currency? But while his concern was understandable, the real question was, If we have such favorable conditions and if the four Asian Tigers had managed it, why couldn't we? Why wouldn't we be able to compete?

There were two obstacles: the system of foreign trade, and state-owned enterprises. In order to carry out the coastal development strategy, foreign trade had to be reformed and those involved in trade needed to be granted responsibility for their profits and losses. At the time, I was proposing allowing "huge volumes of imports and exports without delays." The system of foreign trade had to remove barriers to allow for greater volumes of imports and exports.

The other issue was how to reform the state-owned enterprises. It wouldn't be easy to change the habit of "eating from one rice bowl" or "taking the profit but sharing the losses." I emphasized first the development of township-owned enterprises in the coastal regions. These enterprises were flexible and easier to deal with. I had looked into many township enterprises and saw that they delivered on time, paid attention to quality, and had very good reputations.

There was a third concern, held mainly by academics and scholars involved with planning and foreign trade. They pointed out that the Asian Tigers were very small while we were so much bigger and with a much larger population. They wondered whether all of our products could be sold abroad.

This issue should have been considered in this way: as long as the products were of good quality and low in cost, they would find their place in the market. The market was not frozen or static in a fixed size where, once you'd had your share, there would be no more. Certainly, there was no vacuum in the international market and no commodity that the international market was lacking. The issue was market share: how much you took up and how much I took up. The total volume would grow with world economic development and growth. However, market share is variable and depends on competition. That is why developed countries had stopped producing labor-intensive products and adjusted their industries. Once the emerging economies took off, their own labor costs rose, and they gradually lost their advantage. For example, Japan moved its labor-intensive production to the four Asian Tigers, but now the Asian Tigers have lost their advantage on this front.

A country like China has the advantage of enormous labor resources. There is no need to worry about the future. Once the first step is taken, we can take a second and then a third. As long as we started exporting labor-intensive products, we would accumulate capital and more advanced technologies, and we could then compete internationally on capital- or technology-intensive products.

But that was a question for future development, and there was no need to be afraid. This was just the beginning. We were not instantaneously pushing 200 million people to face direct international market competition. This was a process of development.

There were also some people who were reluctant to give up the pretense of being a world power. They questioned how a socialist People's Republic of China could emphasize labor-intensive production and rely on exports from rural township enterprises. They believed the right way was to organize giant enterprise groups to produce and export products with highly advanced technologies.

This was totally unrealistic for our country. What were we exporting at the time? They were mainly agricultural products, not industrial products, and much of it was raw materials. We were a developing country, and no matter how much we might have wanted to pursue high-tech products, doing so in large volumes was impossible and therefore couldn't improve the unemployment issue in the coastal regions. We needed to start with labor-intensive products with huge export volumes. After the economy stabilized and became more robust, we could return to the goal of exporting advanced high-tech products and those with a higher added-value.

There was another kind of objection. Some cadres in the central and western regions, or who were involved in planning and macroeconomics, questioned why we would want to further develop the coastal regions when they were already ahead of the inland provinces. Wouldn't the discrepancy become even greater? Comrades from the inland provinces believed that developing the coastal regions would make the rich richer. They wanted to know: Why not make the poor richer?

In fact, the acceleration of development along the coast would not only benefit the coast but also drive the economy of the whole nation, including the inner provinces. Without the development of the coastal regions, where would all the migrant workers find employment? If the coastal regions developed, the laws of labor-intensive production would also apply within the country and shift to places where labor was even cheaper. As the cost of labor started to grow in the coastal regions, they would be forced to make adjustments in their production. Therefore, we could not develop at a uniform speed and we needed to proceed with one area driving and promoting another. Uniform moves would mean neither could move faster. The coastal regions were part of China; if their strengths were utilized, it would be beneficial to the whole nation, including the central and western regions. From the point of view of overall development, it was necessary to make development of the coastal regions a priority.

Despite the many concerns, the development strategy of the coastal regions was passed by the Politburo and implemented. After June Fourth, the strategy was no longer mentioned by name, but in reality it has continued. It was because of the sustained development of the coastal economy that the nation reached large export volumes in just a few years and foreign reserves grew to a huge amount. It was all because of having taken this path, was it not? Of course, after June Fourth, no one could talk about this strategy as a policy, which undermined even more active implementation of this strategy.

I once spoke to a wealthy businessman from Taiwan, Chang Yung-fa, chairman of the Evergreen Group. He was as famous in Taiwan as Wang Yung-ching [the onetime chairman of Formosa Plastics]. During the conversation, I said to him, "It is not a trivial thing that you in Taiwan have been able to accumulate several tens of billions [of dollars] of foreign reserves; for such a small region, how did you accomplish this?"

He said, "This is not difficult. Just continue your current policy of reform and openness and develop foreign trade. It won't be long before you will have large amounts of foreign reserves. If Taiwan could do it, the mainland can also do it." He said this very optimistically and confidently.

At the time, I had doubts. Could it really be that easy? It now appears that it indeed was not all that difficult. The key was to embrace openness. I mentioned this many times before to illustrate this point: so long as we implemented the Reform and Open-Door Policy, our economy would be able to develop rapidly.

From autumn of 1987 to January 1988, I traveled to Fujian, Guangdong, Zhejiang, and Jiangsu for long inspection tours and held talks with local cadres at county, municipal, district, and provincial levels. I also exchanged views with relevant central government agencies, after which I proposed the strategy for coastal region development. The most important point of the strategy was to develop an export-oriented economy in the coastal regions to fully take advantage of opportunities offered by a global economy in transition. The plan covered a region along the coast that included between 100 million and 200 million people. The following items were included:

1. The development of the coastal region will essentially be the formation of an export-oriented economy. Taking advantage of the opportunity offered by the structural adjustments of the global economy, concentration will be placed on developing labor-intensive production, or production that is both labor- and technology-intensive.

2. Huge volumes of imports and exports must be achieved with "two ends extending abroad." Capital, equipment, and product sales will be made on the international market to attract international investment and to import equipment and raw materials. Processing will occur domestically and then the products will be exported. Huge volumes of imports and exports should be allowed without delay.

3. When developing the export-oriented economy, the full potential of township enterprises must be realized and they should become a major or even dominant force. That means utilizing the full potential of township enterprises and using them as a vehicle to pave the way to an export-oriented economy. Ultimately, a large portion of rural labor in the coastal regions will be integrated into this export-oriented economy and the international market.

4. In order to adapt to this kind of transformation, centralized imports and exports in foreign trade must be reformed. All entities or enterprises with the capacity to produce for export, and those enterprises that are conducting imports and exports in foreign trade, must be responsible for their own profits and losses while being allowed to conduct their businesses freely.

In summary, this meant allowing the 100 million to 200 million people in the coastal regions, and the enterprises in the regions, to integrate into the global market and participate in the exchange and competition of the international market.

Outside of China, adjustments in the international economic structure were already under way, and in some of the industrialized nations or emerging industrialized nations people's living standards were higher, so the costs of their labor were also higher. This would cause labor-intensive production to gradually move to places where labor costs were lower.

In the Asia Pacific Region, it was the United States that first moved some of its labor-intensive production and manufacturing to Japan. Japan took the opportunity to develop itself. Later the United States and Japan moved some of their production and manufacturing to the four Asian Tigers. As the Asian Tigers developed, Japan and the Asian Tigers are moving some of their industries to the countries of ASEAN [a grouping of ten Southeast Asian nations].

Economic structural adjustments, whether from a global or Asian Pacific perspective, will not stop. This revolving process presents an opportunity for developing countries. In the past, because we had closed our doors to the world and implemented a rigid, highly centralized system without the free flow of information, we had missed many opportunities. We could not throw away another chance!

At the same time, our coastal regions had the right conditions: proximity to coastal ports with convenient transportation, better infrastructure than the inner provinces, and quality labor in both cultural and technical terms. The coastal regions were closer to international markets and had a tradition of doing commerce with the outside world. Having both the opportunity and the right conditions, if we only eliminated the obstacles in our thinking and adopted appropriate policies for guidance, the coastal regions could develop at a fast pace.

If we did not adopt this strategy, the regions would suffer more and more difficulties. If we continued with our old methods, the regions would be limited, primarily because of a lack of natural resources. The highly centralized planned economy looked upon the entire nation as a grand chessboard and relied on the state to invest in the development of natural resources in the western regions and transport them far away to the coastal regions for manufacturing. This path could no longer continue.

Since the inland provinces had become unwilling to sell their resources cheaply to coastal provinces, the conflict between inland and coastal regions had intensified. Therefore, transforming the coastal regions into an essentially export-oriented economy was a major and critical issue.

The proposal had important political significance as well. The highly centralized planned economy made the entire nation develop in a uniform manner so the strengths of the coastal regions could not be utilized. Neither the inland nor the coastal regions could develop at a fast pace. Before liberation, Shanghai was a highly developed metropolis in the Asia

Pacific Region, more advanced than Hong Kong, let alone Singapore or Taiwan. But after a couple of decades, Shanghai had become run-down and had fallen far behind Hong Kong, Singapore, and Taiwan. This made people ask, "What exactly is the advantage of socialism?"

If one area of China, an area with hundreds of millions of people, could develop as quickly as they had, then the situation would be much better and people would not say socialism was a hindrance to the development of productivity. From a political perspective, it would reduce people's doubts and fears of the handover of Hong Kong and Macau* and the unification of Taiwan with the mainland. It would engender in people more enthusiasm for reuniting with the motherland.

I proposed the coastal development strategy after much observation, experimentation, and deliberation. It was also in response to the need for further implementation of reform.

I had worked for many years in Guangdong, which is adjacent to Hong Kong and Macau, so I had an earlier and deeper understanding of the international market and foreign trade. Very early on, I had come to believe that it would be beneficial to allow the coastal regions to utilize international trade to develop their full potential.

For example, if Guangdong were allowed to plant sugarcane, 1,000 catties of sugar could be produced per acre. If the area were made into rice paddies, 1,000 catties per acre of rice could be produced. The value of 1,000 catties of sugar was so much higher than 1,000 catties of rice! The export revenue from 1,000 catties of sugar could import several thousand catties of rice. But in the past, we did not take advantage of international trade. In order to resolve food shortages, we could not expand sugarcane plantations, so there had always been this problem of sugarcane and rice in competition for fields.

There was also a variety of high-quality rice in Guangdong that could be sold at high prices on the international market. One catty of this variety could bring in as much as several catties of ordinary rice. When I was in Guangdong, I used the method of exporting one catty of high-quality rice to buy back one catty of ordinary rice plus several catties of fertilizers, and then using the fertilizer to exchange for more rice domestically. By doing this, we had grain, fertilizer, and foreign currency. But in the past we had mechanically emphasized self-reliance and had not taken advantage of international markets, so we'd undermined our own strengths.

---

* Britain officially returned Hong Kong to China's control in 1997. Two years later Portugal did the same with Macau.

There is huge potential in foreign trade. I thought about this while I was working in Guangdong. If one enterprise or one region were free to import raw materials and export its own finished products, it would have been profitable. The reason that some places around the nation were not able to make products for export was because many of them lacked good material resources, so either the products could not be produced or the quality was not high enough. If we could import raw materials, use our industrial equipment to process them, and export the end product, then not only could we buy back whatever we needed, we could also bring in foreign currency.

In the 1960s, I had written to the Central Committee to propose increasing our foreign trade and using imports to generate export revenue. We had attempted to use this method in Guangdong. With the consent of Ye Jizhuang, the minister of Foreign Trade, we conducted a certain amount of our own imports and exports, and the resulting foreign currency revenue was shared at local government levels. Guangdong's economy recovered relatively fast in the early 1960s, largely as a result of this.

I believed strongly back then that there was huge potential in foreign trade for the coastal regions. Our system and policies had suffocated it. It wasn't for lack of opportunity, or because it had been impossible, but rather because it had not been permitted.

In 1981, when I was on inspection tours of enterprises in Tianjin, this issue also came up. Many of the textile factories in Tianjin lacked a supply of raw materials and were unable to upgrade their equipment, making it difficult to proceed with production. It happened to be during the period of readjustment, and many factories had been compelled to suspend production. I had discussions with them and asked if they had been allowed to import raw materials and whether they could then export their products. They said that of course they could. I wondered what would happen if the coastal regions were all oriented toward developing export-oriented industries. Later, as other issues emerged, this matter was dropped.

After reform was implemented, from 1981 to 1984, Guangdong started the development of "three inputs plus export subsidy." They imported raw materials, samples, and designs, used existing equipment and labor to process it all, and then exported the finished product with subsidies applied. Even though it was a bit primitive back then, standards quickly improved. Guangdong, especially in the areas of Dongguan, Nanhai, and the Pearl River Delta, developed very quickly.

In the beginning, wherever Hong Kong businessmen went, the "three inputs plus export subsidy" policy was put in place, so they eventually moved their production equipment and production bases to the mainland. After Guangdong did this, Fujian, Shandong, Zhejiang, and Jiangsu followed suit. The results were good. All of this had again proven that the potential strengths of the coastal regions were just waiting to be realized.

Of course, this was already happening in the coastal regions during the years of reform. However, as an overall strategy, it was necessary to bring it to the level of strategic thinking and implementation. This was why the coastal development strategy was proposed. It was not without reason, nor was it from a temporary impulse; rather, it was a conclusion drawn from long-term observation, research, and understanding.

12

Coping with Corruption

All government policies, even the successful ones, have costs. One of the costs of China's reform efforts, from the beginning, has been corruption. No reformer could afford to ignore the problem and its potential for provoking a backlash. Zhao argues that corruption is a result of the transition from the old economic system to the new, and that a hard-line response isn't necessary. The answer is to move more quickly with reform of the economic, political, and legal systems.

Corruption was emerging as an important issue in 1988. The challenge was how to interpret and resolve this problem, and how to turn the concerns about corruption and creating a clean government into opportunities to deepen reform—while not giving opponents a chance to exploit this issue and restore the old system.

While spending the 1988 Spring Festival holidays in Guangdong, I read materials that revealed many examples of power-money exchanges. While it could not be assumed that they were the result of reform, we had to acknowledge that this was related to the changing economic environment. We could not ignore the issue. I proposed, "The economy must prosper, the government must remain clean."

I realized more and more that "remaining clean" was a major issue. If neglected, it could provide an excuse to those who opposed reforms, while making the people disgruntled. The consequences could be dire. At the same time, we could use the anti-corruption issue as an opportunity to deepen reform. Because these problems emerged in the new environment, they could not be solved using old methods. First, the causes of these problems had to be understood. Only then could we find effective ways to resolve them.

For example, in Hong Kong, corruption was very serious in the 1960s. The law enforcement agencies had become seriously corrupted. Then, in the 1970s, the Independent Commission Against Corruption was established. There was even a film made, called *The Storm Against Corruption*. After this the situation evidently improved.

Corruption often occurs when the economic culture develops to a certain stage; but later, when the quality of civil servants and law enforcement personnel improves, and their wages and compensations rise, the situation changes. Today's Hong Kong is very different from before. Similar situations have existed in other developing countries. The early stages of a market economy involve exchanges of power and money. As the economy develops, with the refinement of the legal system and establishment of a democratic system, the situation improves. Some ASEAN countries had similar experiences.

In January 1989, *Ta Kung Pao* [newspaper] in Hong Kong published an article with a title along the lines of "An Attempt to Analyze Corruption in the Mainland." It was a systematic analysis of our corruption problem. I forwarded it to [Director of the Political Reform Research Institute] Bao Tong with a message: "This is an article studying corruption. We need to organize a group specifically dedicated to the research and analysis of the corruption problem, then propose our strategy and explain it in some persuasive articles."

At that time, I believed the issue needed to be systematically studied. Only after investigating it clearly could we propose a solution. The reapplication of old tactics would not work. Returning to the highly centralized planned economy would be no good, even if it were for the sake of fighting corruption. That would be like never eating again for fear of choking. Using the methods of mass campaigns and class struggle, as we did in the early years of the People's Republic, for example, by executing people, would not work.

This kind of corruption emerges during an economic and social transition process. The old system has weakened and is disintegrating, but the new system has not yet been established. That is why further economic and political reform is necessary in order to resolve this problem fundamentally.

Take power-money exchanges as an example. Now that the economy is freer, with commodities and markets, many enterprises and entities are subject to market competition. But power is still monopolized in the hands of government agencies. In other words, economic reform has not completed the shift to free markets. Many residual elements from the era of the planned economy still exist. If certain participants in the market competition get favors from agencies with power, they can gain huge profits under conditions that are not equal to those of their competitors.

For example, by converting supplies from inside the planned economy to outside of it—that is, buying commodities at a controlled low price from within the planned system from supply agencies and then selling it at market prices—huge profits can be obtained. Another example is the situation where whoever can obtain permits for exporting or importing certain goods can take advantage of the price discrepancy to make huge profits. Under these conditions, power and money are linked and exchanged so that some businesses profit from unequal competitive conditions. Part of the huge profits obtained in this way can then be used for bribes.

The only solution for resolving this issue is continued deepening of reform to separate government and enterprise, to hand down powers currently held by the government to administrators of the industries, and to resolve the issue of monopolies or the overconcentration of power. Doing this limits the environment for power-money exchanges. Such problems can only be solved through further reforms.

Another imperative is building institutions. A commodity economy requires appropriate institutions: a tax affairs office, police departments, bank branch offices, and various agencies to enforce and execute regulations. If procedures were all transparent, and if the results were made public, there would be fewer attempts to engage in corrupt activities.

I heard that there was a place in Heilongjiang where a bank's agriculture loans were announced publicly every year: who got loans and what were the returns. This let the people participate and check on power. The less transparency, the easier it is to cheat. This is the issue of building institutions to fight corruption. Dongcheng District of Beijing Municipality has a good record in this aspect. This way of doing things easily gains public support.

To fight corruption, reform of the political system must be carried out. Emerging nations have periods of widespread corruption in the early stages of their development. The economy is growing at high speeds while political power is highly concentrated. The behavior of officials is not checked by public opinion. If a political party has no check on its power, its officials easily become corrupt. The situation will eventually improve with the building of democratic politics, a wider variety of political activities, a wider slice of the populace participating in the process, and checks on power by public opinion. Some of the ASEAN countries, as well as

Taiwan, have gone through this. As the economic base changes, the political system also needs to be reformed.

Another important issue—in fact the most essential—is the independence of the judiciary and rule of law. If there is no independent enforcement of law, and the political party in power is able to intervene, then corruption can never be effectively resolved.

I pointed out all of these issues at the Central Committee Secretariat meeting. However, it appears that up to this day, the problems have not been resolved.

After June Fourth, when Li Peng and his associates were criticizing me, they accused me of saying that corruption was unavoidable in the reform process and therefore that I had a laissez-faire attitude toward corruption. They never seemed to run out of words to use against me in groundless accusations!

In fact, tackling corruption was very much on my mind. I talked about the issue of anti-corruption at both the Second Plenum of the 13th Central Committee in March 1988 and at the Politburo meeting in June. I also held several symposiums specifically for hearing about the experiences of people at lower administrative levels. I was actively studying anti-corruption in hopes of finding a solution that would truly resolve the problem. It was utterly unjust for Li Peng and his associates to take my quotes out of context in order to incriminate me.

It appears that this problem continues to this day.

WAR IN THE POLITBURO

I

Hu Yaobang "Resigns"

Just how the opposing forces in Chinese politics have maneuvered against each other has long been a puzzle. Zhao lifts the veil on the Machiavellian scheming by the revolution's Old Guard, who want to protect the Communist Party's power and the legacy of Mao Zedong.

Zhao also sheds light on supreme leader Deng Xiaoping's decision in 1987 to force out Hu Yaobang, the liberal leader of the Communist Party. Hu inexplicably failed to take seriously Deng's warnings to deal with a growing liberal trend in society. But in the end, Hu's fatal error appears to have been an interview he gave to a Hong Kong journalist, in which he almost seemed to be rushing Deng into retirement. Zhao takes over as Party chief and tries to manage the conservatives' wrath. The elders launch an Anti-Liberalization Campaign* as Zhao struggles to protect reforms in the economy.

[H]u] Yaobang was forced to resign in January 1987. There has been a lot of talk about this issue. One version has it that Deng, under pressure from Party elders, was forced to abandon Hu in order to protect Zhao. I don't think this was true. Certainly there were people fomenting trouble between Deng and Hu by making accusations against Hu in Deng's presence. However, I don't think it was the main reason.

The reason that Deng Xiaoping abandoned Hu Yaobang was not that

---

* The Anti-Liberalization Campaign, also known as the Anti–Bourgeois Liberalization Campaign, was launched by Party conservatives in 1987 to combat a growing liberal tide among China's intelligentsia.

he was misled or that he had to compromise under outside pressure. Rather, Deng's attitude toward Hu gradually changed until he finally lost trust in Hu.

From 1980 to 1986, Deng grew to feel that Yaobang was increasingly at odds with him concerning the liberalizing trend among intellectuals. The differences between them grew wider over time. Starting from 1980, whenever Deng came out to condemn liberalization or propose campaigns against it, he was almost always responding to reports he had received from [influential leftist leaders] Hu Qiaomu and Deng Liqun. However, it was a fact that Deng and Yaobang held sincerely different views on this matter. Even without people brewing trouble between them, their conflict was bound to grow more serious. The end result was unavoidable.

Here are some of the things that happened over those years.

Deng gave a report at the Theoretical Discussion Meeting for upholding the Four Cardinal Principles* in 1979. Ever since, it was clear that Hu and Deng held differing views on the issue of liberalization.

As the years went by, their differences grew more obvious and their positions moved further apart. In July 1981, Deng Xiaoping accused the theoretical front† of being "lax and weak" and spoke on the matter. In October 1983, at the Second Plenum of the 12th Central Committee Deng said the theoretical front should not be involved in any "spiritual pollution." He made these comments because he felt that the liberal trend among intellectuals had been gaining ground, and he believed Hu Yaobang should be held responsible for it, since this realm was under Hu Yaobang's management.

Hu Yaobang himself never raised such questions, nor did he ever report to Deng on issues of this nature. Rather, Deng sensed it for himself or heard about it from Hu Qiaomu or Deng Liqun, so he felt compelled to intervene. This naturally implied a dissatisfaction with Hu.

I would like to specifically mention the matter of the Anti–Spiritual Pollution Campaign.‡ I feel that the way Hu Yaobang handled this matter

---

*   The Four Cardinal Principles, introduced by Deng in 1979, stressed that there could be no questioning of the four pillars of the state: the socialist path, the people's democratic dictatorship, the leadership of the Communist Party, and Marxist–Leninist–Mao Zedong thought.

†   "Theoretical front" refers to the various Party institutions that come up with theoretical arguments to back up policy. It was often the battleground of conservatives and reformers.

‡   The Anti–Spiritual Pollution Campaign was launched in 1983 to weed out Western influence in society. The original name, Cleansing Spiritual Pollution, was uttered by Deng Xiaoping, and implies more severe punishment.

aggravated the conflict between them a great deal. This ultimately played a key role in the final rift between the two.

After the Second Plenum of the 12th Central Committee, Deng's Anti–Spiritual Pollution Campaign was disseminated nationwide. "Leftist" thinking made a comeback, not only in the cultural, metaphysical, and economic arenas, but also in people's daily lives. Even the hairstyles and fashion of female comrades fell within the control of the Anti–Spiritual Pollution Campaign, and another Cultural Revolution almost seemed to be on the horizon. Strong reactions came from intellectuals across China and international commentators.

I was visiting the United States that winter, and everywhere I went I had to respond to people's questions about it and ease their concerns. The momentum of the campaign was strong enough to threaten economic policies and reform.

[Vice Premier] Wan Li and I announced that the Anti–Spiritual Pollution Campaign would not be applied to economics or agricultural matters, so as to avoid a disruption to the economy. We also proposed that the campaign should not touch the realm of lifestyle habits. This had the effect of cooling the overall atmosphere. Since anti-liberalization was unpopular to begin with, if we indicated that the economic, agricultural, and science and technology arenas were "off limits," the movement would lose momentum even in the metaphysical and cultural arenas. Even Deng became worried about the way things were going and revealed some of his feelings about this. So the Anti–Spiritual Pollution Campaign was not going to last long.

Yaobang always doubted the campaign. He apparently wished to ease the anger of intellectuals and reduce the negative impact on international opinion. While visiting Party chiefs in Shanghai in February 1984 and again when meeting Japanese visitors, he said that the phrase "Cleansing of Spiritual Pollution" was inappropriate. He said that the phrase led to overreaching in the campaign and that it would not be used again.

This was a very sensitive issue. As soon as word spread of what he had said, people, especially intellectuals, had the impression that the Cleansing of Spiritual Pollution Campaign had been wrong. Yaobang had specifically explained that "Xiaoping originally called for 'Anti–Spiritual Pollution,' but the media campaign had distorted it into a 'Cleansing of Spiritual Pollution,' therefore resulting in an overreaching." In other words, it wasn't that Deng had been wrong, but rather that it had been executed incorrectly. In fact, the campaign was based on Deng Xiaoping's speech, so when it was printed in the newspapers, or mentioned by leaders in speeches, the word "cleansing" was used many times. Everyone knew that the campaign was waged according to Deng's remarks. So Yaobang's explanation could not reduce Deng's responsibility in people's minds.

Deng was not happy with this kind of talk from Yaobang. Even though Deng did not say anything at the time, he did not back down an inch from his previous stand, whether you call it "anti–spiritual pollution" or "anti-liberalism."

On January 15, 1987, at the Party life meeting* that concluded the case of Hu Yaobang, [Politburo member] Hu Qili disclosed that on June 28, 1984, Deng had spoken alone with him. Deng had said, "The main reason I have asked you here today is to talk about Yaobang. Not only in the way that he dealt with Guo Luoji, Hu Jiwei, and Wang Ruoshui,† but with the upholding of the Four Cardinal Principles and in anti-liberalization efforts; as the party's General Secretary, Yaobang has displayed a weakness that is a fundamental shortcoming." Deng didn't talk to Yaobang directly, but asked Hu Qili to relay his message, even harsh wording such as "weakness against liberalization is a fundamental shortcoming in a General Secretary."

This evoked a question: If Yaobang could not change in a fundamental way, was he still suitable for the position of General Secretary? Hu Qili told Yaobang what Deng had said, word for word, but even after this, Yaobang did not pay attention or respond seriously to the matter. This was in 1984.

In July 1985, Deng Xiaoping asked Hu Qili and [Vice Premier] Qiao Shi for a talk. Again he pointed out that the real problem was the growing trend of liberalization. Deng said, "Some people (he meant people like Wang Ruoshui) encouraged Yaobang while using Yaobang's name to oppose our domestic and foreign policies. You should ask Yaobang to raise the issue of anti-liberalization more often." Qili and Qiao Shi did as Deng instructed and relayed the message to Yaobang and to me at Beidaihe [the beach resort where Party officials gather each summer].

I thought then that because Deng was repeatedly emphasizing this

---

*   A "Party life meeting" (*dangnei shenghuo hui*) is held for members of the Communist Party to "exchange ideas and experiences, and conduct criticisms and self-criticisms." According to the Party Charter, such meetings are to be conducted two to four times a year by Party branches.

†   Liberal scholar Guo Luoji published a controversial 1979 article in *People's Daily* arguing that people should be allowed to openly debate political issues. Hu Jiwei was the paper's chief editor, and Wang Ruoshui its deputy chief editor. Hu Yaobang was criticized for not punishing them as Deng had requested.

issue, the Secretariat needed to hold a meeting to discuss it seriously, as an appropriate response to Deng. I suggested this to Yaobang, but when [Hu] Qili asked Yaobang when the meeting would take place, Yaobang's only reply was to say that he was about to leave for Xinjiang. Later, he did indeed go to Xinjiang, so the matter was postponed. Yet he should have dealt with the issue before leaving for Xinjiang; he did not view it as important.

In 1985, Xiaoping spoke of the matter again. Why? I believe it had to do with the fourth Congress of the All China Writers' Association in December 1984.

That meeting was held after the Cleansing of Spiritual Pollution Campaign had been unceremoniously ended amid negative domestic and international responses. In accordance with Yaobang's suggestion, the message from the Central Committee to this meeting made no mention of anti–spiritual pollution or anti-liberalization. When the message was being drafted, Yaobang said that he would like to see the phrase "anti-liberalization" gradually fade away. It was also decided that the Department of Organization would not interfere in the leadership of the Writers' Association, allowing the group to elect its own leaders. Full creative freedom was emphasized.

All of these were right to do. The problem, however, was that under the circumstances, those who had been criticized or punished through the Anti–Spiritual Pollution Campaign would then feel free to unleash their anger in meetings of this kind, sometimes making extreme or inappropriate comments against those who had actively participated in the campaign. As for the leadership, almost everyone who was a "leftist" or had been active in the campaign lost in the elections.

Of course, this embarrassed [conservative ideologues] Hu Qiaomu and Deng Liqun while provoking the displeasure of Party elders. Ultimately, it left Deng Xiaoping the impression that Hu Yaobang had encouraged people in the literary and artistic realms to unleash their dissatisfaction with Deng's Anti–Spiritual Pollution Campaign. That is why he repeated his request to Qili and Qiao Shi to relay his message to Yaobang, asking him to speak more about anti-liberalization. The wording that he used was very harsh; he said that some people had opposed China's domestic and foreign policies in the name of Yaobang, in other words, "using Yaobang's name to oppose Deng Xiaoping."

However, Yaobang did not take the matter seriously. On issues such as this, there ordinarily would have been a meeting of the Secretariat; Yaobang would have delivered a speech and then afterward gone to Deng for a talk. At the time, it was impossible to take a position opposed to

Deng Xiaoping's. Of course, various opinions could be voiced and issues could be discussed with Deng.

The question I still can't answer is: Why did this not get Yaobang's attention? Why did he not take it seriously? It is possible that he believed Deng's method was inappropriate, that he himself had not done anything wrong and was therefore not willing to change course. And he may have believed the issue would not have been resolved by talking to Deng, that Deng would not have accepted his position—and so he avoided the issue. All of this aggravated Deng's sense that Yaobang was moving further and further away from him on the issue of anti-liberalism.

From October 1983, when Deng proposed the Anti–Spiritual Pollution Campaign, to July 1987, when Deng suggested that some people were pursuing liberalization in Yaobang's name, the dispute centered on the correctness of the campaign. Their disagreement grew increasingly obvious and intense; they became increasingly confrontational.

The last debate on the Anti-Liberalization Campaign before Yaobang stepped down erupted at the end of the Sixth Plenum of the 12th Central Committee in September 1986, when the Central Committee was passing the "Resolution on Building a Spiritual Civilization." The first draft was written under Yaobang's supervision. There was no mention of anti-liberalization. When the draft was discussed at Beidaihe, Hu Qiaomu and Deng Liqun proposed adding a reference to anti-liberalization, and most people, including myself, agreed. Yaobang made a concession by accepting the addition.

However, when it came up for discussion at the group level at the Sixth Plenum of the 12th Central Committee, Lu Dingyi [a liberal writer in the Party's ranks] and a few others said they did not agree with such content. When the resolution was put up for a vote, Lu Dingyi gave an impromptu speech, in which he said, "The Gang of Four used the term 'bourgeois liberalization' during the Cultural Revolution as a way to punish people, and it is therefore inappropriate." Lu's speech won some applause from those attending the meeting.

[Conservative elders] Wang Zhen and Bo Yibo gave speeches insisting that anti-liberalization be retained, and also won applause. Yaobang gave an ambiguous response. I also made a simple statement, saying that the draft had been discussed many times over, and since most people supported keeping the phrase, I agreed that it remain unchanged.

Then Deng Xiaoping spoke extremely seriously. He said, "I have talked about anti–bourgeois liberalization more than anyone, and have been the most persistent. Not only must we mention it now, but we will continue to mention it for the next ten, twenty years. It doesn't matter when the phrase was used and who used it in the past. That is not important." That was it; he had made it final. The plenum passed the resolution with all participants raising their hands.

Since the meeting was chaired by Yaobang, the General Secretary, and his ambiguous stand had caused Deng to directly intervene at the last moment, Deng's dissatisfaction with Yaobang was undeniable. When reports about the meeting were later circulated, Yaobang arranged for dissemination only of the passed resolution, without mention of the discussions that had taken place or Deng's speech. Later Bo Yibo attacked Yaobang on this issue, asking why Deng's speech had not been disseminated.

On the surface, the debate at the meeting concerned Deng's criticism of Lu Dingyi's speech. But it was clear that Deng was actually criticizing Yaobang, because he knew Lu's views represented Yaobang's.

However, the actual debate during the Sixth Plenum of the 12th Central Committee had no significant influence on Deng's attitude toward Hu. Before this incident, Deng had already made up his mind to remove Yaobang. Deng had been planning for a smooth transition with a reshuffling of the leadership at the 13th Party Congress, and not the route that ended up being used. So even though Deng showed dissatisfaction with Hu at this meeting, it had no bearing on whether he wanted Hu to continue on as General Secretary.

There were other aspects of Hu that Deng criticized. For example, Deng believed that Hu was not prudent enough. (Before he made Hu General Secretary, Deng had already perceived this as a failing.) On foreign policy, Hu had been too warm toward [North Korean leader] Kim Il Sung and had granted North Korea's demands too casually: for example, the demand for China to supply jets, to train Korean pilots at Chinese air force bases, and to deploy the Chinese air force in an emergency. Immediately upon his [Hu's] return to Beijing, Deng rejected the proposal. And when visiting Japan, Hu had invited three thousand Japanese youths to visit China without having first discussed it. Deng felt discomfited. Yet Hu was General Secretary and had already extended the invitation, so it was difficult to change it. Yaobang exchanged personal correspondences with Japan's [Prime Minister Yasuhiro] Nakasone and held a banquet for him at his home. Deng was also displeased with this, saying, "China never engages in personal diplomacy. It appears that some of us lack the ability to deal with Nakasone properly."

Nevertheless, I believe that none of these issues had any significant impact on the relationship between Deng and Hu, since Deng had always been clear about Hu's merits as well as his shortcomings. Even though

Deng criticized Hu about these matters, they did not affect his basic trust and judgment of Hu.

In addition to liberalization, the issue that did affect Deng's relationship with Hu was a January 1985 interview Yaobang granted Lu Keng [a well-known Hong Kong journalist]. In a meeting with Qili and Qiao Shi in July 1985, Deng said that Yaobang's talk with Lu Keng had been highly improper. Lu Keng had disparaged our domestic and foreign policies, but disguised his comments as flattery of Yaobang. Yaobang had responded frivolously, not choosing his words with care; in fact Yaobang had encouraged him. I was not told about this at the time.

During the summer of 1986, Deng Xiaoping said to [China's president] Yang Shangkun, "Do you know about Yaobang's talk with a journalist?" He asked Yang to find the minutes and read them. Shangkun told me about this when he returned from Beidaihe and said that Deng thought Yaobang's talk with Lu Keng was way out of line, and he was very angry about it. Shangkun later asked the General Office to send me a copy.

Lu Keng was a senior journalist who had once been branded a "rightist." He applied for entrance to Hong Kong in 1978, and had become the chief editor there of *Bai Xing* [Ordinary People] magazine. When he interviewed Yaobang, he said that one aim of the talk was to allow the world to get to know Hu Yaobang better.

Lu said that the nation's image was closely related to that of Yaobang. He praised Yaobang as an enlightened, honest, and straightforward political leader; one who never plotted conspiracies, was generous, open-minded, understanding, full of vigor. Besides praising Yaobang, Lu Keng also asked him, "Why don't you take over the Central Military Commission while the old man Deng is still alive? If you do not, how will you handle the situation if, in the future, the military commanders oppose you? Would you be able to take things under control?"

Yaobang responded by saying he'd never considered the issue: "[Zhao] Ziyang and I are busy with economic and Party affairs. The army is a place for the observance of seniority, so right now with no war to fight, let Xiaoping have this position. That way, Ziyang and I can concentrate on managing the economic and Party affairs."

During the interview, Lu Keng also made derogatory comments about Chen Yun, Wang Zhen, Hu Qiaomu, and Deng Liqun.

The talk was sure to provoke Deng's displeasure. The reference to the Central Military Commission position especially displeased him. Deng could have interpreted this to mean that deep in Yaobang's heart, he agreed with what Lu Keng had said.

When Deng spoke to Qili and Qiao Shi in July 1985, in order to send a message to Yaobang, Deng mentioned the Lu Keng interview. In the summer of 1986, at the meeting at Beidaihe, Deng again mentioned this talk and discussed this matter with Party elders such as Yang Shangkun.

My speculation is that Deng, already unhappy with Hu Yaobang's views on liberalization, was galvanized by the Lu Keng interview and decided to remove Yaobang.

Yaobang resigned in January 1987, but as early as the summer of 1986 at Beidaihe (or even earlier), Deng had made up his mind. Deng's criticisms of the talk between Yaobang and Lu Keng became widely known. When Yaobang visited Europe, reporters asked about a leadership reshuffle and whether Comrade Xiaoping would be retiring. It was Yaobang's habit to let down his guard and speak freely. Some of the things he said were not appropriate. Some Party elders began openly speculating that Yaobang was creating the public impression that Deng would retire. This also affected Deng's view toward Hu.

For all these reasons, Deng told Yang Shangkun and other elder comrades in the summer of 1986 at Beidaihe that he had made a big mistake: that he had misjudged Yaobang. This remark was a decisive one. He then revealed to them that by the 13th Party Congress, Hu would no longer be General Secretary. In other words, the decision that Yaobang would no longer be General Secretary had been finalized by Deng and Party elders in the summer of 1986 at Beidaihe.

How and exactly with which Party elders Deng discussed this, I don't know. But after that, it was clear that some Party elders, including Yang Shangkun and Bo Yibo, had changed their attitudes toward Yaobang. Before that, even though they criticized Hu and disagreed with some of his remarks, they still showed Hu some amount of respect. After, their disrespect, displeasure, and disregard all rose to the surface.

This all took place while Yaobang was drafting the "Resolution on Building a Spiritual Civilization" for the Sixth Plenum of the 12th Central Committee. The draft failed to pass during discussions. Not only were there requests for minor revisions, but many people felt it was fundamentally inadequate, and some even raised doubts about whether the resolution was necessary at all. [Conservative ideologue] Deng Liqun gave a long speech at the discussion and put out a revised draft that was drastically different, quoting Deng Xiaoping at great length. Deng Xiaoping disagreed with Deng Liqun's speech and his revision. He said, "Even though Deng Liqun used my remarks, his aim was to push us toward the left." Yet a majority disagreed with the original draft and it failed to pass.

After returning from Beidaihe, Yaobang told me through his secretary Zheng Bijian that he believed it was still necessary to have such a document, but the fact that there were so many disagreements put him in a difficult position. He wished to hear my opinion. I said that I had always wondered whether we even needed the resolution, but if Yaobang believed it necessary, I would support it. As for the opposing comments, we could adopt whatever could be adopted, and use persuasion to get it to pass. I was now prepared to actively support the resolution. After several revisions, it did finally pass.

When the resolution was discussed at the Sixth Plenum of the 12th Central Committee, it was discussed whether to add a line about "training people to have a communist conscience," which implied a nationwide program for the education of communist ideology. Both Hu Qiaomu and Deng Liqun proposed adding it in and Chen Yun noted his agreement. Yaobang and the comrades on the drafting committee disagreed. They believed that conducting a "communist education program" among the general population (as opposed to just within the Communist Party) was unrealistic and impractical. However, since Chen Yun had expressed agreement, it was a difficult matter to handle.

I suggested quoting Chairman Mao's "On New Democracy" [1940] to support the idea of omitting the clause. Chairman Mao had said, "Our system is that of the communist, but our current policies are that of a new democracy." Comrade Hu Yaobang agreed with this, so we cosigned a letter and sent it to Deng Xiaoping and Chen Yun. Deng was quick to reply that he was in agreement with us, so Chen Yun did not insist. The matter was thus resolved.

During this period, comments from Party elders critical of Yaobang's working style and his efforts in the areas of foreign policy, economic policy, and Party reorganization were becoming public. This traced in part to what happened at Beidaihe. They also said Hu was not concentrating on the administration of the Party, but rather was overly involved in economic affairs. They said a Communist Party's General Secretary should not be so enthusiastic about visiting capitalist countries. And they scoffed at the press coverage that claimed he had replied to several thousands of letters from ordinary people and visited many rural counties in a few days.

During this time, Yaobang could not do anything right. Most of Yaobang's suggestions at Secretariat meetings were resisted and rejected by the elders. His work as a leader had already become very difficult.

Shortly after the Sixth Plenum of the 12th Central Committee, Yaobang told me that Comrade Xiaoping had spoken with him. Deng said that he was going to resign from the Politburo Standing Committee and from his position as chairman of the Central Advisory Commission. He wanted Yaobang to succeed him and to allow a younger person to take over as General Secretary. Deng told Hu that if this happened, it would lead to a great number of retirements among the Party elders. Yaobang also told me that he had suggested me for the position of General Secretary, since I was younger than him, while people even younger were not yet ready for the position.

Since Deng had never spoken to me about whether he would retire or not, or what responsibilities Yaobang would have, I could not comment at the time. As for recommending me for the position of General Secretary, I replied to Yaobang, "I have said many times that among the leaders between the ages of sixty and seventy, you are the only appropriate one. You and I are within the same age group; if you were to retire, how could I be the successor? If it is to be done, then it should go to someone younger."

I also said, "If you think there is no younger person who is ready, a vacancy can also be considered for the General Secretary position. The Politburo Standing Committee [PSC] and the Politburo can be chaired in turn by the different members of the PSC. This could help to train the younger comrades."

Yaobang said that my suggestion would be considered. At that moment, I spoke casually because it was not a formal discussion and was in the context of his merely relaying to me what Deng had suggested and how he had responded. More important, I in fact did not want to be General Secretary, but wanted to continue as Premier to manage economic reform. When Hu related what Deng had said, he seemed calm and showed no signs of being upset.

After the Sixth Plenum of the 12th Central Committee, Comrade Yaobang appeared to be in very good spirits and excited about his work. He visited Jiangsu Province, Shanghai, and many other places. He gave speeches and enjoyed prominent exposure in the newspapers. I felt that he had interpreted Deng's talk simply as a proposal "to make the leadership younger," that Deng would retire and he would succeed Deng in his current position so as to impel a bunch of Party elders to retire. It is possible that he interpreted it in this way without noticing that Deng's attitude toward him had fundamentally changed.

In December 1986, student demonstrations broke out in several cities. In Shanghai, they were very large. Not only were there street protests, but demonstrators stormed the municipal government building.*

This incident shocked Deng Xiaoping. On December 30, he called Yaobang, Wan Li, Hu Qili, Li Peng, [Vice Minister of the State Education Commission] He Dongchang, and me to his home to speak about the student protests. He said, "The student demonstrations that have taken place recently have not happened by chance. They are the result of the lax control over bourgeois liberalization." He named [dissident astrophysicist] Fang Lizhi and [liberal writer] Wang Ruowang, then blamed Yaobang for neglecting to expel Wang Ruowang from the Party. He had asked him to do so long ago, why had it not been done? As for the demonstrations, he proposed firm measures to quell them, even if that meant resorting to the means of dictatorship.

Deng in fact was assigning all responsibility for the student demonstrations to Yaobang. The emotional outburst revealed the increasingly deep rift between him and Hu on the issue of liberalization. The transcript of Deng's speech was immediately printed and disseminated to various levels of administration, so many people knew about it.

On January 4, I received a notice calling me to Deng's home for a meeting. When I arrived around 10 A.M., Chen Yun, Wan Li, Yang Shangkun, Bo Yibo, Wang Zhen, and Peng Zhen were already there. After everyone had arrived, Deng pulled out a letter to show us.

It was Yaobang's letter of resignation, addressed to Deng. The general idea of the letter was that he [Hu Yaobang] had not been cautious enough in his leadership, that he had done a lot of foolish things concerning domestic and international issues. But mainly he said that he had been weak in upholding the Four Cardinal Principles and the Anti-Liberalization Campaign, had been ambivalent in his attitude, and had therefore caused a flood of liberalization and become a protective shield for some villains. Since the mistakes he made were grave, he was asking permission to step down in order to review his thoughts and give a proper accounting to the Party.

After everyone in the meeting had read the letter, Deng said that the resignation should be accepted. Nobody expressed disagreement. Deng said that after Yaobang stepped down, Zhao Ziyang, Bo Yibo, Yang Shangkun, and Wan Li should be in charge of the affairs of the Politburo Standing Committee until the 13th Party Congress. I suggested that Hu

---

*   A disputed local election triggered student protests in more than a dozen cities in 1986. Demonstrators called for greater political freedoms, though their protests resulted in the accelerated removal of liberal Party chief Hu Yaobang.

Qili be included, since he was standing secretary of the Secretariat in charge of daily affairs. Deng agreed.

That became the Five-Person Group that I was in charge of, which took over the daily affairs of the Politburo Standing Committee until the 13th Party Congress. Deng said that soft methods could be used to deal with Yaobang's affair. His membership on the Politburo Standing Committee could be retained so as to minimize the impact on domestic and international affairs. He also said that the Central Advisory Commission could call for a Party life meeting to conduct a criticism and correction of Yaobang, and then announce Yaobang's resignation at an enlarged Politburo meeting rather than in a Central Committee plenum.

At the time, I thought that the reason for not holding a plenum was to reduce the shock and allow for softer measures, rather than out of concern that it might not pass. Of course, the measure was not in line with proper Party rules, but his intention was to resolve the matter while reducing the impact. After Deng spoke, no comrades voiced any differing opinion.

Chen Yun was more active than the others at this meeting. He seemed very attentive to organizational principles and proper procedure. He was afraid there would be comments, both domestic and international, about the acceptance of the General Secretary's resignation at a Politburo meeting, so he made it a point to announce that it was legal and in line with proper procedures.

Deng himself never took such matters seriously. Of course, the way Yaobang's case was handled, especially the criticism of him in the Central Advisory Commission's Party life meeting, did trigger some domestic and international criticism that the change of leadership had involved illegitimate means.

During the meeting at Deng Xiaoping's home, [Party elder] Li Xiannian was in Shanghai. After the meeting, Deng Xiaoping immediately sent Yang Shangkun to Shanghai to inform him and ask his opinion. After Yang Shangkun briefed Li Xiannian on what had happened, Li, of course, wholeheartedly agreed with the outcome; it was like a dream come true. He said to Yang, "I've known all along that this guy was no good!"

He also suggested that Hu was silver-tongued and full of tricks. Li said that when Yaobang recently came to Shanghai, Li requested to meet with Yaobang, who had the nerve to refuse him. Li continued to vent his anger toward Hu. He also agreed with the move to make me Acting General Secretary, but told Yang Shangkun, "Ziyang has learned too much foreign stuff. Continuing in this is unacceptable. You should tell him that."

On January 7, 1987, Bo Yibo, Yang Shangkun, Wan Li, Hu Qili, and I held our first Five-Person Group meeting to discuss the specifics of the Party life meeting. We made the decision to conduct the meeting in as moderate a tone as possible.

At the time, Peng Zhen, Bo Yibo, and other elders wanted to accuse Hu of having promoted a "clique" of cadres, the so-called "Youth League Faction."* I felt that this was not advisable, that the consequences would be serious and lead to a widespread sense of insecurity, repeating the pattern of implicating people by association. After I raised my concerns, everyone expressed their consent, so we agreed not to raise the issue of the "Youth League Faction" and "clique of cadres."

The night before the Party life meeting, I went to Yaobang's home to tell him how the meeting would be conducted. I also told him how the discussion went at Deng's house and that his membership on the Politburo Standing Committee would be retained.

I also raised some questions. I said, "Deng gave you several messages on the issue of anti-liberalism. Why didn't you take this seriously? Were you intentionally keeping your distance from Deng?" He said that that had never occurred to him.

I also said, "After your resignation is made public, it is possible that some people will make trouble in the name of supporting you." I truly anticipated that such things could happen, so I wanted him to be aware of this and be prepared for it.

He replied that he would resolutely stand by the Party. Later, at the Party life meeting, I reported everything that we had said in this conversation.

The Party life meeting was held on January 10 under the name of the Central Advisory Commission. Bo Yibo chaired the meeting, which took place over six consecutive mornings (including one session that lasted the entire day). Participants included the members of the Standing Committee of the Central Advisory Commission, Politburo members, secretaries of the Secretariat, State Council members, the vice chairman of the Party Committee of the NPC, the vice president of the Chinese People's Political Consultative Conference, various department heads of the Central Military Commission, and various department heads under the Central Committee. Deng Xiaoping and Chen Yun did not participate. Li Xiannian was in Shanghai.

Deng Liqun delivered a long speech systematically criticizing Yao-

---

*   Hu Yaobang served for more than twenty years as first secretary of China's Communist Youth League.

bang for not heeding Deng Xiaoping's directions, and for being lax about or even encouraging bourgeois liberalization over a long period of time. Other speeches followed the traditional pattern of the Party, taking different angles from which to criticize Hu. [Second Secretary of the Central Discipline Inspection Commission] Wang Heshou revealed in the meeting that when he went to Hu's home to see him, Yaobang was very upset and had complained that some Party elders were preparing to attack him. The intention had been to conduct this meeting in a moderate fashion, but when Wang Heshou spoke, the atmosphere became more tense. We immediately warned Wang Heshou not to continue on about this. Fortunately, while he was talking, some of the Party elders were not there.

The most surprising statement at the meeting was from [influential military veteran] Yu Qiuli. Yaobang and Yu Qiuli had been very close in those years. In preparations for the 12th Party Congress, Hu Yaobang had put Yu Qiuli in charge of rearranging the leadership positions. Back then, I was in the State Council and did not handle such matters. I did not know why Yu Qiuli should be put in charge of making the leadership arrangements for the 12th Party Congress, but it indicated his [Hu's] trust in Yu Qiuli. In those years, not only did Yaobang visit border regions and inspect troops with Yu Qiuli, but because Yu was in the army and was the director of the General Political Department, they also visited factories and oil fields together. During Secretariat meetings, Yaobang often asked for Yu Qiuli's opinion on economic issues, then praised his views. Perhaps Hu had trouble getting support on economic issues; Yu's views were in line with his, so he was using Yu Qiuli's remarks as a way to express his own opinion, or to gain consensus. Their relationship had been quite intimate.

However, at the Party life meeting, Yu Qiuli unexpectedly delivered a harsh speech against Yaobang. He had collected Yaobang's remarks on whether Deng and Party elders would retire, and asked Yaobang in an accusatory tone, "What was your motive? Why did you say that?"

Yu Qiuli thus revealed himself to be a man who ordinarily appeared to be honest, but at the critical moment engaged in backstabbing to protect himself. It was a singular exposure of his true nature. Perhaps he felt that the two of them had had a close relationship, so if Deng had decided to part with Yaobang and remove him from office, if he [Yu] were seen to be close to Yaobang, perhaps he would also be implicated. So he wanted to take the opportunity to extricate himself.

At the end of the Party life meeting, Yaobang gave a self-criticism speech, admitting to having made serious political mistakes. Toward the end of his talk, he became extremely emotional, weeping openly.

At the enlarged Politburo meeting, on January 16, Yaobang's resignation was passed by a show of hands. I was appointed Acting General Secretary. Even though I had repeated on various occasions that in the age group between sixty and seventy, Hu Yaobang was the only one suited to be General Secretary, on both January 4, at the meeting in Deng's home, and at the enlarged Politburo meeting, I did not oppose the decision to accept Yaobang's resignation, but only made the remark that I was not suited for the position of Acting General Secretary and hoped a more appropriate person would be found soon. I did not refuse.

The reasons for this were, first, that the matter had already been decided by Deng and other Party elders in the summer of 1986. Though I did not participate in the decision, I had heard about it, and as I mentioned before, Deng had spoken with Yaobang, and Yaobang had agreed—even though he didn't know the true reason Deng was having him removed from his position. In other words, Hu was eventually going to step down, only it happened a few months earlier than it would have.

The second reason is that after Deng made his remarks about the student demonstrations on December 30, Yaobang had been unable to continue working. As I mentioned before, after the summer of 1986 it became difficult for Yaobang to manage the work of the Central Committee. Many Party elders no longer paid him any heed. Many of his suggestions failed to win support, especially after Deng attributed the student unrest to bourgeois liberalization and blamed him for not expelling so-and-so from the Party after he'd asked him to. The speech had been transcribed and distributed to a circle of officials. Since it was difficult for Yaobang to lead, he was left with no choice but to resign.

Another point is that in Yaobang's case, Hu Qili had also been affected [because he was a close associate of Hu Yaobang (no relation)]. Having Hu Qili join the Five-Person Group would keep him from being implicated, which was the best scenario under the circumstances. It was impossible to have Qili succeed Yaobang. It was difficult to find a suitable candidate on such short notice. Under the circumstances, it was neither easy nor appropriate for me to refuse to accept the role of Acting General Secretary.

There has been public hearsay accusing me of writing a letter to Deng Xiaoping bringing charges against and making malicious remarks about Yaobang. Some even say that I urged Deng Xiaoping to finish him off. There is no truth to this at all. In 1984, I wrote to Deng Xiaoping once about perfecting the system of the central leadership; that is, how to really establish democratic centralism within the Central Committee, especially within the Politburo and its Standing Committee. A copy of the letter was sent to Comrade Chen Yun. It had nothing to do with Yaobang whatsoever. The contents of the letter are as follows:

Comrade Xiaoping:

I am forwarding to you a copy of a suggestion from Comrade Chen Junsheng [the Party secretary] of Heilongjiang Province. Please read it for reference.

Though his suggestion would not necessarily tackle the fundamental problems, he does raise the extremely important issue of how to preserve long-term peace and good governance in our country.

Currently, various aspects of the situation are improving and seem certain to continue on this trend. However, this does not mean the issue of long-term peace and good governance has been fundamentally resolved. Maintaining the stability of the fundamental laws of the nation is certainly one aspect; however, since we are a socialist state under the leadership of the Communist Party, I am concerned that it is not enough to consider the issue only from the point of view of the constitution. I believe that fundamentally and most importantly, we must tackle the system of the Party leadership. Only by doing so can the problem be truly resolved.

With both you and Comrade Chen Yun still energetic and in good health, and with major and fundamental policies already set down, various tasks have been steered onto the right tracks under your guidance and because of your decisions. The current period is no doubt one of the best in our Party's history. Precisely because of this, I sincerely hope that you will put more energy and concentration on resolving this major and important issue that will affect our Party and our country for generations to come: that is, to establish a much-needed system of leadership for our Party and then to personally inspect and seek compliance so as to make it a custom and culture that will not shift according to the changing of individuals, so it will pass on through the generations.

Please take my suggestion into consideration.

I herewith offer my salute!

Zhao Ziyang

It was May 26, 1984, before a visit to Europe.

This was the only letter I sent to the Central Committee or Deng Xiaoping in reference to the issue of the central leadership. I wrote the letter and sent it together with Chen Junsheng's suggestion.

The reason for the letter was that during the years just after the Gang of Four* had been smashed, while the central leadership was reviewing the atrocity of the Cultural Revolution, we had often discussed how such a tragedy could be prevented from happening again. We saw a need to resolve issues of our Party's system of leadership to prevent concentration of power in, and arbitrary use of power by, a single person.

However, after the 12th Party Congress, because both domestic and international conditions were good and were improving, the discussions about these issues dwindled. But even though we had proceeded with reform—our economy had grown rapidly, people's living standards had improved, and our democratic culture had strengthened within the central leadership—the problem of the system of leadership, whether in the plenum, the Politburo, or the Politburo Standing Committee, had not been resolved. They all remained more or less as before.

As a result, I felt it was necessary to raise the issue again. If the matter were not resolved while conditions were relatively good, it would still be difficult to guarantee that there would be no problems with future leaders.

My letter was written from that perspective, and was not in reference to any specific leader. I did not feel that there was any major problem with the leadership. The situation was relatively good. However, current good conditions did not guarantee future good conditions, since the systemic issue had not been resolved. I wasn't referring to any problems in the leadership, nor was I pointing to Yaobang or any other leaders.

The letter was not meant to imply that because there was an issue with Yaobang, the system of leadership was being raised. However, it also did not mean to imply that because Yaobang was relatively enlightened, there was no need to improve the system of the central leadership.

Yaobang was amiable and open-minded and was able to listen to different opinions. He was very generous to people and did not like giving people a hard time. People could argue with him and even quarrel with him. I have said many times, just because he was open-minded by nature did not mean that we did not still have to consider the issue of the system

* The Gang of Four referred to an ultraleftist Communist Party faction that controlled key organs of power and culture during the Cultural Revolution.

of leadership. Since he was already seventy years old, after the Party elders were gone, who knows how long he would be able to lead?

In my speech at the Party life meeting, I said that we must rely on a system, not on individuals, since people could change. Without a good system, even great leaders such as Stalin and Chairman Mao had problems. I mentioned my letter to Xiaoping without explaining the contents of the letter. Moreover, my criticisms of Yaobang also touched upon the obeying of the rules of democratic centralism and Party discipline. Therefore, it is possible that my comments about Yaobang were interpreted as having also been the contents of the letter. This is probably how the rumor spread.

There was another rumor, which was not as widespread. I heard it much later. Yaobang had often spoken about the issue of Party elders possibly retiring before the 13th Party Congress. So there was a rumor that Deng Xiaoping once said in front of Yaobang and me that he would retire at the 13th Party Congress. Hu Yaobang purportedly responded that he would "lift both hands to approve," while I replied, "You cannot retire, absolutely not!" This incident supposedly made Deng feel that Yaobang was up to no good. This is an entirely fictitious story.

Before Yaobang stepped down, Deng had never expressed in front of me, let alone in front of Yaobang and me, whether he would retire. The first time I heard of Deng saying he would resign from the Politburo Standing Committee and as chairman of the Central Advisory Commission was after the summer of 1986, when Yaobang told me about his talk with Deng. There was no occasion where Deng asked both of us for our opinions.

I indeed asked Deng to retain his official position, asking him not to resign from the Politburo Standing Committee. That was in 1987, after Yaobang had stepped down and I was already Acting General Secretary. Since Deng was still going to be in charge, I preferred that he do so from within the Party Standing Committee.

There is one other event worth mentioning. At a Politburo Standing Committee meeting in March or April 1983, Comrade Chen Yun's criticism of Yaobang caused a small disturbance. Even though this incident had nothing to do with Yaobang's resignation in 1987, rumors about the incident spread, some of which involved me.

At that meeting, the main agenda was to report to Deng and the Politburo Standing Committee about work on the economy. Deng Xiaoping felt at that time that annual target levels had been set too low for two consecutive years. The result was a huge overshooting of the target, which Deng disapproved of. But the comrades on the Planning Commission and

I all felt that there would be no benefit at all to setting the target too high. It was better to have room to maneuver. The report was meant to explain our reasons clearly.

Yao Yilin and Song Ping then reported on behalf of the Planning Commission. After they gave their report, I spoke. In addition to agreeing with their assessment, I talked about the fact that there had been a big drop in the ratio of financial revenue to gross national product. This was normal, since we were paying back debts. But it could not go on for a long period of time or else finances at the central level would run into trouble.

After I finished speaking, without a chance to discuss what I'd said, Comrade Chen Yun pulled out a prepared speech, specifically raising many points about some of Yaobang's recent remarks on economic issues. The criticism was very harsh. For example, Yaobang had said that the Ministry of Finance exaggerated a deficit year after year just to frighten people. Chen Yun said that the reported size of the deficit claimed was in fact real. He also criticized Yaobang for saying that the first Five-Year Plan had managed big enterprises but neglected small and midsize firms.

Since Yaobang had not anticipated this, after Chen Yun's speech he made no rebuttal and only responded that he had made many mistakes and would carefully reconsider them. It appeared that Chen Yun had vented anger with Yaobang that had been accumulating over a long period of time.

Comrade Xiaoping was not willing to criticize Yaobang in this kind of setting and did not want to debate the issue. He seemed displeased. He said that discussion of such things could be put off for some other time, and that we were primarily there to hear the report. Because of this, the discussion did not continue.

It was difficult for others to give their opinions after Comrade Chen Yun made his speech. Hu Qiaomu, however, stood up and spoke. He said that the remarks made by Yaobang and criticized by Comrade Chen Yun had been spread widely and had caused huge disruptions to economic policies. He suggested calling for a meeting at the provincial and municipal levels to inform them of Chen Yun's criticism. At the time, Deng Xiaoping had no choice but to say, "Very well, why don't you discuss this later."

A day or two later, Hu Qili suddenly appeared at my home and told me what was happening. Without telling anyone, Deng Liqun had already disseminated the Chen Yun criticism of Yaobang at the Politburo Standing Committee in a national conference held by the Xinhua News

Agency. Hu Qili and I felt that this action was really harmful. This could cause nationwide confusion.

Since it was difficult for Yaobang to say anything, I had to intervene. I called Deng Liqun, criticized him for doing the wrong thing, and asked him to have Xinhua News Agency retrieve his speech and not distribute or disseminate it. That is what happened.

I then went to Tianjin. After I returned, Yaobang came to my home and said Deng Xiaoping had reconsidered the proposal for provincial and municipal level meetings and had decided they would not be held after all. I surmise that Xiaoping believed if the meetings were to take place, the impact would be even greater.

At the same time, Yaobang said that there were rumors of changes in the central leadership. I wondered whether Yaobang was being oversensitive. I told him, "You shouldn't listen to those rumors. As far as I can see, Comrade Chen Yun only wanted to vent some of the anger he had accumulated all these years over some of the things you'd said. After the outburst, it will be over. Also, you should not read too much into it. Now that we are in the same boat, we should cross the river together. I don't believe Hu Qiaomu and Deng Liqun have any other ambitions."

That's what I thought at the time. I said, "They are intellectuals. As for Chen Yun, he's even less likely to have ambitions. We must stick together and not worry too much."

Yaobang agreed with what I said. Later, I met Hu Qili, who immediately told me that after having spoken with me, Yaobang was in good spirits, and told him, "What Ziyang said was very good. What we must do now is cross the river together on the same boat."

That is what happened. Perhaps there were rumors in public that people had criticized Yaobang at the Politburo Standing Committee meeting. In fact it was not like that. Chen Yun was the only one to give a speech, and because it was directed at Yaobang, no one was able to comment one way or the other. Originally, I too had some reservations about Yaobang on economic efforts and also had critical views about the way he went around making careless remarks. However, I did not think it was appropriate to raise such issues under the circumstances, so I didn't say anything.

A few days later, Deng Xiaoping asked Yao Yilin and me over for a talk. Deng said that initially there was to be a meeting about Yaobang. But after considering the impact that would have, the meeting was canceled. He said that Yaobang had a lot of personal shortcomings but still needed to be supported.

I immediately voiced my agreement. Xiaoping then criticized Yao Yilin, because before this incident, Yao Yilin and Song Ping had written a letter addressed to the Politburo Standing Committee and Deng Xiaoping in which they accused Yaobang of making careless remarks that were not in line with the spirit of the 12th Party Congress. As a result, the Planning Commission was having difficulty carrying out its work.

Deng accused Yao Yilin, "You were venting your anger in the letter!"

Yao Yilin immediately replied, "Yes, I was."

2

Zhao Walks the Line

As the new acting Party General Secretary, Zhao faces a daunting challenge: directing Deng Xiaoping's campaign against "bourgeois liberalization" without throwing economic reforms off course. Zhao devises intentionally confusing jargon to describe his policies since he is now charged with spearheading a campaign he has every intention of subverting. It's not clear whether Deng is aware of Zhao's tactics. What is evident is that Zhao can play politics with the best of them.

In the 1980s, our reform was in the difficult stage of laying its basic foundations. The events of that period had a significant impact on the modernization and development process and are worth remembering. Here I will recount some of those events, in bits and pieces. If I ever get the chance, I would like to recount more.

First, I will talk about the Anti-Liberalization Campaign* that occurred after Yaobang stepped down in 1987.

On January 4, 1987, Deng Xiaoping called a meeting at his house and the decision was made to accept Yaobang's resignation. From January 10 to 15, a Party life meeting, carried out by the Central Advisory Commission and chaired by Bo Yibo, was held for the purpose of criticizing Hu Yaobang. On January 16, an expanded Politburo meeting was held to announce the acceptance of Yaobang's resignation. Subsequently, a nationwide Anti-Liberalization Campaign was launched.

The broadly sweeping campaign began with a reemphasis on the Four Cardinal Principles and evolved into an Anti-Liberalization and Anti-

---

* Also known as the "Anti–Bourgeois Liberalization Campaign."

Rightist Tendencies movement. It ended with the 13th Party Congress [in late 1987], which emphasized reform and opposed "ossification" and leftist tendencies. Over the year, the political climate made a complete 180-degree turnaround. Of course, the route actually taken was a tortuously winding one.

My activities in 1987 can roughly be divided into two major phases. From January to April, when I had just succeeded Yaobang as [acting] General Secretary, I took on the designated task of waging a nationwide Anti-Liberalization Campaign. Most of my energy and concentration was focused on figuring out how to prevent the campaign from overreaching, to control and limit the "left wing" who were hoping to use the campaign to oppose reform. This "left wing" struggle was in essence opposed to the principles set forth at the Third Plenum [in 1978].

The second phase ran from May until the beginning of the 13th Party Congress [in October]. During this period, I reemphasized reform, tried to prevent a swing to the left, and opposed ossified thinking—all with the preparation for the 13th Party Congress in mind.

The Cleansing Spiritual Pollution Campaign of 1983 had taught us that people like [conservative ideologues] Deng Liqun and Hu Qiaomu must be prevented from seizing opportunities to launch overzealous campaigns. From the beginning, I made strict stipulations on the nature, scope, key points, policies, and methods of the campaign. In the drafting of the document "The Chinese Communist Party Central Committee's Notice Regarding Several Issues in the Current Anti-Liberalization Campaign," which I supervised, I defined the campaign as focused on resolving issues of basic political principles and policy direction. This campaign was to be applied only within the Party and within the realms of metaphysics and politics. It was not to touch rural policies, or science and technology. Nor was it to have any bearing on issues of literary or artistic style. This campaign would not be conducted in the countryside, and only positive educational activities were to be carried out in enterprises and government organizations. And even within the metaphysical and political arenas, the campaign was to be limited to educational activities about political direction and principles. The Anti-Liberalization Campaign was to be conducted in accordance with the principles of the Third Plenum, and none of the old leftist methods were permitted.

Because the Spring Festival of 1987 fell on January 29, the notice issued by the Central Committee would have had to have been approved by the Politburo meeting scheduled for the afternoon of January 28. Hence it was impossible to disseminate before the Spring Festival. Yet the custom of visiting friends and relatives during the Spring Festival would make for the most effective way to spread the news.

To let people know about the rules regarding the campaign, I delivered a speech at a January 28 meeting in Beijing of senior cadres from the Central Committee, various organs of Party administration, government, and the military. The speech identified the scope, policy, key issues, and methods for the campaign, outlining the Central Committee's approach so that the news could spread through the Spring Festival activities.

I specifically stated that "The Third Plenum resolved that there would be no more mass campaigns. However, people are accustomed to the old ways, so whenever we oppose anything, these methods are still being used. Now, in our approach to defeating liberalism, to avoid these mass campaign methods it is very important from the beginning to be alert to possible biased tendencies, especially 'leftist' ones. We cannot do what we did in the past, placing emphasis only on proceeding boldly and firmly while ignoring all policies and limits. The result of that would be mistakes being made from the start and an overreaching that in the end will only require correction. This time we will take a distinctly different approach from the past mass campaigns. From the beginning we will clearly define what can and cannot be done and declare specifically what the limits are. That's how to avoid another mass campaign." (At the time, the momentum had already begun, and we couldn't halt the campaign altogether.)

My speech and the Central Committee's "Notice Regarding the Anti-Liberalization Campaign" were derided as chains by those who had hoped for a full-blown campaign, such as Deng Liqun, Hu Qiaomu, and Wang Renzhi. They felt that this notice [popularly known as the Number Four Document] had bound them hand and foot and protected bourgeois liberals. They opposed the document, but because it defined the scope, key points, and policy from the start, the campaign ended up hurting few people. There was no nationwide shock, no disruptions to the economy, and no great harm to reform. The overall result was quite good.

During this period of time, whenever I received foreign guests or spoke in public, I repeatedly confirmed that the principles set forth at the Third Plenum would not be changed. (There were doubts both at home and abroad, because when people heard "anti-liberalization" they thought it meant retrenchment in reform.) I emphasized that reforms would not backtrack, but rather would only improve. I reiterated that current urban and rural policies would not change; the overall approach to reform would not change; the policy of opening up to the outside world would not change; the drive to reenergize the domestic economy would not change;

and the policy of rewarding individual knowledge and merit would not change. Moreover, we would attempt to build on these efforts.

In response to those who were worried about the campaign spreading to Hong Kong, I told some Hong Kong visitors that while the mainland was compelled to uphold the Four Cardinal Principles and to oppose liberalism in its pursuit of socialism, the meaning of "One Country, Two Systems"* was to allow the capitalist system to continue in Hong Kong and Macau, and to allow liberalism there. How could we possibly carry out the Anti-Liberalization Campaign in Hong Kong or Macau?

The main idea I put forward was this: "There are two basic points to the principles of the Third Plenum. One is the upholding of the Four Cardinal Principles, and the other is the Reform and Open-Door Policy. We cannot neglect either one. Omitting either one would result in the failure of 'socialism with Chinese characteristics.' In an earlier period, we neglected the Four Cardinal Principles, so now we are reemphasizing them. However, if we give up the Reform and Open-Door Policy, we will veer in another wrong direction."

I hoped first to relieve the doubts people were having, and second to prevent anyone from accentuating the Four Cardinal Principles while resisting reform. The Anti-Liberalization Campaign caused great misunderstanding because people did not grasp the true meaning of the Third Plenum principles. Some believed that they only stood for reform, so when the Anti-Liberalization Campaign was proposed, it seemed to constitute a change in policy. I made clear that the Third Plenum principles included the two basic points. These talks had the effect of calming the public and greatly reduced the range of activities that pitted left against right and set anti-liberalization against reform. The forces behind ossified thinking and dogmatism, led by Deng Liqun, Hu Qiaomu, and Wang Renzhi, were highly displeased by my strategy. They attempted to sway public opinion and assert pressure in every way possible to disrupt and change the Central Committee's way of deploying the Anti-Liberalization Campaign.

From the start, when Wang Renzhi succeeded Zhu Houze as Director of the Propaganda Department, I told him to remember that there were two basic points and not to neglect the other when carrying out the Anti-Liberalization Campaign. I also told him that when carrying out his work,

* One Country, Two Systems is the formulation that describes how Hong Kong and Macau can be loyal parts of China despite their vastly different social, economic, and political systems.

he should think for himself—meaning that he shouldn't just obey [former Director of the Propaganda Department] Deng Liqun—and should respect the policies of the Central Committee.

However, in a meeting of provincial and municipal level department heads of propaganda, Wang Renzhi said, "The Anti-Liberalization Campaign marks the second 'restoring of order from chaos' since the fall of the Gang of Four." His meaning was obvious, that the first case involved restoring order after the leftist chaos brought on by the Gang of Four; this time, order was being restored from the Third Plenum and reform. When this was reported to me, I reproached Wang Renzhi and asked him if Deng Liqun had asked him to say such a thing, but he refused to answer directly, conceding only that he'd expressed "undeveloped thoughts." I had never had a bad impression of Wang before. When he was at the State Planning Commission, he was decent and honest in his economic research, so I had hopes that he might keep some distance from Deng Liqun. Therefore, I only criticized him orally and did not pursue it further. Nor did I reveal to the public what he had said or how I had criticized him, hoping to give him another chance.

Around the summer of 1987, Wang Ruilin [Deng Xiaoping's secretary] forwarded me a letter from Wang Daming [a former Deputy Director of the Propaganda Department]. It claimed that some bureau chiefs in the Department of Propaganda, upon hearing Deng Xiaoping's statement that the main agenda in the immediate future was to oppose the left, reacted with inappropriate emotional remarks, such as "We must hold out and resist!" and "There is still no telling who will win!"

On July 11, after Hu Qili had taken over the propaganda front, I called comrades from the front to a policy briefing that was also a work transition meeting. At the meeting, I harshly criticized Wang Renzhi and Wang Weicheng [a Deputy Director of Propaganda], according to what had been reported in this letter.

I said that the Department of Propaganda was in a bad state. "As soon as you heard that Deng Xiaoping was opposing the left, you all reacted as though the sky had fallen, and appeared grief-stricken as though your parents had just died. How can you possibly implement the policies of the Third Plenum correctly with this kind of attitude?" I demanded that they make real changes to the Department of Propaganda's position, but they expressed no remorse, and only evaded the issue by disclaiming any knowledge of it.

In March 1987, a conference was held in Zhou County, Hebei Province, for a discussion of theory. Attending were the three organizations under the control of the left wing, led by Deng Liqun and Hu Qiaomu: *Red Flag* and *Literary and Art Theory and Criticism* magazines and the paper *Guangming Daily*. [Xinhua News Agency director] Xiong Fu and others took a stand to "restore order" from the "chaos" of the Third Plenum of the 11th Central Committee, complaining that the eight years since the Third Plenum had been a nightmare. During those years, Marxists had been under pressure and a fierce struggle was being waged between anti-liberals and liberals.

Everyone knew Xiong Fu had been the main drafter of the "Two Whatevers."* He portrayed people like himself as heroes of anti-liberalism and denied that anything positive had occurred in the eight years since the Third Plenum. Xiong Fu had been criticized by some cadres at the Third Plenum. Although Deng Liqun had opposed the "Two Whatevers," his way of thinking had much in common with Xiong's, so Deng Liqun befriended him and entrusted him with important responsibilities.

At that time, Deng Liqun, Hu Qiaomu, Wang Renzhi, and others who were influenced by them criticized the Central Committee's Number Four Document, which they said "bound the hands and feet of the Anti-Liberalization Campaign and strangled the activists' fighting spirit while increasing the worries of those who opposed liberalism." They also said the restrictions outlined in the Number Four Document emboldened those who were involved in liberalization. Some even complained that the Number Four Document had "poured cold water" on the Anti-Liberalization Campaign. The earlier Anti–Spiritual Pollution Campaign had lasted only twenty-seven days; this campaign, these people said, would not even last that long.

Their goal was to pressure me to revise the approach and let them proceed without the restrictions. They also complained that "criticizing those who speak of liberalization is allowed; criticizing those who actually *do* liberalization is not allowed." They labeled liberals in the ideological and theoretical arena as "speaking liberalism" and those carrying out economic reform as "doing liberalism." They said, "Liberalism in ideology and theory involves the superstructure, and liberalization in the economic area involves the base that is its source. If we cannot touch liberalization in the economic arena, then the basic problem cannot be resolved."

They actively tried to breach the boundaries set by the Number Four

---

* The Two Whatevers was a leftist philosophy, first published in newspaper editorials in 1977, whose followers pledged to uphold whatever decisions Mao made and to follow whatever instructions Mao gave.

Document and attempted to spread the Anti-Liberalization Campaign into the areas of economic, agricultural, and science and technology policies. They tried to criticize and retaliate against reform on all fronts.

During the New Year and Spring Festival activities and during talks with foreign guests, I proposed the idea of the "two basic points" of the Third Plenum principles. It was not long before someone suggested that the "two basic points" could not be considered on the same level: the Four Cardinal Principles were principles; reform was only the means.

The person who proposed this was Lu Zhichao, the leftist bureau chief at the Theoretical Department of the Department of Propaganda. Deng Liqun approved of him and had on several occasions proposed making him Deputy Director of Propaganda. But since I always opposed it, he had never made it to this position. I later insisted on his leaving the Department of Propaganda. [Director of the Organization Department] Song Ping discussed it with Deng Liqun, and they had him placed in the post of deputy general secretary of the Chinese People's Political Consultative Conference.

The leftists organized a conference for theoretical discussion through the education department head of the Central Party School, Jiang Liu. The agenda was to discuss the "principle versus means" issue concerning the Four Cardinal Principles and the Reform and Open-Door Policy. The discussion was meant to point out that I had made the two ideas parallel—or degraded the principle by overemphasizing the means. They hoped to downgrade reform in the name of upholding the Four Principles. When I heard about the event, I asked the president of the Central Party School to investigate. When the conference was held, Jiang Liu found an excuse to not participate. Nothing came of it.

Faced with such resistance from the left, I spoke at a national meeting of Propaganda Department leaders of provincial and local levels on March 13, 1987, and stated that we must further unify our views on the Central Committee's Number Four Document and should completely, carefully, and accurately carry out its spirit. I criticized statements that had characterized the Number Four Document as restrictive, and spoke out against efforts to expand the Anti-Liberalization Campaign into the economic arena.

Since the timing was not yet right, my criticism of such incorrect thinking remained vague and lenient. I thought at the time that in order to turn things around, I would have to find the right opportunity to strike back forcefully. I needed to resist these forces to contain the Anti-Liberalization Campaign.

Another issue was how to deal with people implicated in all of this.

The Anti-Liberalization Campaign was not just a theoretical issue. My biggest headaches came from the issues of whether to punish people, how to reduce the harm done to people, and how to contain the circle of people being harmed. From the beginning of the campaign, some Party elders were also very enthusiastic and wanted to punish a lot of people. Deng Xiaoping had always believed that those who proceeded with liberalization within the Party should be severely punished. Wang Zhen and other elders believed this as well. People like Deng Liqun and Hu Qiaomu were even more eager to take the opportunity to destroy certain people and take pleasure in the aftermath.

Under these circumstances, it was difficult to protect certain people, or limit the number being hurt or even to reduce the degree of harm that was done. Hence when it was drafted, the Number Four Document set strict limits on the punishment of those designated by the campaign as having made mistakes. The document defined this as: "Punishments that will be publicized and administrative punishments must first be approved by the Central Committee, and are to be meted out to those few Party members who openly promote bourgeois liberalism, refuse to mend their ways despite repeated admonitions, and have extensive influence." The document also stated, "For those who hold some mistaken views, criticisms by fellow Party members may be carried out in Party group administrative meetings. They should be allowed to hold to their own views and the method of carrying out the criticism must be calm."

At the meeting of national Propaganda Department leaders and on other occasions, I also spoke on how to win over the vast majority of people in the theoretical and cultural domains. I suggested we cooperate even with people with biased or false ideas. I pointed out, "Among Party members working in the theoretical and cultural fields, there are those who clearly uphold the Four Cardinal Principles but are a bit conservative and rigid; some are enthusiastic about reform yet have made statements that are inappropriate. We cannot just label the former as dogmatic or the latter as pursuers of liberalization. We should educate and cooperate with them all."

When proceeding with the Anti-Liberalization Campaign, I had intentionally emphasized that we should classify those who had taken faulty liberal actions as well as those who were too conservative and rigid into the same group of people who were too biased. The purpose was to avoid or reduce the harm being done to people.

Deng Xiaoping suggested making a list of liberals, and punishing them one by one. In addition to [liberal editor] Wang Ruowang and [dissident astrophysicist] Fang Lizhi, whom Deng had long wanted to expel from the Party, the first draft of this list—which included [prominent economist] Yu Guangyuan—was proposed by Deng Liqun and Hu Qiaomu. I suggested that according to the spirit of the Number Four Document, the criticism of Yu Guangyuan should be done at a Central Advisory Commission Party life meeting, with no administrative punishment. On March 2, 1987, Deng asked me at his house how the case of Zhang Guangnian [a prominent poet and literary critic] should proceed. I replied that I thought it would be best to employ the same method used with Yu Guangyuan. There were others on the list, but they did not pass through the approval process.

Some people in the Central Discipline Inspection Commission remained fervent about punishing people for liberalism, and Deng Liqun cooperated with them. He had help from the Research Office of the Central Committee Secretariat. They gathered materials and compiled a record of things people had said as evidence of their incorrect opinions. They then drew up a list of names that was sent to the Central Discipline Inspection Commission for comments and then forwarded it, in batches, to the Central Committee Secretariat.

If this were to continue, batch after batch, one could just imagine how many people would be punished. I had no option but to deal with this by stalling. Since these lists had to be discussed by the Secretariat, I would hold meetings infrequently and discuss only a few cases at each meeting. Differences of opinion inevitably arose during the discussions. If a discussion was inconclusive, the case would continue to be discussed at the next meeting. Not many people were punished, and the cases that were never discussed disappeared into oblivion.

During the campaign, the Secretariat decided to expel from the Party [influential journalist] Liu Binyan and [liberal intellectual] Zhang Xianyang. [Playwright] Wu Zuguang was originally marked to be expelled from the Party but ended up being "persuaded to quit." [*People's Daily* deputy chief editor] Wang Ruoshui was originally marked to be "persuaded to quit" but ended up being discharged. [Liberal intellectual] Su Shaozhi was originally marked for expulsion but I proposed removing him from his post as director of the Institute of Marxism–Leninism–Mao Zedong Thought but retaining his Party membership.

[Intellectual] Sun Changjiang was marked to be expelled, but because Marshal Nie [Rongzhen] spoke up for him, he was not punished. Marshal Nie did a good thing. When he learned that Sun Changjiang's case was being discussed at the Secretariat, he wrote a note to Chen Yun praising Sun's work at the *Science and Technology Daily* and suggesting he not be punished. Chen Yun, who was at the time the secretary of the

Party Discipline Inspection Commission, agreed with Marshal Nie. I took the opportunity to comment on the document along these lines: "The treatment of other cases shall be dealt with in the spirit of Marshal Nie and Chen Yun's directive," meaning they would be dealt with as Sun Changjiang had been. After that, the punishments practically came to an end.

On the issue of whether or not to publicize the names of people being criticized, the Number Four Document set limits and preferences: articles containing personal attacks or abusive language were not to be allowed, and inundating the media with meaningless assertions must be avoided. Inappropriate use of the Cultural Revolution–style language of past mass campaigns was prohibited. If those who were being criticized provided concrete and reasonable rebuttals, they should be published as well. Any publications unrelated to the campaign should avoid publishing articles of this kind.

However, as soon as the campaign started, Deng Liqun organized a group to employ the methods used in the mass criticisms of the Cultural Revolution: collecting articles and speeches of those they deemed as having made the mistake of liberalization; compiling digests of their so-called "incorrect opinions," which were printed into booklets; making attacks on remarks taken out of context; distributing this material to staff writers of relevant organizations, inviting them to write their own criticisms according to the compiled digest. They published article after article, taking on the form of mass criticisms by quoting out of context and exaggerating a person's offenses—all in an arbitrary and tyrannical manner.

At a Secretariat meeting, I criticized Deng Liqun and asked this group to stop this behavior. In a later meeting of provincial and municipal propaganda heads, I praised only articles by [Heilongjiang Party secretary] Chen Junsheng and [political reform think tank head] Bao Tong. I believed their articles were carefully reasoned and had a positive effect, unlike others that failed to lay out reasons, were simplistic and rough, and attempted to pressure people by labeling them.

I said that in the future, when publishing any critical article, the effect needed to be considered; that is, whether it had the power of persuasion and whether people could bear reading it. The articles written by Deng Liqun's group were in general not welcomed, as they were infused with methods of Cultural Revolution mass criticisms. As a result, articles criticizing liberalism appeared less and less often.

After the resignation of Yaobang, another issue emerged in the Anti-Liberalization Campaign: "guilt by association." Many people, including Party elders, had long objected to the promotion decisions Yaobang had made. They accused him of promoting people based on their skills without regard for their [political] virtue. In addition to preferring smooth talkers, he had also promoted people in the "Youth League Faction" to important positions. In the Party life meeting to criticize Hu, some elders raised the issue of the so-called "Youth League Faction," accusing Yaobang of favoring this group.

I thought that if this issue were allowed to stay on the agenda, the effect could be excessive. So I recommended that no matter what, they should not raise the issue of a "Youth League Faction," of Yaobang attempting to build a faction. I explained that the case was very difficult to judge, given that the Communist Youth League was the organization responsible for training and supplying cadres for the Party.

However, the issue never dissipated. In March 1987, even Deng Xiaoping remarked that Yaobang seemed to have promoted cadres from a certain faction. In the Number Four Document and in many of my speeches, I stated that we would absolutely not find people guilty by association; we would not do as was done during the Cultural Revolution, labeling people because of their connection to someone else. I raised the issue with Deng Xiaoping and suggested that we minimize the changing of personnel in this campaign. In any case in which the existing situation was tolerable, we would avoid reshuffling. Even if reshuffling were found to be necessary, we would do everything possible to delay the change and proceed slowly, so as to reduce the shock. Deng agreed.

It was Hu Yaobang who had proposed Wang Meng for the position of Minister of Culture. Deng Liqun and his associates had always seen him as a representative of liberalism. Naturally, they wanted to force him out. As soon as Yaobang resigned and the Anti-Liberalization Campaign was started, this change was proposed. I was firmly opposed. I told Deng Liqun and Wang Renzhi that Wang Meng would not be removed. The president of the *People's Daily*, Qian Liren, who himself had been promoted from the "Youth League," was relatively progressive, so Deng Liqun wanted to take the opportunity to remove him as well; I also objected to this. Bo Yibo told me that Shandong Party Committee secretary Liang Buting was a member of Yaobang's faction and maintained a close relationship with Yaobang; since Shandong was a major province, he needed to be replaced. I found an excuse to object to this change.

It was impossible to prevent all the personnel changes. Zhu Houze, the Director of Propaganda, was in a very sensitive position, so his removal was unavoidable, as was that of Wei Jianxing, the Director of Organization, and Ruan Chongwu, the Minister of Public Security. For these sensitive bodies, the elders were extremely intent on having people in charge with whom they were familiar. In these situations, there was no choice but to make the changes. I did my best under the circumstances to arrange other positions for them. A female party secretary in Jiangxi was also removed, mainly for incompetence unrelated to the campaign. Also, Zhang Shuguang, Party secretary of Inner Mongolia, was removed because he had made some inappropriate remarks and, after Yaobang resigned, had exhibited attitude problems that triggered a lot of criticism. All of these terminations were handled with caution and new positions were arranged for all of them.

In general, throughout the campaign, excessive harm and major reshuffles were averted. The old habit of implicating or labeling people solely because of their associations was not repeated.

Even though there was no choice but to carry out the Anti-Liberalization Campaign, the above measures largely contained the attempts made by Deng Liqun, Hu Qiaomu, and other elders to expand it. However, open disapproval of reforms continued in the name of the campaign. The campaign still had the loudest voice in the nation's media, while the voice of reform was still extremely weak. The majority of cadres who were at the forefront of reform were in a difficult position. With the 13th Party Congress only several months away, I sensed it would be difficult in the existing political climate to make it a congress that supported reform. It was time to decisively change the situation.

On April 28, 1987, I had a long talk with Deng Xiaoping. I reported to him that after several months of the Anti-Liberalization Campaign, the prevailing climate had changed. The situation that existed before, in which the media had been taken over by supporters of liberalism, had been turned around. However, certain people were using the campaign to resist reform. This attitude was incompatible with the goals of making the 13th Party Congress a meeting that supported reform, so it was important, if we wanted the 13th Party Congress to be successful, for us to start right away to highlight reform in the media.

Deng supported my view. He asked me to carefully prepare and deliver a speech on this matter soon.

On May 13, 1987, I spoke at a meeting of cadres involved with propaganda, theory, and media, and from the Central Party School. At around that time, Deng Xiaoping told foreign guests that socialism did not just mean being poor, and that the mistakes of being too far to the left were the most important lessons learned in China's pursuit of socialism. Because of his remarks, my speech had much more impact. In the meetings of the Secretariat and the Politburo, in addition to harshly criticizing the disturbances caused during the Anti-Liberalization Campaign by attempts to use the left against the right to ignore the limits set by the Number Four Document, I reiterated the following:

First, after several months of effort, the overall climate has changed. The spreading of liberalization has successfully been stopped. From this point on, we must emphasize reform. The 13th Party Congress must be a meeting that supports the Reform and Open-Door Policy. We must make preparations for a successful 13th Party Congress.

Second, this campaign was meant to resolve the problem of the spreading of liberalization. Spreading could have been avoided from the start; it was only a case of a failure in leadership. It is not a difficult matter to resolve.

But after we have resolved the problem of spreading, the next step is to look to long-term efforts. First, we must depend on education; and second, we must rely on continued efforts in reform. Only with the reform programs will productivity develop and people's living standards rise, so people can see the advantages of socialism—and then the influence of liberalism will naturally wane. From this point of view, only reform can deliver the aims of upholding the Four Cardinal Principles. Failure to carry out reform will ultimately end in the overturning of the Four Cardinal Principles.

Therefore, we cannot rely on the repeated waging of campaigns to resolve the fundamental problems of liberalization. We cannot let the issue of spreading liberalization change our resolve to develop productivity through the reform programs. To resolve the problem of spreading liberalization, it was right to take time to root out the disturbances from the right, but from a long-term and fundamental viewpoint, the barriers against reform have come from the left.

Third, the Four Cardinal Principles are the basis of our political system. Reform is our general direction and policy for the building of socialism with Chinese characteristics. The characterization of the Four Cardinal Principles as the principle and the Reform and Open-Door Policy as only the means was an attempt to overturn reform in the name of upholding the Four Cardinal Principles, that is, to denounce the new policy set forth at the Third Plenum of the 11th Party Congress in the name of upholding the Four Cardinal Principles. If the reform is only a means and only a specific tactic, then what is socialism with Chinese characteristics? We should not treat reform as though it were liberalization, nor should we uphold the Four Cardinal Principles in a dogmatic manner. We must use the concept of reform to interpret the Four Cardinal Principles. Otherwise, the result will be the overturning of reform, and a falling into the trap of leftist dogma. If so, "upholding" would have only a utopian meaning and the resulting socialism would be Soviet-style, not one with Chinese characteristics.

Fourth, we must understand the importance of productivity. Gains in productivity are the standard for judging whether a society is progressing or in recession. Especially in our country, which is in the initial stage of socialism, increasing productivity is a must. The leftist viewpoint prolonged its existence for a long time with talk about production relations, without actually developing productivity.

As for what socialism is, there are many attributes that have been attached to it over the years. For example, the Soviet-style economic model was in fact an economic model for times of war, but we took it on as though it were economic planning intrinsic to socialism. In theoretical studies, some have branded the methods that are beneficial to the development of productivity and socialist modernization as capitalist, while labeling other methods that prevent the development of productivity as socialist. Even now these viewpoints that are disconnected from reality and rigid in their reasoning remain prevalent in the theoretical realm. We must further emancipate our minds and advocate bold explorations.

After my speech, most of the cadres showed support and the prevailing climate turned in favor of reform. This made for a successful drafting of the 13th Party Congress report.

3

The Ideologues

Even with the support of Deng Xiaoping, the economic reform program remains politically vulnerable. After all, it is ultimately inconsistent with the Communist Party's proclaimed ideology. Two influential leftists, Hu Qiaomu and Deng Liqun, try to exploit this vulnerability, with backing from powerful Party elders. Zhao actively works to keep them out of the propaganda sphere. But in doing so he becomes Enemy No. 1 among the Party's conservative elders.

Even before the Anti-Liberalization Campaign, Hu Qiaomu and Deng Liqun's situation was not good. Starting in 1986, Deng Xiaoping had distanced himself from Hu Qiaomu and had not met with him for a long time. Hu had made several attempts to arrange appointments but was turned down each time; this made him very worried. He had asked [China's president] Yang Shangkun to speak to Deng on his behalf.

Deng Xiaoping treated Deng Liqun a little better, but had noted that he liked being involved in left-wing type activities. Deng once commented on how Deng Liqun had proposed a revision to the draft of the "Resolution to Build a Spiritual Civilization" at the Beidaihe discussion. He had quoted Deng Xiaoping extensively but had actually been attempting to effect a major turn to the left. Deng was still referring to this in a talk with me as late as March 1987. Deng said Deng Liqun was very stubborn, like a Hunan mule.

At the time, amid the general climate of reform under the advocacy of [Hu] Yaobang, Zhu Houze headed the Department of Propaganda and consistently promoted a tolerant and relaxed environment for intellectuals. People in the intellectual realm dared to voice their opinions and

197

ignored the leftists. For a period of time, the forces of conservatism, rigidity, and dogmatism represented by Hu Qiaomu and Deng Liqun were marginalized.

. However, after Yaobang resigned and the Anti-Liberalization Campaign began in earnest, they [Hu Qiaomu and Deng Liqun] were suddenly anti-liberalization heroes and posed as victors. They hoped to take advantage of the situation by venting their suppressed fury. While Yaobang was in charge of the work of the Central Committee, I was busy dealing with economic and foreign affairs, and had very little involvement in the theoretical and metaphysical arena.

Frankly, I had no interest in it. I felt Yaobang was wrong to ignore Deng Xiaoping's directions. I believed he had not considered the big picture, and that his actions had not helped the overall situation. And it had not been good for Yaobang himself. Therefore, I was in a relatively neutral position in the struggle between Yaobang and Hu Qiaomu and Deng Liqun.

Nor did Hu Qiaomu and Deng Liqun regard me as a rival, even though I had opposed their attempts to spread the Anti–Spiritual Pollution Campaign into the economic arena. In the economic arena, I had always advocated emancipating minds, being bold in exploration, and eliminating restrictions. But I was rarely involved in the cultural realm, so did not have any direct confrontations with the two.

After Yaobang resigned, however, I was in charge of the Central Committee's work. The situation soon changed, as I tried to cool down the Anti-Liberalization Campaign and proceed moderately. I tried to ensure that the fewest possible people were harmed and actively protected reform. Hu Qiaomu and Deng Liqun wanted to go all out, making direct confrontation difficult to avoid. They soon came to regard me as their principal rival.

In March, I suggested to Comrade Xiaoping that Li Ruihuan be moved from Tianjin [where he was Party secretary] to the Department of Propaganda to assist Deng Liqun in theoretical work; Deng Xiaoping approved. With two people in charge, different opinions could be heard. Issues from the lower levels could be reported, unlike when one person was in charge. However, Chen Yun opposed the idea, so it was not carried out.

Later, I felt that a resolution of this matter was necessary because reforms urgently needed new theories and guidelines. Theoretical studies needed to proceed alongside the actual practice of reform. However, with Deng Liqun in charge, nothing would get done in this area; on the contrary, he was a counterproductive force. I expressed my view that if Deng Liqun were to continue to head theoretical studies, not only would there be no progress in the development of theories, but there could be extra barriers to their development. Therefore, I proposed at the 13th Party Congress that Deng Liqun be made a member of the Politburo to give him a position from which he could speak out and voice his opinions—but also to remove him from the Secretariat so he would no longer head theoretical and metaphysical work.

While this matter was in planning stages, Comrade Li Rui [a pro-reform elder] wrote a letter to me to report that while in Yan'an,* Deng Liqun had exhibited disreputable and immoral behavior and was therefore unfit to lead work in ideology and propaganda. I forwarded the letter to Deng Xiaoping, who responded by issuing a decree that Deng Liqun should no longer be in charge of propaganda. Both were forwarded to Chen Yun and Li Xiannian to read. They both wrote comments praising Deng Liqun but were unable to directly object to Deng Xiaoping's decree that Deng Liqun be removed from his post in charge of propaganda. So the decision was finalized.

On July 7, 1987, Deng Xiaoping held a meeting in his house of the Five-Person Group [set up to exercise the power of the Politburo Standing Committee until the 13th Party Congress] and formally announced his decision. I suggested Hu Qili take over this work, and everyone agreed. A decision also was made to dissolve the Research Office of the Secretariat, of which Deng Liqun was chief, since it had been producing public commentaries casting doubt on reform. Deng said that Deng Liqun should continue to be a member of the Politburo in the 13th Central Committee. The changes took effect immediately. [Party elder] Bo Yibo was assigned the task of talking to Deng Liqun. All of the arrangements proceeded according to Deng Xiaoping's wishes.

As it turned out, because Deng Liqun's opposition to reform made him unpopular, he lost in the election for members of the Central Committee of the 13th Party Congress. When Deng Xiaoping learned about this, he said he would respect the outcome of the election. As such, it was impossible for Deng Liqun to be a member of the Politburo. I suggested to the presidium of the 13th Party Congress that Deng Liqun be listed as a

* Yan'an is a remote mountain town in Shaanxi Province where leaders of the Communist Party retreated in 1937 at the end of the Long March and remained until 1947. Though conditions were dire, it was also a period noted for the idealism, self-sacrifice, and discipline of Party members.

candidate for the Central Advisory Commission, so he could be a member of the Standing Committee of the Commission. The result was that he was elected into the Central Advisory Commission, but lost again in elections for its Standing Committee.

For the 13th Party Congress, we had slightly reformed the way in which elections were held, giving some democratic rights to the representatives. Representatives consequently used their rights to make this choice.

Removing Deng Liqun from his position as the head of propaganda, dissolving the Research Office of the Secretariat, and halting the publication of *Red Flag* magazine—all of this made some elder comrades, including Chen Yun, Wang Zhen, and Li Xiannian, displeased with me. It seemed to them that the things Hu Yaobang had wanted to do but couldn't had finally been carried out by me. I had done what Yaobang had not been able to do. Therefore, they directed their antagonism toward me.

At the time I did not realize that these circumstances would have such profound ramifications. But when problems emerged with consumer prices in 1988, with the buying frenzy, bank runs, and inflation, they carried out a campaign against me, with the Party elders accusing me of wrongdoings and even calling for my impeachment, all of which was very much related to the above incident.

Deng Liqun was extremely close to Chen Yun, Li Xiannian, and Wang Zhen. He was highly regarded by them and won their positive recognition. In 1980, Deng Liqun actively promoted Chen Yun's thinking and proposals in economics through the Research Office of the Secretariat under his control. Deng Liqun promoted Chen Yun's economic ideas in an obvious attempt to use them to resist Deng Xiaoping's ideas of reform.

As I mentioned above, in 1987, I suggested that Li Ruihuan be brought in to assist Deng Liqun in managing ideological studies. Chen Yun did not immediately comment, but after a day's consideration, he told me through his secretary that it was better that the work be managed by Deng Liqun alone. He [Chen Yun] had turned down my suggestion.

On July 3, he [Chen Yun] spoke with Bo Yibo and published a speech titled "Those with significant responsibilities had better study some philosophy." It was intended for my ears. Bo Yibo took notes and forwarded it to me. On the face of it, it was a suggestion for me to learn dialecticism; in fact, it was a criticism of me. He believed that I was unable to tolerate opposing opinions.

The main cause of this was my forcing Deng Liqun from the propaganda front as soon as I had taken power. Another issue was criticism I had made of the left. In particular was my May 13 speech, in which I had criticized Hu Qiaomu and Deng Liqun's remarks. When the minutes were printed and sent to Chen Yun, he disagreed with my remark: "In the 1950s, the economic model copied was in fact a temporary economic model intended for times of war."

After Deng Liqun lost in the 13th Party Congress elections, Comrade Chen Yun gave special instructions to ensure that all of Deng Liqun's political privileges and living arrangements remained unchanged.

Deng Liqun was also an important associate of [Party elder] Li Xiannian. Li Xiannian had been in charge of the Fifth Office of the State Council, where Deng Liqun also worked. He participated in decision making and the drafting of Li Xiannian's documents. In 1987, Deng Liqun was personally in charge of the group set up to edit and publish Li Xiannian's selected works. When Deng Xiaoping's decree to remove Deng Liqun from his position in charge of propaganda was circulated, Li Xiannian wrote, "Deng Liqun is a good comrade. We still need to fully utilize his skills."

The relationship between Deng Liqun and Wang Zhen went even deeper. As far back as the establishment of the People's Republic, Deng Liqun was the Propaganda Division head of the Xinjiang Bureau under the Central Committee that Wang Zhen headed. Wang Zhen later was criticized by the Central Committee for recklessly forcing the husbandry industry into collectives. Deng Liqun stood by him then and tried to defend him. Since then, Wang Zhen always trusted him, and they were very close. After the Third Plenum of the 11th Party Congress, when Deng Liqun needed something to be said that he found difficult to say publicly, he often called on Wang Zhen to voice his ideas for him.

It was around the summer of 1987 when [son of Marshal Ye Jianying] Ye Xuanning called me to say that Wang Zhen wanted to have a talk with me, so I went to Wang Zhen's home. Wang Zhen advised me, "You shouldn't accept the position of General Secretary. There is a great deal of work to be done by the State Council that cannot be done without you, while there is not a lot to do at the Secretariat. We could ask Yao Yilin to take charge instead." Ye Xuanning was in attendance when we had this talk.

At the moment, I was not really interested in the post of General Secretary, either, so I asked Wang Zhen to persuade Deng Xiaoping. Later, I learned that, in fact, Wang Zhen was actively promoting a motion to nominate Deng Liqun for the position of General Secretary. The move caused concerns among many people, who all warned me that no matter what, I should not yield the position to Deng Liqun, thus arousing my own sense of vigilance. These events are why it was not at all surprising that the Party elders deepened their disapproval of me after Deng Liqun lost in the elections.

4

Preparing for the Main Event

Zhao's preparation for the 1987 Party Congress—the critical Party sessions held every five years—further demonstrates his skills as a politician. He uses his newfound power as Party chief to advance his agenda by devising unassailable theoretical arguments to support economic liberalization. His deft political wordplay continues to sparkle: he persuades the Congress to endorse the idea that China is only in the "initial stage of socialism," a purely rhetorical invention to excuse China in the near term from having to abide by orthodox socialist policies.

There were two main issues in preparing for the 13th Party Congress: the first was drafting the Political Report, the other was filling leadership positions. The Political Report was to be drafted by the group organized before [Hu] Yaobang resigned. When he stepped down, its work came to a standstill. I gathered the group together and assigned Bao Tong as its leader, to work under my supervision.

As early as May 21, I wrote to Deng Xiaoping regarding ideas for drafting the Political Report. I proposed using the concept the "initial stage of socialism" as the theoretical basis of the report. The report would systematically cover the theory, principles, and tasks of building socialism with Chinese characteristics. Beyond that, it would emphasize the two basic points defined by the Third Plenum of the 11th Party Congress [in 1978]: upholding the Four Cardinal Principles and upholding reform to reenergize the economy. The report quickly won the approval of Deng, who said the outline was great. Because of the improved political climate, the drafting process went relatively smoothly.

I would like to comment on two phrases in the Political Report: "initial stage of socialism" and "one central focus, two basic points."

Many people were under the impression that I first coined the phrase "initial stage of socialism" in the 13th Party Congress report. That's not accurate. As early as the Sixth Plenum of the 11th Party Congress [in 1981], a resolution on historical issues contained the phrase: "Though the socialist system of our country still remains in an initial stage of development. . . ." Hu Yaobang in his Political Report at the 12th Party Congress [in 1982] reiterated that "the socialist system of our country still remains in an initial stage of development."

Yet these two assessments had not elaborated on the meaning of the phrase or its implications. Instead, they emphasized the following viewpoint: "There is no doubt that we have already established a socialist system and entered the socialist stage of society. Any views that deny such a reality are incorrect." In other words, the phrase was intended to indicate that although we were still in the initial stage, we had already established a socialist system and should be able to create an advanced socialist spiritual civilization while building the material civilization. The purpose was to answer doubts some people had about whether our nation was socialist, or whether we were pursuing socialism.

At the Central Committee's Theoretical Discussion of 1979, an important question was raised as the meeting was reviewing leftist mistakes the Party had made. Namely, since China's past was semifeudal and semicolonial, once the revolution had been victorious, were conditions right for the establishment of a socialist system? Should we proceed with a "new democracy"? The Central Committee was critical of such doubts at the time.

Statements about the "initial stage of socialism" were meant to help counter such doubts. But the concept had not yet attracted much attention. Then, in September 1986, the Central Committee's "Resolution Regarding the Establishment of a Socialist Spiritual Civilization" said that since our nation was still at the "initial stage of socialism," we could allow various types of economic elements under the dominant system of public ownership. We would allow a portion of the populace to get rich first. This was intended to make a connection between the assessment that we were still in the "initial stage of socialism" and the policy of reform we were pursuing.

This document was mainly focused on the "Establishment of a Socialist Spiritual Civilization" and it did not elaborate further on the issue. I don't remember any follow-up discussions on the phrase those first three times it was used; nor was there much public attention paid to it.

The phrase only triggered strong domestic and international reactions when it appeared in the 13th Party Congress Political Report, as the theoretical basis for carrying out reform.

As I started to organize the drafting of the 13th Party Congress Political Report, my vision was to further advance major policies and strategies for reform, but also to formulate a theoretical basis for carrying it all out. Since the reforms had been put into practice after the Third Plenum of the 11th Party Congress, productivity had grown, the speed of development had increased, people's living standards had risen, and our nation had become much stronger. These were widely accepted facts.

Yet what was the theoretical basis for carrying out reform? There had been no explanation, and many cadres and citizens were concerned. On the one hand, they did their best to support reform and to actively carry it out, but on the other hand they did not feel secure, fearing that policy could swing in another direction. Reform needed to be powerfully backed up with theory.

In practice, the reform of those years was, to be frank, the rejection and correction of the planned economy, the exclusivity of public ownership, and the single method of wealth distribution that had been enforced since the 1950s. The practice of reform had proven that this had been correct and necessary. It had also proven that the practice of implementing orthodox socialist principles in the style of the Soviet Union was excessive for China's level of socioeconomic development and productivity. This was a leftist mistake. Only if we restored appropriate policies and approaches more suitable for China could we save China. This was the essence of the matter.

Nevertheless, we had practiced socialism for more than thirty years. For those intent on observing orthodox socialist principles, how were we to explain this? One possible explanation was that socialism had been implemented too early and that we needed to retrench and reinitiate democracy. Another was that China had implemented socialism without having first experienced capitalism, and so a dose of capitalism needed to be reintroduced.

Neither argument was entirely unreasonable, but they had the potential of sparking major theoretical debates, which could have led to confusion. And arguments of this kind could never have won political approval. In the worst-case scenario, they could even have caused reform to be killed in its infancy.

While planning for the 13th Party Congress report in the spring of 1987, I spent a lot of time thinking about how to resolve this issue. I came to believe that the expression "initial stage of socialism" was the best approach, and not only because it accepted and cast our decades-long implementation of socialism in a positive light; at the same time, because we were purportedly defined as being in an "initial stage," we were totally freed from the restrictions of orthodox socialist principles. Therefore, we could step back from our previous position and implement reform policies more appropriate to China.

Most important, it was not a new statement. As I mentioned above, it had already been quietly accepted without controversy in the resolutions of the Sixth Plenum and the 12th Party Congress. It was now merely being used as the basis for the theoretical articulation of reform. It would not provoke fierce debate and should be easy to accept.

The first time I revealed these ideas in a public context was at a Central Committee Secretariat meeting in May 1987. I said that we must pay attention to the assessment that we are in an "initial stage of socialism." All policy issues of reform could be resolved in accordance with this.

Later I formally asked the drafting group to use "initial stage of socialism" as the theoretical foundation for the 13th Party Congress report. Then I wrote a letter to the Politburo Standing Committee and the Five-Person Group about this approach. This was the same letter I mentioned above that I sent to Deng Xiaoping outlining the idea. Deng Xiaoping, Chen Yun, and Li Xiannian all replied or phoned to express their approval.

The basic approach for building socialism with Chinese characteristics was embodied in three things: making economic development the central focus, upholding the Four Cardinal Principles, and upholding the Reform and Open-Door Policy. They were the three components that formed the general direction after the Third Plenum. During the process of drafting the report, it was proposed that we sum up these priorities with the colloquial phrase "one central focus, two basic points."

The idea of making economic development our "central focus" had already been asserted at the Third Plenum of the 11th Party Congress in 1978: "From this day forward, we renounce class struggle as the central focus, and instead take up economic development as our central focus." This had been reiterated in Party documents and speeches.

The concept of "Upholding the Four Cardinal Principles and Upholding Reform" had also been consistently emphasized since the Theoretical Discussion Conference of 1978 and the Third Plenum of the 11th Party Congress, but never before were these three things connected together as the major components of the Party's general direction. Upholding the Four Cardinal Principles and upholding reform had already appeared as two separate components in the draft of the "Resolution to Build a Spiritual Civilization" in 1986. Most people had the impression that the principle of the Third Plenum was reform. I proposed a revision to the principle of the Third Plenum of the 11th Party Congress so that it would include the Four Cardinal Principles; we should not give attention only to one side while overlooking the other. The phrase "two basic points" had not yet come into use.

The first time I formally stated that these two principles were interconnected and couldn't exist without the other was in my speech at the Celebration Assembly of the Spring Festival on January 30, 1987. Before this, I had used the same language in my talk with leaders of the Hungarian Communist Party on January 19, 1987, which had been released to the press.

The intention of my speech at the Celebration Assembly was to ease fears that the Anti-Liberalization Campaign would reverse the principles set by the Third Plenum. In order to extinguish such fears, I said that the Third Plenum had included both aspects: the Four Cardinal Principles and reform. Anti-liberalization had a specific meaning: to oppose the abandonment of the Four Cardinal Principles. Therefore, the campaign did not imply any change to the Third Plenum principle and was in fact meant to implement it more thoroughly. This time, the "two basic points" were meant to underline that the Party's principle defined by the Third Plenum of the 11th Party Congress had also included the Four Cardinal Principles, so we should not talk only about reform.

To my surprise, my speech at the Celebration Assembly on the "two basic points" was opposed by some people, particularly those who were relatively conservative or rigid in their thinking. They said we could not set the Four Cardinal Principles on the same level as reform, making them equally "two basic points." The Four Cardinal Principles were the basis and reform merely the tactic and means.

I mentioned above that a cadre, Lu Zhichao in the Department of Propaganda, even assigned the educational chief of the Central Party School to convene a meeting to discuss the idea of the "two basic points," with the intention of criticizing the formulation. This campaign caused quite a commotion.

I was compelled to criticize this opinion at the May 13 meeting of the departments of propaganda, theoretical research, and media, along with the Central Party School. And earlier, at the meeting of the Central Committee Secretariat and the Five-Person Group, I stated that we were discussing not the direction of socialism in general, but rather the direction of socialism with Chinese characteristics. The Four Cardinal Principles provided the basic principle and foundation of our political system while reform was our general approach. Both were foundations on which we based our policies. Taking one as a principle and the other as a means was in fact a way to detract from the importance of reform. Without the approach set by the Third Plenum, with only the Four Cardinal Principles, where would socialism with Chinese characteristics be? The Four Cardinal Principles continue to be one of our basic principles, even as reform has been added.

After my speech of May 13, attacks on the "two basic points" were more restrained. At that point, the phrase "one central focus, two basic points" could be listed together in the Political Report of the 13th Party Congress as the three basic components of our general approach. The colloquial formula "one central focus, two basic points" was coined by Bao Tong and the rest of the drafting group during the writing process. Deng Xiaoping was impressed with this phrase, and said on many occasions, "This phrase, 'one central focus, two basic points' is very well put!"

There was still the question of political reform. Deng Xiaoping had said some very positive things about reforming China's political leadership system in the past, and in 1986 even proposed proceeding with political reform. However, during the drafting of the Political Report for the 13th Party Congress, he repeatedly warned, "No matter what, there should not be anything resembling a 'tripartite separation of powers' " and even said there should not be even "a trace of it." During this period, when he was receiving foreign guests, he said things like "a tripartite separation of powers means each is restricting the other" or "such a system is inefficient and cannot get things done."

Frankly speaking, if there was anything new in the area of political reform in the Political Report for the 13th Party Congress, it certainly was not because of Deng. On the contrary, he did everything possible to eliminate any traces of congressional politics and checks and balances in the Political Report. He made such comments every time we sent a draft to him for review. Even when our report no longer contained any of those things, he still repeated his warning each time. If not for Deng's intervention, the contents on political reform could have been written much better.

The other critical issue during preparation for the 13th Party Congress was the appointment of new leaders. Even before Yaobang had resigned, Deng Xiaoping had appointed a group of seven people to be in charge of the proposal for leadership changes for the 13th Party Congress. The most critical arrangements were planning the future of some of the elders and naming the new Politburo Standing Committee [PSC].

Many people, including me, believed that Deng needed to continue as a member of the PSC because it would be difficult, while so many other elders were still alive, for it to establish its authority without him. I believed that, as long as Deng's position in the Party as ultimate decision maker was continuing, it would be better for him to exercise his power legitimately from within the PSC rather than from outside of it.

Deng, however, insisted that if the positions of Chen Yun as first secretary of the Central Discipline Inspection Commission, Li Xiannian as President of the republic, and Peng Zhen as National People's Congress chairman remained intact at the 13th Party Congress, it would be seen as a setback, or as the foreign media would say "a victory for the conservatives." No matter what, we should not give people this impression. This was what Deng told me during a conversation in March 1987. However, if they were all asked to retire, it would be difficult for Deng to justify remaining in the PSC.

Deng proposed that one of them be retired completely and the other three moved into semiretirement status. That is, Peng Zhen would retire, while Deng, Chen, and Li would semiretire. What this meant for Deng was that he would be out of the PSC but continue as chairman of the Central Military Commission, Chen Yun's position would be changed to chairman of the Central Advisory Commission, and Li Xiannian would become chairman of the Chinese People's Political Consultative Conference. Only one was a position with real power while the other two were honorary positions.

At first, none of these people—Chen Yun, Li Xiannian, and Peng Zhen—were willing to accept the proposal. Deng then asked [another elder] Bo Yibo to mediate with these elders. It wasn't easy at first. It was not until July 3 that Chen Yun expressed his consent to Bo Yibo, saying that he would follow the arrangements made by the Party. Once Chen Yun conceded, the others were easier to persuade. The proposal was accepted.

After that, Deng Xiaoping met with Bo Yibo and Yang Shangkun to discuss whether, after leaving the PSC, the three elders would still manage any affairs at all or participate in making decisions on crucial issues. I don't know the details of their discussion, but I did hear of one suggestion: that there should be only one "mother-in-law" for the PSC; there could not be several "mothers-in-law." That is, after the three retired, only Deng should act as a "mother-in-law," which characterized the relationship pretty accurately. Deng's position was not to change; he was the "mother-in-law" of the PSC, but the others should not assume that role.

Later, however, as new situations emerged, it turned out that Deng had to consult with Chen Yun and Li Xiannian on all major issues (especially with Chen Yun). As to how Bo Yibo actually negotiated with Chen Yun and Li Xiannian, I don't know. It wasn't until July 7, 1987, that the issue of whether the elders should remain in power was finally settled at the meeting of the Five-Person Group held at Deng's home.

It was in this meeting that Bo Yibo suggested I give a speech at the First Plenum of the 13th Party Congress to announce that we would continue to seek Comrade Deng Xiaoping's guidance on major issues, and have Deng make final decisions. When Bo Yibo spoke of this, Deng expressed his view that as long as the international community knew that he would remain the decision maker, they would feel reassured, because his continuance would be taken as an indication of China's stability. That's why I announced to the First Plenum of the 13th Party Congress that we would continue to seek Deng's opinion and ask him to make the final decisions.

In the same meeting of the Five-Person Group held in Deng's home, appointments for new PSC members, President of the People's Republic, Premier of the State Council, and chairman of the National People's Congress were also finalized. As for the PSC, the initial proposal had included seven people, and the number had remained seven up until this meeting.

There were objections to Wan Li. He was sometimes not very careful and had offended some people, so the elders had objections about him. I heard that when the [PSC] list was being drawn up, Yao Yilin mentioned that Wan Li was the kind of person who would jump on the bandwagon in a crisis. In other words, he was a factor of instability. During the Five-Person Group meeting, Bo Yibo spoke as a representative of the Seven-Person Group, saying that the group "does not approve of Wan Li being appointed to the PSC." Yao Yilin then identified Tian Jiyun as a problem, saying there were reports that Tian had promoted a relative who was proving problematic. Bo Yibo also identified some unresolved issues with Tian Jiyun. Under the circumstances, there was no time to investigate further. After hearing these opinions, Deng said, "Wan Li and Tian Jiyun will not be in the Standing Committee, so the list of seven people will be changed to five."

It was at this meeting that I started to realize that Yao Yilin, who ordinarily gave people the impression of being upright and honest and had always seemed objective and fair, was in fact a calculating schemer who played nasty tricks. He did not raise the issue of Tian Jiyun earlier or later, but right at the moment when a decision needed to be made. Since doubts had been raised, the issue could only be shelved.

It was also in this meeting that the decision was made to appoint Yang Shangkun President of the People's Republic. Deng proposed Wan Li for the position of chairman of the National People's Congress. Wan Li modestly replied that he was no expert on law. Deng said, "You certainly can learn! Also, you can ask others to assist you." After the decision was made, Deng was afraid that some people would not accept Wan Li as NPC chairman, since many of the elders had objections to him. He even had a talk with Wan Li to suggest that he visit the elders, one by one, to do some self-criticism and win their support. Wan Li did as Deng suggested.

The candidacy for Premier took a long time to finalize. People were worried that Li Peng was not up to the responsibility, especially in the area of economic reform, since he had previously worked in engineering, technology, and electricity generation, and had very little experience in economics. In economic reform, he had no experience whatsoever. However, Chen Yun and Li Xiannian were both very supportive of him.

Another proposal being considered was to have Yao Yilin act as Premier for a two-year transition period, since he was more familiar with economic affairs, and people had good impressions of Yao Yilin. But Deng found this unacceptable, saying that Yao was suffering from bad health and had a very narrow field of experience, as he had worked mainly on finance and trade. At the time, it was difficult to find anyone new, and they most likely would not be accepted by Chen Yun and Li Xiannian anyway. So in the end, there was no other choice but to go with Li Peng.

Since Li Peng was not familiar with managing the economy and had no experience with economic reform, Deng made a decision: "For the time being, after taking the post of General Secretary, Zhao will continue to manage economic affairs and continue to head the Central Economic and Financial Leading Group." Deng also mentioned that Li Peng had a bad reputation among some people who claimed that he favored the Soviet Union, where he had studied. Once on a visit to Europe, he had, without checking with anyone, taken a detour through the Soviet Union. Because Deng believed that his reputation was not perfect, that he favored the Soviets, he asked that Li Peng make a public statement upon becoming Premier to dispel the doubts that people had.

As far as I know, Wan Li, who was my Vice Premier, was never proposed for the position of Premier. There were two reasons: first, Wan Li had offended a lot of people. Second, Deng wanted to find someone younger to be Premier.

When the 12th Party Congress was being planned, [Party functionary] Yu Qiuli was in charge of the leadership appointment group, under

Yaobang's leadership. All issues were reported first to the Secretariat, directly managed by Yaobang, and then reported to the elders. But things were different with the 13th Party Congress's leadership appointment group, which was headed by Bo Yibo with the participation of Yang Shangkun, Wang Zhen, Yao Yilin, Song Renqiong, Wu Xiuquan, and Gao Yang. It was directly controlled by Deng Xiaoping. Before his resignation, Yaobang did not intervene in these matters. Afterward, neither did the Five-Person Group. Perhaps the situation was different from the 12th Party Congress because the issue of retiring the elders was at stake. For that reason, Deng took over and implemented his ideas through the Seven-Person Group.

After Yaobang resigned, the Five-Person Group replaced the Politburo Standing Committee, thus making it parallel to the Seven-Person Group. The Five-Person Group managed daily affairs. The Seven-Person Group made preparations for leadership appointments for the 13th Party Congress. It also expanded its powers to take over the Central Committee's role in making general personnel changes.

The Minister of Forestry was removed from office because of a forest fire in Daxing'anling [in Heilongjiang Province] in 1987, so a new Minister of Forestry was proposed. However, because of the intervention of the Seven-Person Group, it failed to go through. At the time, I was on a state visit abroad, leaving Wan Li in charge at home. Wan Li objected to what had happened and reported to Deng Xiaoping.

Deng announced that the Seven-Person Group should be led by the Five-Person Group. Day-to-day personnel changes would still be managed by the Secretariat and the State Council. Bo Yibo had no choice but to agree. However, he continued to overreach. He often asked the Director of Organization [Song Ping] to report to him; he would then relay his opinions to Song Ping and ask him to carry things out accordingly. Bo Yibo said that because the leadership appointments for the 13th Party Congress included the evaluation of all provincial, municipal, and ministerial leaders, the Department of Organization must consult the Seven-Person Group before deliberating the reshuffling of cadres.

Before the 13th Party Congress, he also conveyed a suggestion to me through Song Ping: that it would be preferable for the existing Seven-Person Group to continue in some form after the 13th Party Congress in order to assist the Central Committee in managing personnel work. The original purpose of the Seven-Person Group was to make arrangements for the leadership of the 13th Party Congress, but now he was proposing that it continue even beyond the Congress. It was obvious that they hoped to control the management of personnel indefinitely.

I could not agree with that. I told Song Ping to relay my message that we would stick to the original decision—that after the 13th Party Congress, the mission of the Seven-Person Group will have been accomplished. As for how to utilize the effectiveness of the elder comrades with regards to personnel management, this was something we could discuss at a later date. Bo, a person who had always been keen to grab power, must have been deeply displeased when I rejected his idea.

A TUMULTUOUS YEAR

I

After the Congress

By his own account, 1988 is the most difficult year in Zhao's entire political career, a time when things take a dramatic downward turn. The 13th Party Congress has been a success, and Zhao even manages to win approval for a political reform plan. But a series of conflicts and crises lies in store.

The 13th Party Congress met with good reactions both at home and abroad, and was highly praised. Above all, it made people across the country feel hopeful. It is fair to say that it renewed people's enthusiasm.

The economic situation in 1987 was also better than it had been in past years. Not only was the nation's economy continuing to grow at a fast pace, but the signs also seemed to point to a smooth and stable development. The balance among the various parts of the nation's economy was also good, except in agriculture. We had an abundant harvest, but problems arose due to stagnation in the sector in the prior few years. But money supply had remained within the plan, foreign reserves had greatly increased, and foreign trade was healthy.

Efforts to control macroeconomics while freeing microeconomics had also improved. The macroeconomics had not gotten out of control, and the microeconomics had not been stifled. The problems of economic overheating and excessive money supply had all been eased.

In the few years prior, problems had occurred when we tried to bring the macroeconomic situation under control while making improvements to the mechanism. From our experiences of 1987, stabilizing the economy and growing at a certain pace can happen concurrently. Bringing the macroeconomic situation under control can be done at the same time as freeing activities at the microeconomic level.

After the 13th Party Congress, the general political and economic situation was good. If we had continued to adapt the measures and policies learned from the successful experiences of the past few years, the situation in 1988 could have continued to improve.

However, that is not what happened. Instead good became worse and in the end was quite bad. There are a lot of lessons that can be drawn from what happened.

2

Panic Buying and Bank Runs

Freeing up prices represents one of the thorniest challenges for China's economic reformers—and one of the most critical. After all, freely set prices instantly transmit vital information on the real demand for commodities, a fundamental part of the efficiency of a market system. In the early reform era, China has a dual-price system: both government-set prices and market-determined prices exist for the same goods. Exploiting the difference between the two creates widespread opportunities for corruption. Reformers feel an urgency to fix this volatile situation, but in their haste make some fatal mistakes. The result is panic buying and bank runs as the public anticipates what will come next.

Rising prices was a hot issue in 1988; it was inevitable during the reform process. The 7 percent rise in 1987 was not very high, but higher than in the few years prior.

In the first quarter of 1988, prices continued to rise, especially for food. The cause was the mediocre agricultural output over the previous few years. At the same time, our approach had been problematic, as we had not followed market rules. Grain prices had been raised, but meat and egg prices had not, resulting in shortages. During the Spring Festival of 1988, some cities were considering a return to the ration system. If we had immediately adjusted prices of agricultural produce to lift that sector, and at the same time provided compensation to urban residents, the problem could have been resolved.

However, there were concerns. Prices were rising every year, and the cumulative rise was significant. People were complaining, and we were reacting by making further adjustments—yet the overall pricing system had still not been straightened out. We considered quickly raising prices to their correct levels within a few years, enduring the pain for the sake of breaking through the difficulties of reforming the system. At the same time, we would raise workers' wages.

With the benefit of hindsight, however, this idea was not practical. In those years, the coexistence of two markets, with a two-track pricing system, created so much friction and corruption that it was impossible to institutionalize the market. We wanted to come up with a coordinated plan to eliminate the coexistence of two systems as soon as possible.

We also believed that the reforms to date had been relatively easy, and while the results had been good, the things left to accomplish were more difficult. The task at hand was to tackle the thornier issues and achieve a breakthrough; if we shied away from confronting them, things would not improve, and might get worse.

In moving from a planned to a market economy, we had always taken a gradual approach, especially when adapting new elements. The nation's economy was divided into two sectors. We were increasing the market sector and gradually weakening the planned sector. These two efforts were coordinated.

The government did not directly intervene in the market sector, especially not through administrative means. Production was self-initiated and prices were freely set according to market forces. In the market sector, family enterprises, privately operated firms, and joint ventures were all self-initiated and responsible for their own profits and losses.

The planned sector was basically under the control of the state, and here the state set prices. Some products in this sector also were put on the market, but they mainly did not respond to market mechanisms. The state-owned enterprises had no real autonomy.

In the market sector, enterprises were free to set their own prices. In the planned sector enterprises' prices were set by the state, or at least the state retained authority over the process. The same was true for wages. In the market sector, enterprises were free to set wages themselves. In the planned sector, wages were set by the state or, even if the state ceded some of this power to the enterprises, it still retained ultimate control. The market sector in those years grew out of nothing, from infancy to maturity, while the planned sector gradually shrank. Still, in 1988, the planned sector accounted for more than 60 percent [of the economy].

Though the two-track system caused friction and created opportunities for corruption, overall it brought vitality to the economy, especially the market sector.

It was not possible to transform large and midsize state-owned enterprises into market entities through a one-time reform of the system, prices, and wages. They could only be transformed bit by bit through gradual reforms to the planning, pricing, and ownership systems. The gradual approach was more stable, less risky, and easier for society to accept. We had been proceeding this way all along, though not consciously.

We knew that pricing reform was critical. And we always thought that at some point conditions would be right to take measures, all at once or in several steps, to transform the state-owned enterprises. This implied that the development of the market sector was a prelude to a final breakthrough.

In May 1988, I gave a report to a Politburo meeting titled "Establishing the New Order: The Socialist Market Economy," in which I said the task was to reform the pricing system in the next few years while raising workers' wages appropriately. We believed this was the decisive battle in the transformation to a market economy: ending the coexistence of the two systems and the two-track pricing system.

The existence of these concerns indicated that price reform was not a simple problem. After August, I concluded that the success of price reform and wage reform depended on deepening the entire reform. If price and wage reform ultimately required us to transition all medium and large state-owned enterprises toward a market model, then there was a feasibility question. It was difficult for the plan to work.

There also were tactical problems, specifically involving price reform. The original plan was problematic—but it was highly publicized before implementation, without consideration for people's psychology. Economic conditions were good in 1987, but in 1988 there were tensions in the market.

Abroad, this is known as the psychological anticipation of inflation. If people know that the state will raise prices, even if they know there will be government compensations and that their living standards will not drop, they will be concerned about preserving the value of their savings.

Because we did not raise the banks' interest rates in time to address the issue of preserving the value of savings, people started panic buying and hoarding to preserve the value of their money. This was primarily psychological. Even though we announced repeatedly that the price hikes would not lower people's living standards, we had overlooked the issue of people's savings. It was common sense, but we lacked experience at the time.

In August, we discussed the issue of pricing reform at Beidaihe. Immediately the newspapers began publicizing the breakthrough, reporting that there had been a decision to raise prices. People started to panic.

They rushed to banks to make withdrawals and frantically bought up commodities. Suddenly there were shortages, and it seemed as if the economic situation had worsened.

In fact, the economic situation in 1988 was not bad; there wasn't an excessive supply of money. The main issue was the psychological factor: people were in a panic. Of course, there still was some hangover from the overheated economy and excess currency of earlier years. People's buying power had not yet materialized in the form of large amounts of savings. There was perhaps 1 trillion yuan deposited in banks; once people panicked they withdrew their funds and started buying.

The issue was the improper publicizing of price reform. If we had announced a cessation of price reform and then raised interest rates and promised value-guaranteed savings, people would have felt more secure. If we had then scaled back the tens of billions of yuan being spent on infrastructure, saving several million tons of steel, the economy would not have suffered any problems.

Back then, the Central Economic and Financial Leading Group repeatedly proposed to the State Council that interest rates be raised as quickly as possible and that value-guaranteed savings be put into practice. However, at the State Council, Li Peng and Yao Yilin worried that if savings' interest rates were increased while interest rates on loans to the state-owned enterprises could not be raised accordingly, that would put too much burden on the banks. They were indecisive for a time, before eventually putting value-guaranteed savings into place.

In fact, as soon as value-guaranteed savings were in place, savings deposits rose again. That started in the fourth quarter of 1988 and accelerated in the first quarter of 1989. The situation quickly stabilized. This proved that the economy did not have any serious problems. Inflation was not higher. But when people were in a panic, they withdrew cash that amounted to years of savings to purchase commodities, making it appear that inflation was getting worse. In fact, inflation had gone down after 1987, though it had not fully subsided.

3

A Series of Missteps

Zhao further analyzes the events that led in 1988 to panic buying and bank runs. The political fallout is far worse than the actual effect on the economy. Many people now believe the reform program is a failure, and control over the economy reverts to leaders who want to reassert administrative controls. It will be years before things recover.

The bank runs and hoarding of commodities led to an overall panic, which arrived with the force of a tidal wave. Every major city was in a tense situation. Criticisms within and outside the Party grew, and people at all levels of authority were under pressure.

This caused us to overestimate the seriousness of the economic problems and believe that inflation had soared. We did not use the term "runaway inflation" but called it "high inflation." In fact, we had not actually analyzed the inflation.

We decided to reassert order over economic affairs in 1988. We started to shift emphasis away from reform and toward "adjustment and reorganization." The intention was to assuage people's panic, but the effect was extremely negative and in retrospect things should not have been handled this way.

We should have stabilized the economy by getting control over infrastructure spending and money supply. If we had done this, the economy could have been stabilized. There was no need for a major reorganization and contraction. If we had deepened reforms, which would have meant further reducing the planned sector while developing the market sector, the situation would have developed smoothly. One goal of the proposed "adjustment and reorganization" was to quickly create conditions for an-

224 PRISONER OF THE STATE

other attempt to reform the pricing and wage systems, to end the two-track pricing system. But I now realize that this idea was not realistic.

People like Li Peng and Yao Yilin had always had misgivings about reform, so as soon as the slogan "adjustment and reorganization" was proposed—and with direct management of economic affairs under their control—they tightened on all fronts. They restored the old methods, making major cutbacks through administrative means. Powers that had been handed down to lower levels were reclaimed. Measures that had relied significantly on market mechanisms were abolished.

After a few months of this, the economy slowed down; the contraction would continue for two to three years. This shows that there had not been a problem with the Chinese economy; otherwise, why would these weaknesses occur only after administrative controls were put in place?

The end result of "adjustment and reorganization" was not good. My intention had been to use the slogan to quickly stabilize the situation and create the right conditions for reinitiating price and wage reforms, and continue with the original plan. In retrospect, however, this was a mistake.

The economy wouldn't show signs of vitality again until Deng Xiaoping took his southern tour in 1992. At that time, he criticized "adjustment and reorganization" and suggested that we take advantage of opportunities to speed up development and reform. This won the people's approval and further proved that the single-minded cutbacks and contractions had not been in line with China's reality. If the Chinese economy had really been in a critical condition and inflation so serious, it would have been impossible for the economy to recover so quickly in reaction to Deng's remarks in the south.

There are two important issues from this period that need to be revisited. One concerns reform: under the existence of the two-track system, the only way to reform matters was to make gradual transitions, incrementally expanding market-adjustment mechanisms while progressively reducing the planned economic sector. We had to proceed step-by-step in expanding the market sector. It would have been impossible to transform the planned economy into a market economy in one blow. In retrospect, the "all at once" method had not been appropriate; the basic approach was wrong.

Another issue was that when bank runs and panic buying occurred, the seriousness of the situation had been overestimated. Necessary measures could have been applied, but it was inappropriate to move in a new direction. Rather, actions to deepen reform should have been taken to stabilize the situation. If we had done that, the panic buying of 1988 and the stagnation and setbacks of the next few years could have been avoided.

The problem was with how we were thinking about pricing reform. We did not follow the path that we had taken in the few years before that, but instead had attempted to use brute force to make the breakthrough, believing that the market transformation would complete itself afterward. It was in fact a treatment of shock therapy.

Next, the timing and the publicity of the price reform policy were mistaken. In spring of 1988, the nationwide problem of price hikes was not due to the economic overheating of 1987, nor was it triggered by currency oversupply. The main cause was that when we set prices for agricultural products we did not handle things appropriately. The prices of meat, vegetables, and eggs were all raised; rising prices were already a focus of attention. So when we then made plans for pricing reform, the timing was ill chosen and naturally caused panic. Publicizing the plan was especially inappropriate; we suffered a great deal as a result. This was the main reason for the panic buying: people were not buying products for consumption, but rather for preserving the value of their savings.

Throughout the process of designing, discussing, and finalizing the price reform plan, newspapers continuously published articles. Some reported on what Deng Xiaoping had said; others included remarks made by me. It put a spotlight on the issue. They said that the easiest part of reform had already been done, and that now we would tackle the problem with prices.

These factors together made people panic. The situation, therefore, was caused by the inappropriate measures we had taken. When the bank runs and panic buying started, we didn't make a coolheaded analysis. We rushed too quickly to propose "adjustment and reorganization," and the result was that those who had opposed reform were given a chance to cause several years of economic decline.

4

The Problem with Prices

Zhao expounds on the political circumstances surrounding the attempts to dramatically reform the pricing system. The plan has the solid political backing of Deng Xiaoping, who wants to eliminate the billions in subsidies that support the dual pricing system. In the end, however, Zhao chokes under the pressure and pulls the plug on price reform. He takes full responsibility for the failure.

The attempt to achieve a breakthrough in pricing reform went as follows.

In May 1988, I issued a report at an enlarged Politburo meeting, "Establishing a New Economic Order: The Socialist Market Economy." I proposed that within five years we should adjust prices and the inappropriate wage levels, at the cost of having to suffer price hikes each year. It was resolved at the meeting that the State Council would draw up plans. [Vice Premier] Yao Yilin and his associates drafted the detailed plan. It was discussed once at Beidaihe, after which they made revisions and it came back to the Politburo for consideration.

While we were discussing the issue, the incidents of panic buying had become widespread. People expressed concerns in the discussion that pricing reform would cause problems. I said at the Politburo meeting that when implementing this reform, each step must not be too big; at the same time, we should cut tens of billions in infrastructure spending to reduce market demand for steel and other resources.

The timing was perceived to be relatively favorable: the economy was growing, and people's incomes were increasing. Plus, we had some backup measures on reserve. For example, we had large amounts of public housing that could be sold in order to take some currency out of circulation. We could also sell some small and midsize enterprises.

Our main objective with price reform was to correct price levels and make enterprises meet market conditions through fair competition, so as to improve their efficiency.

In August, regional authorities, especially in Tianjin and Shanghai, were concerned, but none expressed their opinions clearly. And so at Beidaihe, the plan was approved. In the process of carrying it out, there were no obvious disagreements, even from Yao Yilin and his associates at the State Council, as they had drawn up the detailed plans.

Comrade Deng Xiaoping had always believed in price reform. In 1988, he commented several times that price reform had proceeded too late, and that things would have been better if it had been done a few years earlier.

At the enlarged Politburo meeting in May, I proposed that we make significant progress in price reform over the next few years. I had discussed this with Deng Xiaoping beforehand, and he had been very supportive. Later, he said publicly that price reform needed a breakthrough and that we should overcome the difficulties. He also said that our problem was not that we might take too bold of a step, but rather that we might vacillate, and when faced with problems, hesitate or back down.

I believe that Deng Xiaoping's understanding of price reform was based mainly on concerns about the losses at state-owned enterprises and his hopes for reducing state subsidies. He often said that, because of incorrect pricing, we were spending tens of billions of yuan on subsidies. He asked Yao Yilin several times, "If we proceed with this reform, how many billions can we save in subsidies? If we don't proceed, how much will they increase?"

He was very firm in supporting price reform. He liked taking bold steps, and he encouraged anything to do with reform.

Of course, if we believed something was too difficult to carry out, he would not insist. Therefore, for the attempt at price reform in 1988, the responsibility was not his, but primarily mine. I had proposed all of it. The entire process from design to discussion in the State Council was chaired and approved by me. At the last moment, when we faced difficulties, I proposed delaying implementation, with his [Deng's] agreement.

In the end, I decided to stop price reform and turn to "adjustment and reorganization." Just before making the decision in September, I spoke with Yao Yilin. I said that we should all unite to delay price reform. He said it could be postponed for several months, until the latter half of

1989, when we could reevaluate. Later, because of the repercussions of price reform and the tense situation in so many places, I concluded that we had to delay the implementation and concentrate on improving the economic environment and easing people's fears. We could fight this battle later. After I made my decision, I spoke again with Li Peng and Yao Yilin, and they agreed with me.

I felt it necessary to report to Comrade Deng Xiaoping. Just before I had made my decision, Deng Xiaoping had spoken with Li Peng and encouraged us by saying, "Don't be afraid." He said there were risks involved with price reform, but these were risks that had to be taken. If anything happened, he would take responsibility.

Given this, if I were to halt price reform, I felt compelled to report that to Deng. The issue was very difficult to explain; it involved a change in direction that was not easy to express in a few sentences. Plus, Deng Xiaoping's hearing was poor. So I asked [Deng's secretary] Wang Ruilin to come to my office and outlined the situation in detail for him. I explained why I had decided to delay the plan, and why it would be bad if we did not delay. I asked him to relay this to Deng Xiaoping, because he worked closely with Deng and could clearly explain the issue. After it was reported to Deng, the decision was finalized in the Politburo meeting.

5

Reforms Take a Hit

The failed attempt at pricing reform allows Party conservatives to seize the opportunity to reverse many successful attempts at liberalizing China's economic system. Ambitious plans like the coastal development strategy are scrapped altogether. Zhao is powerless, as Li Peng and his team roll back the clock.

We had planned for great advances in 1988 in reform and openness. At the end of 1987, it was proposed that Hainan be established as a separate province and be designated a Special Economic Zone (SEZ) with provincial level administration, making it the largest SEZ. The drafting of the Enterprise Law began. In March 1988, the National People's Congress passed the proposal to establish Hainan Province as a SEZ as well as the Enterprise Law and regulations on private enterprises. The Congress also made amendments to the constitution regarding the rights of land use and the development of private enterprises.

In the Enterprise Law, ownership and managerial authorities were separated. The point was to emphasize the authority to use and manage a property, as distinct from the rights of ownership. It was recognizing the enterprise as a legal entity. The state was giving its property to the enterprise to use and manage. According to the new law, the state was no longer permitted to interfere unduly in the affairs of enterprises, thereby reducing the importance of the state's right of ownership. We also established the "factory director responsibility system," which emphasized the central role of the director as the legal representative of the enterprise.

The document also adopted the policy that formally permitted family businesses and private enterprises to exist and grow. They were given lawful status. Amendments to the constitution also included the rights of land use, which allowed land to be leased out. All of these were part of furthering reform.

Many important ideas on enterprise reform were formulated at this time. In 1987, we promoted the contract-out scheme, which was also intended to separate the two authorities. In 1988, we introduced competition mechanisms into the contract-out scheme. Later we proposed introducing the approach of rural enterprises [that is, with a great deal of freedom from state control] into state-owned medium and large enterprises. We implemented the shareholding system for medium and large enterprises. We proposed the "grafting method" for adopting foreign systems of finance, technology, management, and marketing. In fact, we used the mechanism of joint ventures for state-owned medium and large enterprises. That is, we borrowed an approach and "grafted" it onto the enterprises to transform them.

I later saw news about five state-owned enterprises that had adopted a free style of management in Lanxi, in Zhejiang Province, and it was quite evocative. Thereafter, I proposed letting medium and large enterprises adopt the free style of management and take responsibility for their own profits and losses.

The so-called "free style of management" meant government agencies would no longer intervene in the management of enterprises. The enterprises would decide everything: prices, what to produce, profit distribution, and all other matters of running a business. As long as they did not violate the law, they could independently manage their affairs.

In August and September, I viewed the concepts of "free style of management" and "responsible for one's own profits and losses" as important aspects of enterprise reform. I emphasized that they were two inseparable parts of a whole; only if we allowed free management could the enterprises take responsibilities for their own profits and losses; only when they took responsibility for that could they truly be free to manage well. Otherwise, we could experience a situation of "profits enjoyed by the enterprises and losses being suffered by the state."

Some people said these businesses were "enterprises with no higher authority." That saying was not right. They really were enterprises not under government administration. All of these approaches were aimed at improving efficiency and enabling enterprises to apply proper management and strengthen their ability to adapt during price reforms.

After price reforms were proposed, I felt that they ultimately depended on the efficiency and flexibility of enterprises. Only then could we avoid a return to the old pricing system. We needed to deepen reform, especially enterprise reform.

During this period, I was also very interested in the shareholding system. In September 1988, I met the famous American economist Milton Friedman. I said, "Our biggest problem is that everything is owned by the state, yet management authority is unclear. Is it mine? Or is it his? It could mean that no one assumes responsibility." Enterprise reform at that time touched upon the problem of ownership rights. The shareholding system was proposed to tackle this problem, to deepen reform.

In the winter of 1987, the coastal development strategy was also proposed. It was an extremely important issue. I also proposed making the entire province of Guangdong a testing ground for reform policies, where everything could be launched first.

If all of these efforts had been allowed to proceed smoothly, reform and openness would have advanced. All the right conditions were in place. Following the successful 13th Party Congress, reform could have taken a giant step forward.

Regrettably, because of the missteps on price reform, the entire reform effort not only could not be advanced, but actually suffered a setback that ended with "adjustment and reorganization." When I think about it now, I still feel profound regret.

Some of the situations that emerged after the proposal of "adjustment and reorganization" were beyond what I had anticipated. In the State Council, Li Peng and Yao Yilin used "adjustment and reorganization" to fully restore the old methods and completely roll back reform.

They issued many rules, laws, and regulations and placed controls on infrastructure spending. They abolished most measures that had been adopted in recent years to revitalize enterprises. They took back the powers that had been handed down to local authorities and enterprises.

The rise in the consumer price index in 1989 was not larger than it had been in 1988, and hit the target I originally had planned for. But they [Li and Yao] turned the target into an order and made all of the administrative levels responsible for it. That meant some of the commodity pricing that had been freed up was again firmly under administrative control.

For a time, rural regions had been free to make their own choices about crops after fulfilling the state procurement quotas: whether or not to plant, how much to plant. These rights were also abolished. All of this reverted into the state planning sphere. The coastal development strategy that had just been proposed and was about to be launched was entirely scrapped.

It marked the complete comeback of the old system and a great setback for reform. Power was concentrated in a few hands at the State

Council and a few agencies of the Central Committee. For example, in order to control loans and credit, withdrawals on ordinary people's savings were frozen; only deposits were allowed.

As they proceeded with this form of "adjustment and reorganization," the economy quickly went into a dive: markets slumped and production stagnated. If not for the non-state-owned sector of family businesses and joint ventures, the entire national economy could have fallen into extreme adversity.

6

Zhao in Retreat

*With the brakes applied to reforms, Zhao's authority fades. He tries
to keep his hand in the running of the economy but is ignored.
There are widespread rumors that he is about to lose his job, and
that his family is engaged in corruption. Zhao concludes that he is
the target of an organized campaign: frozen out of power and
pilloried by his foes. Even Deng Xiaoping can't help. The economic
innovations the two introduced are at risk.*

During the process of "adjustment and reorganization" greater power
shifted into the hands of the State Council, and away from me and
the Central Economic and Financial Leading Group. I continued to search
for economic solutions within the group; however, they would not discuss, let alone execute my proposals.

Deng Xiaoping originally suggested the formation of the Central Economic and Financial Leading Group. The purpose was to let me continue
to lead economic development and reform even after I had left the position of Premier. When Li Peng had taken over as Premier, many people
were concerned, because I was more familiar with the issues involved.
Moreover, Li Peng had always been vague about his attitude toward economic reform, so people had doubts. Therefore, Deng Xiaoping designated that I should continue to manage economic affairs, and the group
was established.

When "adjustment and reorganization" began, they believed that my
position in economic affairs had weakened. They took controlling power,
which meant the Politburo Standing Committee, the Central Economic
and Financial Leading Group, and I could no longer run economic affairs.
Thus they were able to restore many of the old methods, in the name of

"adjustment and reorganization," something the Politburo Standing Committee and the Leading Group would never have agreed to do.

As I mentioned previously, people made a run on banks and commodities to preserve the value of their savings. If interest rates had been raised immediately, the problem could have been resolved. At Leading Group meetings, I repeatedly proposed that we raise interest rates on bank savings. Other comrades in the group, such as Zhang Jinfu and Du Runsheng, agreed.

But the State Council kept fiddling, neither raising interest rates nor launching value-guaranteed savings. Although they eventually raised interest rates, the increase was too small to make a difference. The State Council's method was to use administrative means to slash credit quotas. As a result, there was insufficient liquidity, and no funds for procuring agricultural products or upgrading technology for factories. Production stagnated.

Another issue was that while people's savings had decreased, the currency supply had actually grown. Therefore, in the latter half of 1988 and the beginning of 1989, the biggest problem was a severe tightening of credit and loans, which disrupted production and distribution, even as the money supply and currency in circulation had both increased. This proved that the measures taken were a mistake.

I suggested keeping credit under control—tightening it but not so stringently—so that production needs could still be taken care of, while at the same time making efforts to resolve the savings issue to ease people's fears. My proposal was not adopted.

Some senior comrades complained that since I was now the General Secretary and no longer Premier, I should focus on the Party and matters of political theory, leaving economic affairs to the State Council. In fact, it was clear that the State Council was attempting to block my work and evade decisions made by the Central Economic and Financial Leading Group—while spreading such comments to force me to cut back or halt my work on economic affairs. It couldn't have been a coincidence that these two things were happening at the same time.

The campaign was powerful. Hong Kong newspapers said I had been stripped of real power and no longer managed economic affairs. Rumors claimed I would lose my post as General Secretary and become chairman of the Central Military Commission, or the President of the People's Republic. The meaning of all of these rumors was that I was no longer in charge. Once, at a photo session in Huairen Hall for a conference of delegates, Xiaoping asked me, "Why did Hong Kong newspapers report that you no longer manage economic affairs? How can you not be managing the economy anymore?"

Another issue was that "adjustment and reorganization" gave people the impression that economic reforms had run into serious trouble; otherwise, why wasn't "deepening reform" being mentioned as a way to stabilize the economy? This allowed certain people an opening to reverse economic reforms, deny their achievements, and wage a campaign to overthrow me.

Some senior comrades demanded that the Politburo Standing Committee—in fact they meant me—take responsibility and admit guilt. [Vice Premier] Wang Renzhong more than once raised the issue in Politburo meetings of an investigation into who was responsible. He said that, since such a grave situation had emerged, those responsible must take part in a self-criticism.

During this period, I heard from many channels that a group of elders collectively wrote a letter to Deng Xiaoping condemning me, saying I was not qualified and demanding that I step down. Deng Xiaoping said several times during this period that "the structure of the central leadership should not be changed."

Around the end of 1988, a newspaper in Hong Kong reported that when Deng was in Shanghai, Li Xiannian had suggested to him that Deng ask me to step down, but that Deng had not accepted his suggestion. After I read the report, I wrote a few lines to [Deng's secretary] Wang Ruilin and asked him to show it to Deng. I said something like "There have been rumors circulating around the country and abroad. I don't know whether Deng knows about them."

With this campaign, people around the country and abroad worried that I could turn out to be the "second Hu Yaobang."

The State Council and some senior comrades exaggerated the economic problems, presenting them as extremely grave. The State Council repeatedly criticized the so-called "two rushes for results": "the rush to build" and "the rush to reform." There may have been grounds for attacking "the rush to build," referring to infrastructure expenses that had grown too large. But there were no grounds for attacking any "rush to reform." They merely used this phrase to oppose reform and attempt to overturn past policies.

Some Party elders cooperated with Li Peng, Yao Yilin, and the State Council. Just before the New Year's holiday of 1989, the Politburo Standing Committee held a Party life meeting at which Li Peng and Yao Yilin took the lead in criticizing me. By that time, they had already blocked my influence, but in the meeting they accused me of intervening too much, making his [Li's] job as Premier very difficult.

They also asked many odd questions about reforms. Yao Yilin asked, "What does 'price reform breakthrough' mean? How did that come to be proposed?" He had not known at that time that the phrase was proposed not by me, but by Deng Xiaoping. He thought I had invented it and was trying to use it to attack me.

They wanted to settle a score. The intention of the meeting was to blame me for the problems that had emerged because of economic reform.

When I reported to Deng about what had happened at the meeting, he appeared very displeased. He spoke at length in support of reform, and made positive remarks about it. He believed that without reform, there was no hope for China's future.

Yao Yilin had never expressed unequivocal opinions, nor had he ever taken the lead on anything before. This time, however, he was clear, direct, and apparently fearless. His attitude and the attitude of Li Peng seemed to represent a general trend, and somebody was supporting them from behind the scenes. A campaign was under way.

There were also rumors attacking me and my family. Some claimed that my children were profiteering: trading color televisions, automobiles, grain supplies, and alloy steels, and making themselves wealthy. These were all completely fictitious, but they spread far and wide. Later, after I stepped down, they rushed to launch an investigation into the matter, which actually was helpful. After searching high and low, they were unable to find a thing.

Before this, rumors of this kind about me were rare. Why did they suddenly pop up, giving the impression that my family was corrupt, in the latter half of 1988? The emergence of this campaign was not an accident, but rather a concerted attempt to smear me and destroy my image as a reformer.

7

The Campaign to Overthrow Zhao

The Party elders had long opposed Deng Xiaoping's aggressive push to dismantle Mao's economic system. But Deng's clout was such that few dared to challenge him openly. Instead they focused their opposition on his reformist lieutenants. The first to fall was Hu Yaobang, who was toppled in 1987. Zhao Ziyang becomes their next target. Here Zhao details what he knows about the campaign and how certain rivalries would resurface after the turmoil of 1989.

A campaign was growing strong within the Party: opposition to reform, efforts to "Overthrow Zhao," the creation of a public opinion campaign. Behind it all were comrades with deep-seated beliefs in the planned economy, who thought reform was a failure and that it was responsible for problems like the bank runs and panic buying. With these developments, it was easy for the campaign to spread.

But let's step back. Before 1987, I held the position of Premier and was mainly responsible for economic affairs. The policy was, of course, reform and openness. Political affairs—matters relating to politics and ideology—were managed by Comrade [Hu] Yaobang. I had a lot of things on my hands; I often took trips abroad and received foreign guests. I did not often involve myself in political affairs.

Yaobang and I had differing opinions on how to manage economic affairs. I was considered more cautious and did not speak about things so casually. I did not promote unbridled development, I opposed large-scale infrastructure projects and I believed in proceeding methodically. Yaobang was different: he was ideologically liberal and carefree.

There was a conservative faction in the Party that stubbornly opposed liberalization and reform. Among Party elders, it was represented by Li Xiannian and Wang Zhen; in the ideological sphere, it was represented by Hu Qiaomu and, especially, Deng Liqun. Together with their associates and organizations, they formed an influential force.

Yaobang had been the primary target of their opposition. They did not make me a target, as I was viewed as being relatively neutral. They may even have believed I was closer to their side in some areas. Therefore, when Yaobang stepped down and the decision was made to make me General Secretary, they were not opposed.

That said, [influential Party elder] Li Xiannian had objected at first. He said I had learned too much foreign stuff, and demanded that I change my ways. As long as I was willing to change, he would support me to take over from Yaobang. There was no other obvious opposition.

Wang Zhen [another Party elder] had tried to persuade me to remain as Premier while suggesting that [State Planning director] Yao Yilin become General Secretary instead. Since I had never wanted the position of General Secretary and preferred to remain as Premier, I thought that whoever was made General Secretary would be just fine by me. At the time of his suggestion, I had no reason for suspicion. Later, people told me that Wang Zhen had actually wanted to make [ultraconservative ideologue] Deng Liqun the General Secretary, but experienced trouble winning support for the idea.

Once I became Acting General Secretary, the first issue I had to deal with was the Anti-Liberalization Campaign. I believed it should be strictly contained, reduced in scope, and cooled down. I didn't agree with their plan to wage a full-blown campaign to widen its scope. They had drafted a list of names, wanting to criticize this person and that. I suppressed it and made speeches aimed at protecting some of those who were on the list. They also wanted to wage a major criticism campaign in newspapers against Yaobang. I didn't like this Cultural Revolution–like behavior and from the very beginning laid down the rule that there would be no guilt by association in the Anti-Liberalization Campaign, no hunt for "representatives" at various levels. I also blocked the campaign from entering the economic arena.

As a result, after the June Fourth incident [in 1989], I was criticized for having placed these restrictions on the campaign. In fact, the charges were true. The Central Committee had issued a document setting strict rules and limits on the campaign and defined so-called "liberalization" as opposing the leadership of the Communist Party and supporting

·wholesale Westernization. This was done to avert the mistakes of past campaigns.

If the campaign were to continue all the way up to the 13th Party Congress, then the Congress would not be able to proceed. We absolutely had to make it a congress of reform and openness.

The leftist forces—Deng Liqun and his associates—used every means possible to expand the reach of the campaign and restore the old leftist ways. They made every attempt to extend the campaign to the economic arena. Using their terms, they wanted to attack not only those who were speaking liberalization, but those who were "doing liberalization." The term "doing liberalization" was meant to refer to those who were carrying out reform. Under the suggestion of Deng Liqun, some people in the Central Party School opposed the phrase "one central focus, two basic points," arguing that upholding the Four Cardinal Principles could not be placed at the same level as reform, that the former was a principle and the latter just a means. They also said that the rural land contract scheme had damaged the foundations of agricultural cooperatives and had destroyed rural collectivization.

I discussed these issues with Deng and offered him my opinions. I felt that some Party elders were attempting to use the Anti-Liberalization Campaign to oppose reform. An appropriate response needed to be made in order to influence public opinion; otherwise, it would be difficult for the 13th Party Congress to support reform. I was prepared to give a speech about it. Deng completely supported my idea.

On May 13, 1988 [actually 1987], I spoke to comrades working in the area of theory and ideology. I said that after the implementation of the Anti-Liberalization Campaign, the general climate had changed; therefore, the campaign could be brought to a close. The tasks going forward would mainly be in the field of education. I also said that the disturbance caused by liberalization was temporary, while the disturbance caused by leftists was long-lasting and fundamental. I listed many mistaken leftist comments in the theoretical and ideological arena opposing reform.

After the June Fourth incident, they also criticized me for shifting the target of the struggle from the right to the left and, on May 13, turning Anti-Liberalization into Anti-Leftist Dogmatism. This was actually true as well.

This indicates that they had expected me to adopt their ideas in conducting the Anti-Liberalization Campaign. However, my May 13 speech turned out to be not against liberalization but against them. Later, at the 13th Party Congress, I set the tone for the gathering and wrote a report to

Deng that included the phrases "initial stage of socialism" and "two basic points," and in general opposed the leftists. This provoked more antagonism from them.

There was a phrase in my 13th Party Congress report that referred to the market economy, without using those exact words. I stressed that "the state intervenes in the market, and the market drives the enterprises." This is the mechanism of market economics, with the state only playing the role of making adjustments, and then only by using economic means. The market would guide enterprises and production. I also said that market mechanisms were to cover all aspects of society.

Before these points were drafted into the report of the 13th Party Congress, I wrote a letter to Deng Xiaoping, but did not send copies to Chen Yun and Li Xiannian. They were displeased with my ideas, but it was hard for them to oppose them openly.

A few incidents made them particularly unhappy with me. One was removing Deng Liqun before the Party Congress from the role of heading ideological work, and replacing him with Hu Qili. I suggested that Deng Liqun could continue as a Politburo member and participate in Politburo meetings. He had read many books and was entitled to express his opinion. I also said that if Deng Liqun were allowed to continue in theoretical work, not only was there no hope for Marxism to develop in China, but there would be no hope for theories that would benefit reform. He soon heard about my damning remark.

I also abolished the headquarters of the left-wing writers, the Research Office of the Secretariat, as well as *Red Flag* magazine. Of course, Deng made the final decision to shut them down, but the suggestion came from me.

These actions strengthened popular support for reform. Deng Liqun and the left-wing conservatives who opposed the reform agenda were suddenly exposed to the public in China and overseas; they were isolated. We did nominate Deng Liqun during the 13th Party Congress for membership on the Central Committee so that he would have a chance to become a member of the Politburo, but he lost in the election. Later he was nominated for membership on the Standing Committee of the Central Advisory Commission, but he lost again. They thought I had manipulated the results; as a result, Li Xiannian, Wang Zhen, Hu Qiaomu, and even Comrade Chen Yun remained angry with me.

Comrade Wang Zhen actively opposed liberalization but he believed in openness, so I was surprised that he ended up hating me to such a degree. After the 13th Party Congress, Li Xiannian openly denounced me in Shanghai and Hubei in front of local officials. He accused me of not carrying out socialism and of having learned too much foreign stuff. He said that I had no understanding of economics and had brought chaos to the economy. Comrade Chen Yun was more discreet and made reasoned arguments.

They later came to the conclusion that I was "more Hu Yaobang than Hu Yaobang." Things Hu Yaobang had not dared to do or was unable to accomplish, I had managed to pull off.

Before the panic buying, and before "adjustment and reorganization" had been proposed, they had secretly tried to undermine me. When these developments took hold, they believed their chance had arrived, since they thought that I had ruined economic policy and spoiled the reforms. They spread adverse opinions about me and waged a campaign to "overthrow Zhao."

I was not well informed. Since I had spent so many years working at local levels and had recently come to the central leadership, I had fewer channels. Some of the behind-the-scenes dealings remain obscure to me, even now. For example, a group of people wrote a letter to Deng Xiaoping attacking me, but I don't know who they were.

Before the incident of June Fourth, amid the "Overthrow Zhao" campaign, Deng Xiaoping had always firmly supported me and was not moved by their attempts to sway him. This can be seen from a series of incidents.

For instance, Deng said on many occasions that the structure of the central leadership could not be changed. It was obvious that Deng said this in response to the people who wanted to make this change. Deng even said directly to me and to other comrades that I should remain General Secretary for two subsequent terms. Of course, this was only his personal opinion.

After the New Year of 1989, Li Peng and Yao Yilin launched an attack against reform at the Politburo Party life meeting. Deng was upset when he heard about the incident, so Li Peng went to Deng's place to explain and defend himself. During this conversation, Deng told him, "Zhao will be General Secretary for two more terms" and asked him to forward this message to the other members of the Politburo Standing Committee. Of course, Li Peng had to tell me what Deng had said.

Before June Fourth, just before my North Korea trip, I paid a visit on Deng. He told me that after my trip, he wanted to discuss my continuing on for two additional terms as General Secretary. A list of names had been prepared to participate in a discussion of this. In addition to the members of the Politburo Standing Committee, some of the Party elders were included. He also told me then that Chen Yun and Li Xiannian had agreed. As for how that discussion had gone, I don't know.

During the Spring Festival holiday in 1989, just before departing for Shanghai, I had made another visit to his home. That discussion had gone even further. He said that he had been thinking for some time, but had not told anyone and wanted to discuss with me first, that he wanted to resign as chairman of the Central Military Commission and wanted me to take over. He said that if he did not entirely retire and still kept the position, it would be difficult to persuade other elders to stop intervening. He said this seemed the only way. It was obvious that he felt that the elders had been too intrusive and had made it difficult for me to manage. Perhaps he considered this move after the elders had gone to him to express their opposition to me. In order to allow me to work unfettered, he had decided to relinquish his position.

When he suggested he retire, I firmly disagreed. I said, "With the economic problems we are now encountering, people are talking. If you retire completely, it will be very difficult for us to manage. Politics in the East differs from the West; here in the East, your retirement would not stop the interference, nor would the fact that they no longer held any official positions. As long as these heroic founders of the nation are still alive, it will be impossible to persuade them to stop interfering in state affairs. If you were to stop intervening, but they continued to, it would be even more difficult for us to manage. With you in charge, it is still easier for us to get things done." I suggested to him, "No matter what, you really must not raise this issue again for at least a year."

After I said this, he paused to think for a moment. Then he replied, "Very well. I will do what you have suggested. I will not mention this for another year."

This talk with Deng made me realize that some people, perhaps many of the elders, had been putting pressure on Deng, bad-mouthing me. Deng openly expressed that he would not be influenced by them. He rejected their pressure. From the moment I was made General Secretary in 1987, a conservative force had gradually formed to oppose me. Though they were aggressive in their opposition, utilizing all sorts of tactics, without Deng Xiaoping's support they were unable to succeed.

This situation only changed after the political upheaval of 1989. Because Deng and I disagreed over how to deal with the student demonstrations, and because I refused to execute his decision, Deng's attitude toward me changed. When that happened, the elders who had opposed me for more than a year were finally able to share a consensus with Deng. United, they made the decision to remove me from office.

Here I'd like to talk about Li Xiannian and Deng Liqun. Deng Liqun was the general leading the conservatives in the ideological, theoretical, and propaganda realms. His supporters behind the scenes included Li Xiannian, Wang Zhen, and Comrade Chen Yun. Of course, there were other elders who also opposed reform. Deng Liqun had extremely close relationships with them.

His relationship with Wang Zhen extended back to the early years after liberation, when Wang Zhen was the Party secretary of the Central Committee's Xinjiang Bureau, where Deng [Liqun] was in charge of its department of propaganda. He also had a good relationship with Li Xiannian and had long served as his assistant. When Li Xiannian was in charge of the Fifth Division of the State Council, Deng [Liqun] was his adviser.

Comrade Chen Yun was also very good to him. Deng Liqun held Comrade Chen Yun's opinions on the economy in high esteem. As for Deng Liqun's own views on economics, though of course he didn't approve of the ways of the Cultural Revolution, he very much approved of what had come before the Cultural Revolution, especially the methods of the first Five-Year Plan. At least as early as 1980, he promoted the notion that Comrade Chen Yun's economic ideas were sufficient to guide us in our new economic policies.

He [Deng Liqun] often used his position in charge of [propaganda] to publish collections of essays for Party elders, to flatter them and win favor. Examples include the *Selected Works of Chen Yun* and the *Selected Works of Li Xiannian*. Therefore, when Deng Xiaoping decided to remove Deng Liqun from his position leading ideological and theoretical work, both Chen Yun and Li Xiannian disagreed. They openly expressed this by commenting, "Deng Liqun is a good comrade." However, since Deng Xiaoping had already made the decision, there was nothing they could do to change it.

Immediately after Deng Liqun lost in the elections at the 13th Party Congress, Comrade Chen Yun wrote a letter to safeguard Deng Liqun's salary and other compensation. To this day, Deng Liqun still enjoys the compensation package of a secretary of the Central Committee Secretariat or a member of the Standing Committee of the Central Advisory Commission, even though he was never elected to be a member of the latter group. This is highly abnormal.

In fact, Deng Liqun is the most powerful writer among those who oppose Deng Xiaoping's reforms. It would be wrong to underestimate Deng Liqun's influence. After *Red Flag* magazine and the Research Office of the Secretariat were abolished, Deng Liqun made other arrangements for people who supported his work. Deng Liqun still holds titles in many organizations, where he controls the realm of ideology and theory, especially in Party history and other Party publications.

Li Xiannian was the most prominent elder who opposed Deng Xiaoping's reforms. He hated me because I was implementing Deng Xiaoping's reforms, but since it was difficult for him to openly oppose Deng, he made me the target of his opposition. Li Xiannian claimed that I only listened to what Deng Xiaoping said, while ignoring him. He once relayed a message through [Vice Premier] Wang Renzhong, who in turn sent [Hubei Party secretary] Wang Quanguo to tell me, "You should listen to all Party elders and not be so partial to just one!" In fact, I could not listen to him, because he was opposed to reform.

Another issue was Comrade Chen Yun's insistence on applying the methods of the first Five-Year Plan, which he said should not be criticized. He believed that reform had, in many ways, negated the methods of the first Five-Year Plan, so he was often antagonistic toward reform.

Li Xiannian's opposition, by contrast, was not primarily based on the first Five-Year Plan. Instead he advocated for the policies used during the Cultural Revolution or the three years of stagnation afterward, during which he was in charge of economic policy. When Comrade Chen Yun lost Chairman Mao's favor in 1958, it was Li Xiannian who took over as the Standing Vice Premier of the State Council and for a long time he was in charge of economic policy. He was upset that the records of his economic successes during the Cultural Revolution era and the three years of post–Cultural Revolution stagnation went unrecognized. He often said, "The economic successes are not all the result of reform. Weren't there successes in the past, too? Weren't the foundations laid in the past?"

HOW CHINA MUST CHANGE

I

Deng's View on Political Reform

The modest political reform measures passed by the 13th Party Congress in 1987 are shelved after the Tiananmen crackdown. The effect is still in evidence today: China permits widespread economic freedom but little in the way of political liberty. Zhao, as he languishes under house arrest, turns his thoughts to China's stillborn political development.

His journey begins with a look back at the diverging views that China's top leaders held before Tiananmen. He starts with an analysis of Deng Xiaoping, his onetime mentor, who set China on its current path.

Let me start with a discussion of Deng Xiaoping's view. From 1980 until just before June 4, 1989, Deng repeatedly spoke about opposing liberalization. On the other hand, he also said many times that political reform was necessary, so how exactly was reform to be conducted, according to Deng Xiaoping's idea of political reform?

I believe Deng was somewhat dissatisfied with the existing political system. His belief in political reform was genuine. But the reform he had in mind was not a modernization and democratization of politics. It was rather a kind of administrative reform, the kind of reform that only involved specific regulations, organization, methodology, and general morale. Deng believed that a precondition of reform was an upholding of the Communist Party's one-party rule. Reforms were precisely intended to further consolidate the Communist Party's one-party rule. Deng firmly rejected any reform that would weaken that.

247

The impression most people had of Deng Xiaoping's idea of political reform was from a speech he delivered at the enlarged Politburo meeting of August 1980, titled "On the Reform of the System of Party and State Leadership." He criticized the bureaucratism, overconcentration of power, and patriarchism that were part of the system at that time. He pointed out that these problems were rooted in the existing system and that a good system would prevent unscrupulous people from being able to do whatever they wished, while the unsound system was restricting good people from fully realizing good deeds or was even pushing them to the opposing side. In the speech, he even quoted an expression of Chairman Mao, who once said that an episode such as Stalin's trampling on the socialist legal system could never have happened in Western nations such as England, the United States, or France. Also, when he analyzed the root of the existing shortcomings, he referred especially to the influence of feudalism. He pointed out that even though we worked on building our new democratic revolution for twenty-eight years, and had overthrown the rules of feudalism as well as the feudal ownership of land, we had underestimated the task of cleansing feudalism's influence on political thinking, and we had not completed the task.

The contents of Deng Xiaoping's speech could easily have caused people to believe that Deng was prepared to proceed with political modernization and democratization and to change the fundamentals of the political system. But it wasn't like that. After Deng criticized those shortcomings, he proposed measures that did not exceed the realm of specific regulations, organization, methodology, and morale, and did not touch upon the fundamental system. His reform was to be administrative in nature.

In addition, Deng's speech was made in a particular context: at the time, he was focused on how to deal with Hua Guofeng [Mao's chosen successor]. Both Deng Xiaoping and Chen Yun believed that Hua was an obstacle to carrying out the policy of the Third Plenum of the 11th Central Committee [in 1978, when Deng's reforms were launched]. Chen Yun even believed that since Hua rose to the top from Mao's "rebel factions," he was not to be trusted. Hua's leadership position was unacceptable to both Deng and Chen.

At that time [1980], Hua was Party Chairman, Premier of the State Council, and Chairman of the Central Military Commission, so in his hands were all the powers of the party, the state, and the military. Therefore, when Deng voiced opposition to an overconcentration of power, one of his objectives was to break up Hua's power. Foremost was asking Hua to give up his position as Premier.

A document reviewing lessons to be learned from the Cultural Revolution, "The Resolution of Several Historical Problems," was being drafted around that time. The entire Party was consumed with reviewing how Mao's patriarchal dictatorship had put him above the Party and resulted in the great catastrophe of the Cultural Revolution, in which Deng himself had been severely victimized and had directly suffered. Therefore, when Comrade Li Weihan [vice chairman of the Central Advisory Commission] proposed cleansing out the influences of feudalism, Deng accepted without hesitation.

In June 1986, at a briefing on the economic situation and again at an enlarged Politburo meeting, Deng raised the need to proceed with political reform. He said that if we didn't initiate political reform, we could not adapt to new situations. Political reform should be made a milestone of reform; the success of all other reforms depended upon reform of the political system. In September of that year, at a briefing by the Central Economic and Financial Leading Group, Deng again mentioned political reform and said that a blueprint was needed. In June 1987, in a talk with visitors from Yugoslavia and again in July with Bangladeshi visitors, he repeated that political reform should be an important agenda item. He also said that political reform would be one of the two most important issues of the 13th Party Congress.

However, the meaning of "political reform" in his remarks was even more limited than what he had said in 1980. He was referring only to administrative reform, issues related to administrative organizations and regulations. In his definition of political reform, foremost was the separation of Party and state, aimed at resolving the issue of how the Party might provide leadership and how to lead well. That was the key. Second was handing authority down to lower administrative levels, which would tackle the issue of the relationship between central and provincial governments, and also the issue of provincial governments handing power down to various local levels. Third was reducing the size of the administration. Another point was improving efficiency.

In Deng Xiaoping's speech of September 13, 1986, he said, "I consider there to be three items. First, the Party and administrative bodies and the entire state administrative system must improve their vitality. That means they shouldn't become ossified and must adopt new ways of thinking to deal with newly emerging issues. The second is to truly improve efficiency. Third, we must fully mobilize people, enterprises, and all local level administrations to be more enthusiastic and to have renewed vitality. The most significant issue now is to promote younger cadres. Other major issues include boosting people's enthusiasm and handing more power down to lower levels."

Some people feel that Deng only paid lip service to political reform now and again, in order to give people a favorable impression. Others believed that Deng's political reforms could never be carried out because they were blocked by the [political] situation or had encountered forces of opposition. I believe these two views both lack sufficient evidence.

The essence of the issue is what kind of political reform Deng had in mind. In Deng's mind, there was no contradiction between political reform, upholding the Four Cardinal Principles, and anti-liberalization; they could all exist simultaneously. Therefore, each time he spoke about political reform, he almost always spoke at around the same time or even in the same speech about anti-liberalization and strengthening the people's democratic dictatorship, and so on.

Before he gave his famous August 1980 speech, "On the Reform of the System of Party and State Leadership," at a theoretical discussion in March 1979, he spoke about "Upholding the Four Cardinal Principles"—like issuing a hoop-tightening incantation* just as the theoretical and metaphysical arenas were beginning to enjoy some freedom.

After his August speech, in a talk delivered in December, "Implementing the Readjustment Policy and Safeguarding Peace and Solidarity," he emphasized maintaining the stability and unity of the political scene, as well as strengthening the state apparatus and the people's democratic dictatorship. He pointed out that though class struggle was no longer a major conflict in society, it continued to exist and could not be underestimated. He stressed that organs of the state must use the appropriate laws and rules to ensure that worker and student strikes be mediated and handled in advance, and that street demonstrations only take place after permits have been obtained specifying time and place; no interorganizational or cross-region contacts for cooperative demonstrations would be permitted; activities of illegal organizations and illegal publications were to be prohibited; martial law could be applied if necessary to areas where events of potentially serious consequences were taking place.

The years 1986 and 1987 were the period when Deng Xiaoping was focusing on dealing with anti–bourgeois liberalization. As I mentioned above, at the same time on various occasions he mentioned political reform. This shows that what Deng had in mind for political reform was

---

* A reference to the classical Chinese novel *Journey to the West*, about the Monkey King. His master controls him by reciting an incantation that tightens a golden hoop that he wears around his head, causing severe pain.

different from what most people understood it to mean: modernization of the state and democratization. His idea was mainly to tackle the vitality and efficiency of the Communist Party and the state; in other words, administrative reform.

In June 1987, when Deng spoke with guests from Yugoslavia regarding China's political reform, he said that, in general, political reforms were associated with democratization, but the meaning of democratization was not clear. Democracy was an important means of reform, but how exactly democracy could be carried out was an issue that was new to us.

Deng was particularly opposed to a multiparty system, tripartite separation of powers, and the parliamentary system of Western nations—and firmly rejected them. Almost every time he mentioned political reform, he was sure to note that the Western political system absolutely could not be adopted. This was the foremost component of the "bourgeois liberalization" that he opposed. In September 1980, when Deng said that separation of Party and state must be the first item on the agenda of political reform, he also pointed out that pursuing liberalization and copying the West were absolutely forbidden. The June 1987 talk with Yugoslav guests included a long section in which he said, "The democracy of the bourgeoisie is in fact a democracy for those who have a monopoly on capital, nothing more than multiple parties, elections, and tripartite separation of powers. How could we possibly do that?"

During the drafting of the report for the 13th Party Congress, he warned me several times: "The idea of political reform absolutely must not be influenced by Western parliamentarian political ideas. Let there not be even a trace of it!" Many other times, when he mentioned the functions of the National People's Congress and the Chinese People's Political Consultative Conference, he criticized people who wanted to make the NPC and CPPCC into houses, with the NPC as the lower house and the CPPCC as the upper house.

In 1988, when I proposed expanding participation by other political parties, he opposed allowing them to establish party groups or to conduct activities during the convening of the NPC. As for selecting people from other parties for positions of real power in the government, he said, "They should only be permitted to join the government in a personal capacity, not as a representative of their party." He did not want even the slightest relaxation on this issue.

Deng very much appreciated and liked the political system of socialist countries whereby power was concentrated in the hands of one or a few. He despised systems in which powers were separated by checks and balances. When he was talking to the guests from Yugoslavia, he said,

"One of the greatest advantages of socialist nations is that, as long as something has been decided and a resolution has been made, it can be carried out immediately without any restrictions; unlike the parliamentary democratic process that is so complicated, going back and forth, only talking about it without doing it, concluding without executing. In this respect, our efficiency is higher; we carry things out as soon as we have made up our mind. What I am referring to is the overall efficiency. It is our strength, and we must retain this advantage." Deng regarded a system without restrictions or checks and balances, and with absolute concentration of power, as our overall advantage.

"We absolutely must not adopt the Western system of tripartite separation of powers! We must safeguard the advantages of the socialist system." Deng made remarks like this several times.

I remember once, sometime in the early 1980s, on the topic of the Soviet military intervention in Afghanistan, Deng said, "I would say that the Americans cannot compete with the Soviet Union. The Soviets can do something after just one Politburo meeting. Can the Americans do that?"

Another time, when Deng was speaking to foreign guests, he said, "There are three governments in the United States. When we deal with them, we don't know who can actually make decisions. They balance each other out and wrangle with each other. It is very difficult to get anything done."

That is why whenever he spoke about political reform, he was sure to remind people to maintain and utilize the advantages of the socialist system, to not proceed with anything like the Western tripartite separation of powers, with each restricting the power of the others. Once Deng Xiaoping took over as paramount leader [in 1978], he placed strong emphasis on maintaining political stability. Stability trumped everything else. His belief was that, without stability, in the midst of chaos, nothing could be accomplished. In order to maintain stability, dictatorship was the ultimate weapon.

Deng had always stood out among the Party elders as the one who emphasized the means of dictatorship. He often reminded people about its usefulness. Every time he mentioned stability, he also emphasized dictatorship.

Not only was he opposed to establishing any checks and balances in the political system, he found extremely annoying the use of street demonstrations, petitions, and protests as a way for people to express their views. In fact, he believed in drawing up laws to prohibit people from conducting such activities. Whenever these kinds of incidents occurred, he advocated "using a sharp knife to cut through knotted hemp," in other words, deploying coercive measures to suppress them. In Deng's political reform, dictatorship was the one thing that was not allowed to be changed.

Given the serious lessons drawn from Stalin and Mao Zedong's later years, and from Deng's personal experiences during the Cultural Revolution, Deng was not unaware of the shortcomings of the political system of socialist countries. For that reason, he often mentioned expanding democracy within the Party and the society, abolishing the patriarchal system, and cleansing out Soviet influences.

However, in order to fully resolve these problems, there had to be a change in the overconcentration of power in the political system. Deng's creed was not only that the ruling status of the Communist Party should never be challenged; he also adored the high concentration of power and dictatorship and believed they should be retained.

Therefore, the democracy that he talked about, the removal of special status for the leadership and the cleansing of feudal influences, could never be realized. They were no more than empty words.

2

Hu's View on Political Reform

Zhao next turns to an analysis of the views of his predecessor as Party General Secretary, Hu Yaobang. Zhao surmises that if Hu had not been ousted from power in 1987, he would have guided China more quickly toward democracy.

[Hu] Yaobang was accused many times by Deng of indulging in bourgeois liberalization, and in the end he was forced to step down because of that. People generally viewed Hu as part of the reform-minded and democratic faction. What exactly was Hu's view of political reform? What had he proposed?

Yaobang was a quite generous and tolerant man. He advocated implementing a more tolerant social policy, especially with intellectuals, toward whom he had always been empathetic and tolerant. In past decades, when class struggle and constant political campaigns dominated the scene, he rarely took any extreme actions.

After the Third Plenum of the 11th Central Committee, when he was Director of the Organization Department as well as General Secretary of the Central Committee, he actively overturned cases of condemned rightists, removed the branding of "landlords" and "rich peasants," and reinstated many of the wrongly convicted. Against opposition and resistance, he insisted on overturning all such cases regardless of when they had occurred. When he was General Secretary, whenever social problems emerged, including demonstrations, he always advocated the principle of reducing tensions and opposed heavy-handed measures. Even for cases related to hooliganism and petty crimes, he promoted the use of multiple approaches to dealing with them. He opposed the "strike hard" campaigns that rounded up and detained large numbers of people. He was very much against the frequent use of dictatorial means.

Even though he did not specifically or clearly express his views or his plans for political reform, the ideal he sought was more democracy and freedom in China's socialism—to enable people to live in a democratic and free environment with a spirit of enthusiasm. Just before he stepped down, he was personally in charge of drafting the "Resolution on the Building of a Socialist Spiritual Civilization," which included this paragraph:

> In the history of mankind, in the struggle of the newly emerged bourgeoisie and the working class against feudal dictatorship, the formation of the ideas of democracy, freedom, equality, and fraternity greatly liberated the human spirit. The most important [negative] lessons learned during the development of socialism were: first, neglecting development of the economy, and second, failing to build real democratic politics. After the Third Plenum of the 11th Central Committee, our Party has stressed that without democracy there can be no socialist modernization and it is ready to really promote the democratization of Party and state political affairs. Recently the Central Committee emphasized the issue of political reform, the goal of which is to expand socialist democracy and to perfect the socialist legal system.

From the above, it can be seen that Yaobang undoubtedly sought democracy. Even though he had not yet come up with a specific structure or model for the socialist democracy he had defined, I believe that if he had continued as leader of the Party and state—as situations emerged in our country and abroad, and given the worldwide democratic trend—he would have pushed China's political reform forward along the path of modernizing the political system and democratization.

3

How Zhao's View Evolved

Zhao concedes that political reform was not on his mind when he first came to power. But as he realized that China's political system was blocking the pace of economic change, his thinking began to shift. He began to advocate for "rule of law," instead of "rule by men."

After the Third Plenum of the 11th Central Committee [in 1978], I focused all of my attention for a time on reforming the economic system, ignoring the issue of political reform. Even though as early as when I was in Sichuan, as I had begun experimenting with expanding the autonomy of enterprises, I never thought about how to conduct political reform.

I also felt that history had taught us some lessons and that we needed to overturn the policies that had brought about abnormal events in our Party and society after 1957 and throughout the Cultural Revolution. However, I didn't think we needed major changes to our fundamental political system.

A worker in Shaanxi once wrote me a letter saying that he had read many of my speeches and believed that on economic issues I was a reformer, but that on political issues I was a conservative. This was indeed an accurate description of my thinking at that time and into the mid-1980s. Therefore, Deng Xiaoping's famous 1980 speech on reforming the Party and state leadership did not even catch my attention; even less did it change my attitude. It was not until 1985 or 1986 that my understanding started to change. My attention was aroused somewhat by events in the broader international environment and problems that had emerged in the Eastern Bloc. Yet the main reason for the change was that

I had come to see a need for political reform from the perspective of economic reform.

Until then, I'd believed that political reform in China should neither be exceedingly progressive, nor lag far behind economic reform. As economic reform deepened, the resistance from conservative forces within the Party grew more intense. Yet without political reform it would have been difficult to sustain economic reform. And without reforms in the political arena, the forces of reform would find it difficult to reach their full potential. Besides, social problems had emerged in the process of reform that would be difficult to address properly without political reform. For example, the development of a market economy created problems involving exchanges of power for money and the exploitation of power for personal gain.

After 1987, I became Acting General Secretary and later General Secretary [of the Chinese Communist Party]. As I became increasingly involved with political issues, I developed a strong belief that tensions in the relationship between the Party and the intelligentsia needed to be resolved. Yet without political participation by intellectuals, it was impossible to improve the relationship in a fundamental way.

Of course, the political reform I had in mind for China at the time, up until 1989, was not an adaptation of a multiparty system or the implementation of a Western-style parliamentary system. Nor did I think that the Communist Party's ruling position should change.

My idea was that the Party's ruling status need not be changed, but the way it governed had to be changed. Moreover, in order to realize "rule of law," the existing situation of "rule by men" needed to be changed. Socialist nations should also be nations with rule of law.

I have heard but not read for myself that Gorbachev's memoir states that in our talk during his 1989 visit to China, I hinted that China would proceed toward a multiparty and parliamentary system. I didn't mean to convey any such thing in my comments. I made two points to him: one was that the Communist Party's status as the ruling party would not change, but that its method of governing had to change; the other was that socialist countries should be governed not by "rule by men" but by "rule of law." I intentionally used the word "rule" instead of "system." These ideas accurately summed up my position on political reform at the time, a position I had developed over the prior two years.

We had to change the way we governed, but how were we to make these changes? I had gradually developed some ideas on how to accomplish this.

Given that the Communist Party was the ruling party, how should it govern? My idea was to modernize how it governed, so that it could become more modern, civilized, enlightened, and open. I didn't sense it then, but when I think about things now I realize that my general inclination was to change the methods as well as the system of the long-standing "proletarian dictatorship." The idea included the following:

First, we needed to increase the transparency of Party and state decision making. Gorbachev called this "openness" [glasnost] and we called it "transparency." The major activities and decisions of the Party and the state needed to be made public. This would have changed the long-standing "black-box operation," where the public is only given the final result of a decision. As soon as the government announced a decision, it moved on to implementation, but people were not privy to the process by which the decision had been made. This is very important. People have the right to know.

Next, we needed to establish multiple channels for dialogue—with various social factions, forces, and interests. Decisions on major issues should be made with ongoing consultation and dialogue with various social groups, not just within the Communist Party, and not only after merely consulting once with key figures of other political parties.

Of course, we had to permit social groups to exist; otherwise, how could dialogue be conducted? Most important, we needed to change the situation in which all social groups—including workers' unions, youth organizations, women's organizations, chambers of commerce, and others—were all in monotonous unity with the Communist Party. They should not be treated like the Party's royal instruments. They have to be able to truly represent the people they are meant to represent.

Only dialogue conducted with groups of this kind would carry any real meaning. In other words, their function as intermediate organizations should be fully developed. The Communist Party should not take control of everything or interfere so much in their affairs, and should give them room for independent activities. Under such conditions, the Communist Party should hold dialogues and consult with various social groups, enabling these groups to have real political participation.

We also needed to address changes to our election system: expanding the scope of democratic elections and of "differential quota elections."* At the time, we were contemplating submitting multiple candidates for the leadership of the National People's Congress; the final choice would

---

*   "Differential quota elections" refers to internal Party elections in which voters were presented with more candidates than positions, effectively eliminating the least popular candidates. By Communist Party standards, it was a democratic breakthrough.

be made by a vote of NPC representatives, after the Communist Party had proposed its candidates. At the time, differential quota elections were only available for deputy positions, not for high-level posts in the central leadership. Even though we could not all at once adopt the methods of Western-style elections, the Communist Party could at least increase the number of proposed candidates, including for positions such as the Chairman of the NPC or the Premier of the State Council. With more candidates, people would have a real choice.

Moreover, the ruling party must respect the separation of Party and state. The Party's leadership should be essentially political and not interfere in so many other domains. More tolerance should be shown especially in the realm of culture and the arts; the Party should not be so controlling or so severe.

We also needed to enrich the level of cooperation with other political parties and let other parties enjoy true political participation with functions of dialogue and mutual checks and balances. I also contemplated allowing other political parties to conduct their own activities while the NPC was in session, and to establish their own leading groups. Furthermore, we needed to protect citizens' rights in concrete terms. This was extremely important. Our constitution was a good one, but there were no laws in place to support its implementation. That is why many of the citizens' rights defined in the constitution could not be realized.

I talked about this with Gorbachev. I said, "There are many things that are defined in the constitution but cannot be realized in concrete terms. Therefore, we must establish laws that guarantee the protection of specific aspects, for example, freedom of association, assembly, demonstrations, petitions, and strikes. All these should be protected by specific laws."

We also needed to allow greater press freedom, though under management and leadership. In 1989, I talked to [chief editor of the *People's Daily*] Hu Jiwei about whether we ought to allow independent newspapers. Currently, all news media are monopolized by the Party and the state: this is not right. At that time, I had not considered permitting a completely free press, but wanted to allow a controlled process of opening up. At the very least, material that Party- and state-controlled media were not willing to run could be published by other media. Even in Chiang Kai-shek's era [before the Communist Party took power], independent newspapers existed. Even if we did not allow full press freedom, we should allow the airing of public opinions.

At that time, I was thinking about how to allow more political participation—under the Communist Party's continued ruling position—from various social groups and interest groups, and especially by intellectuals. Even without a multiparty system, we should have expanded various forces of political participation as much as possible.

Some of these thoughts had been included in documents and talks that were written into the Political Report of the 13th Party Congress. Of course, in these texts, some of the ideas could not be expressed as explicitly, and some could not be included at all.

These are the ideas that gradually formed in my mind from 1986 to 1989. The Party's ruling position would not change, but the way it governed had to. That is to say, under the basic framework of the Communist Party's leadership, we would allow more political participation from various social groups; "rule of law" would gradually replace "rule by men"; and many of the wonderful things defined in the constitution would be realized, one by one.

4

The Old Guard Fights Back

Zhao tries to analyze why the drive for political reform never took hold after an initial period of excitement in 1987. For one thing, a period of social calm immediately afterward encouraged intellectuals to speak more freely about politics, which triggered a backlash among Party elders. Such opposition was also hindering economic reform, in particular efforts to make factory managers, not the local Party chiefs, responsible for running their enterprises. Zhao also talks about his enemies' unwarranted attacks against him that were related to a controversial TV series that praised Western ways.

At the 13th Party Congress [in 1987], we discussed not just economic reform but also political reform. It was raised in the context of how to improve socialist democracy. At that time the political environment was relaxed. Metaphysical and theoretical studies, culture and the arts—all were vibrant. At the same time, during the ten years of reform we were being influenced from abroad, by Western values, concepts, and political systems. Moreover, the Soviet Union's policy toward political dissidents had changed through glasnost. All of these things encouraged China's intellectuals, youths, and young workers to demand more democracy.

We should have taken advantage of the situation to carry out the political reform measures that had been approved by the 13th Party Congress: separating Party and state, installing a civil service system, informing people of important developments, consulting with people on key issues, experimenting with democratic procedures in organizations made up of intellectuals, satisfying intellectuals' demands for political participation, and so forth. If we had been able to carry out what had already been decided, we could have won over the vast majority of people who had hoped for more democracy through these channels. We could have expanded democracy via the gradual approach approved by the 13th Party Congress, and strengthened the development of democratic politics. The demands of most people would have been satisfied, leaving only small, insignificant groups of extremists.

However, after the 13th Party Congress, it was difficult to do political reform. First of all, the Party elders, including Comrade Deng Xiaoping, had differing opinions on economic reform but shared one opinion on political reform: they were opposed to changing the basics of the existing system. They feared that any real political reform would lead to challenges to the Communist Party's power, thereby weakening the Party or even causing it to lose its ruling position.

When drafting the 13th Party Congress Political Report, I was repeatedly warned by [Deng] Xiaoping not to be influenced by the Western concept of a tripartite separation of powers. He went so far as to say that not even a trace of this should be allowed to appear in the Political Report. What he intended by "reform of the political system" was in fact merely administrative reforms: simplification of organizations, streamlining of personnel, reduction of bureaucratic red tape, improved efficiency, etc. None of these touched upon the most essential problems in the political system.

I then thought about enriching and improving the system of "cooperation by and in consultation with other political parties under the leadership of the Communist Party." Those other parties could be made truly useful if they were allowed real political participation, if the system were genuinely functional instead of just in name. We could make the other political parties active and truly useful, with their political participation acting as a check. It would allow those people in society who had a strong desire for political participation to fulfill their wishes through joining other political parties, which would not yield when opposing the Party; something that would be outside of any existing framework. Doing this would constitute a kind of distribution of power, so that the Communist Party would not monopolize it all. However, it absolutely would not challenge the Communist Party's ruling position. For this purpose, I proposed changing "multiparty cooperation system under the Communist Party" to "multiparty cooperation system with the Communist Party's leadership." The change was not a major one, but "leadership" was a political matter, while "under" also included an organizational aspect.

I also suggested that skilled people from other political parties be promoted to positions of Vice Minister or even Minister levels in various branches of the State Council. This had been done in the early years of the People's Republic of China. Also, on some issues, other political parties should no longer have to wait to be informed by the Communist Party only after it had made a final decision. We should be able to hear the opinions of other parties before making decisions. This would make it a "consultation" in reality, not just in name. The promotion of members of other political parties to leadership positions in ministries had won Deng Xiaoping's approval, and he had said, "Do it as soon as possible."

Also, there was the issue of how to develop the potential of other parties. As long as there were going to be political parties, they should be parties with real political participation. That meant that they ought to function as real political parties, not just as a single representative at the National People's Congress.

These were ideas that I had in mind at the time, though without resolute certainty.

Some people wondered: If the Communist Party could establish leading groups during National People's Congress sessions, would other political parties be allowed to establish their own leading groups? I don't know how this matter was relayed to Deng, but [his daughter] Deng Maomao sent a message to me via my secretary Li Yong: "When Deng spoke of expanding participation by other political parties, he was just talking. How can this be taken seriously? We absolutely must not allow other political parties to establish their leading groups during NPC sessions." Deng was opposed to this idea and had sent this message.

We could not even complete and bring substance to a system we already had in place, a system that had everyone's approval. Imagine how difficult it would be to put through any other reforms.

On the question of the separation of Party and state powers, many Party members were worried about implementing the factory managers' responsibility scheme—and their resistance was fierce. Many local Party committees were opposed. They were used to the Party committee managing everything, with a monopoly on all powers, over the Party and administration. The final decision maker was the Party secretary.

Implementing a separation of Party and state powers would strip the Party secretary of real power. Therefore, local-level officials refused to make the factory director a principal leader and the legal representative. The result would have been that the Party secretary no longer made all factory decisions, but would mainly be in charge of Party and political affairs.

Separation of Party and state powers and the factory managers' responsibility system did in fact touch upon the issue of the distribution of powers, so those who already had power were unwilling to give it up. The reform was therefore extremely difficult to carry out.

I had said before that we needed to strengthen and reform our political and propaganda work, and that it was a major issue. Strengthening politics and propaganda while implementing reform was of course the right thing to do; the question was how to strengthen it.

If we followed the old methods to implement this, we would end up with the opposite of what we had intended. Even though our politics and propaganda work had achieved positive things in the past, after 1957—for nearly twenty years—our politics and propaganda had been focused on class struggle. The politics and propaganda that had taken class struggle as its central focus viewed people as objects to be changed and controlled. Therefore, political and propaganda work had never used reasoning or tried to persuade, but had relied on coercion and labeling. The class struggle–based politics and propaganda had been seriously damaging and had created some of the worst habits. At the same time, there were problems with political affairs having become seriously bureaucratized. The organization was huge, with large numbers of nonproductive people.

Therefore, I proposed reforming political and propaganda work, which meant fundamentally changing how it had been done—continuing some of the good traditions formed in the war years, while searching for ways to reinvent political and propaganda working methods. Primarily, we needed to search anew and reinvent.

My raising of this issue caused great unrest. Many elder comrades were opposed, as were comrades of Party committees at various local levels. Those who were doing political and propaganda work in the factories, and the large number of people across the country who relied on political and propaganda work for a living, believed that they were about to be pushed aside.

I felt back then how difficult China's economic reform had been at every step, and how little room there had been for taking risks. Any little problem that emerged provoked opposition.

In political reform, however, every step was even more difficult. Because political reform was in certain respects changing the way the Communist Party governed, the way it exercised power, and the way it dealt with things, in the end it had to change the way the Party itself viewed power and its own monopoly on power. Therefore, resistance was tremendous.

The resistance to political reform primarily came from the leadership, at all levels within the Party. If economic reform can be said to have eas-

ily gained the support of the "dukes,"* political reform met with their reluctance and resistance. I felt very strongly that China's top-down and
gradual approach of reforming the economic system was workable, but
for political reform, the situation was truly much more difficult.

However, I also felt that if the political system were not reformed,
economic reform would run into difficulties as it continued to be deepened. For example, the standards for cadre promotions hadn't changed.
Even though China had already implemented ten years of reform, we had
never attempted to resolve the imperative of putting people who supported reform in charge at various levels of leadership. Therefore, reform
could not withstand any rocking of the boat.

Some local authorities had taken pragmatic attitudes in dealing with
reform; they had done whatever was beneficial to them and resisted anything that might harm their interests. They would expand whatever
worked to their benefit, and they would limit in scope whatever worked
against their interests.

There was also the problem of corruption. In 1988, I spent the Spring
Festival holiday in Guangdong. After I learned more about the situation
there, I had a profound sense of how reforming the economy had revitalized it, but also that corruption had emerged. At the time, I proposed that
"the economy must prosper, but the government must stay clean." By
"government" here I meant the cadres, those in power. Afterward, I became increasingly aware that "being clean" was a major challenge.

During the transition period from old to new economic systems, without checks, corruption was bound to grow, in the form of power-money
exchanges, official profiteering, official monopoly of businesses, and bribery. To resolve these kinds of corruption issues, the key was transparency
and democratic supervision, including scrutiny by the press and public
opinion, and an independent judiciary.

In other words, this was the issue of political reform. Without an independent judiciary, the courts could not judge a case with a disinter-
ested attitude, the procurator could not exercise power independently,
and even laws that were in place could not be carried out. This touched
upon the issue of the judiciary's relationship with the Party. I deeply believed that the political system needed to be reformed accordingly; of
course, not via a wholesale copying of the West, but rather, something
appropriate to China's situation: gradually adding democracy and checks

---

* Powerful provincial leaders were referred to as "dukes" because historically, local
dukes of Chinese imperial dynasties often had greater actual power than the central government.

and balances to the Communist Party's way of ruling. Power absolutely could not be monopolized and it needed checks.

Almost no Party elders supported this kind of reform. The reality was that political reform was at a standstill. This created a problem. On the one hand, we had people making increasingly strong demands for democracy and an acceleration of political reform; on the other hand, no action had been taken on political reform since the 13th Party Congress. There was a wide gap between the people's demands, especially the intellectuals' demands, and the Party's intentions.

Because the political environment was still relatively relaxed, people spoke out boldly—unlike after June Fourth, when the political environment became highly repressive. The contrast between reality and public demand only intensified the desire for democracy, to the point that extreme ideas were expressed and actions taken that aggravated the conflict. Suggestions were made that a Western parliamentary system be implemented. A student by the name of Chen Jun, who had been studying in the United States, came back to China to organize well-known intellectuals to demand the release of [prominent dissident] Wei Jingsheng. There was a signature petition campaign in the United States to issue an open letter to Deng Xiaoping demanding Wei's release. Similar activities took place in Hong Kong. In 1989, during the National People's Congress, a Hong Kong delegation demanded human rights and the release of Wei Jingsheng. There were many activities in the universities as well. There were various kinds of salons and forums in which extreme ideas were expressed. Some intellectuals who held extreme views went to universities and colleges to give speeches expressing their disaffection. [Dissident astrophysicist] Fang Lizhi, who was abroad, attacked Deng Xiaoping personally, by name.

All of this offered an excuse to those who opposed reform in the name of anti-liberalization. They used these occurrences to provoke the Party elders and make them and Deng even more anxious, and convince them that not even a shred of relaxation should be allowed in the political realm.

This complicated situation emerged after 1988, amid the more relaxed political situation that followed the 13th Party Congress. Tensions heightened between some intellectuals and the Party. The political upheaval that occurred in 1989 was not completely coincidental. Hadn't Deng Xiaoping stated that it had been caused by the general international climate and the domestic climate? I believe if there was a domestic climate, it was the condition that I described above. Certainly people were disgruntled with rising prices, but what made them even more dissatisfied, especially intellectuals and young people, was the standstill in economic reform and the restoration of the old methods.

They were having doubts about the future of economic reform. Meanwhile, political reform had been silenced and no progress had been made. People were angry about corruption and they believed that without political reform to put checks on the Communist Party's rule, the corruption problem could not be resolved. At its core, the spirit of the student demonstrations was a demand for the deepening of reform and an opposition to the conservative forces. The most convincing evidence of this is the fact that, even as inflation dominated public attention, the students cautiously avoided this sensitive issue, out of concerns that it would only lead to opposition to the reforms. Their primary motivation was to promote reform, to oppose undemocratic ways and oppose official profiteering.

[Party elder] Li Xiannian was very active in the "Overthrow Zhao" campaign, both as a front man and behind the scenes. In October 1988, at the Third Plenum of the 13th Central Committee, there had been plans to approve a public announcement on reorganization until [Party elder] Wang Zhen suddenly launched an attack on *River Elegy** and demanded that the Central Committee issue an official criticism of it. I managed to brush him aside.

After the incident, [son of Marshal Ye Jianying] Ye Xuanning told me that Wang Zhen had ardently denounced [Zhao aide] Bao Tong in his presence, saying that Bao Tong was a scoundrel who had supported the production of *River Elegy*—an allegation Wang Zhen had heard from Li Xiannian.

In fact, this was completely fictitious. Bao Tong never had anything to do with *River Elegy*, nor had he ever spoken to me about it.

There was more that Wang Zhen had not said. When Li Xiannian named "Bao Tong," he in fact was referring to me, implying that I had supported *River Elegy*. It is possible that Wang Zhen himself had been displeased with *River Elegy*, and Li Xiannian had taken the opportunity to link me with *River Elegy* to provoke Wang Zhen's anger against me. In order to provoke dissatisfaction in some elder comrades toward me, Li Xiannian had been willing to go so far as to fabricate a rumor.

After June Fourth, when they published criticisms against me in the

* *River Elegy* was a controversial multipart TV documentary in China, first broadcast in 1988. It criticized traditional Chinese isolation and embraced Western openness. The Party later denounced the broadcast and blamed it for helping to inspire the 1989 demonstrations.

newspapers, *River Elegy* was a major issue. Many of the accusations were entirely fictitious, such as the claim that I had supported the production of *River Elegy*, had ordered x number of copies of tapes to be distributed nationwide, had suppressed criticisms of the production. None of this was true.

5

The Way Forward

Despite spending his career in the Communist Party, Zhao ultimately acknowledges that China's system is far from a democratic ideal and concludes that a parliamentary democracy is the best course for a modern state and should be China's goal. He even suggests that China could learn a thing or two from Taiwan.

After I stepped down in 1989 and with the changes that occurred both at home and abroad, I started to develop a new understanding of China's political reform.

I once believed that people were the masters of their own affairs not in the parliamentary democracies of the developed nations in the West, but only in the Soviet and socialist nations' systems with a people's congress, making the latter system more advanced and a better-realized form of democracy.

This, in fact, is not the case. The democratic systems of our socialist nations are all just superficial; they are not systems in which the people are in charge, but rather are ruled by a few or even a single person.

Of the various political systems that existed in the world during the twentieth century, absolute monarchies and the fascist dictatorships of Germany and Italy have been eliminated. There have been military dictatorships, but they have existed briefly or are losing support. Even though they often appeared in very underdeveloped nations—for example, military rule in South American nations—they have all steadily turned out to be brief episodes in these nations' gradual march toward parliamentary politics. For several decades during the twentieth century, the so-called "new democratic system," the proletarian dictatorship, competed with the

Western parliamentary system. But in the vast majority of these nations, it has since receded from the historical stage.

In fact, it is the Western parliamentary democratic system that has demonstrated the most vitality. This system is currently the best one available. It is able to manifest the spirit of democracy and meet the demands of a modern society, and it is a relatively mature system.

Of course, this system is not perfect; it has many problems. Yet relatively speaking, this system is best suited to a modern civilization, more adaptable to shifts in public opinions and most capable of realizing democracy. Moreover, it is more stable. The vitality of this system has grown increasingly clear. Almost all developed nations have adopted a parliamentary democracy.

In the past few decades, the newly emerging nations with their fast-paced development have illustrated more clearly the trend to converge on a parliamentary democratic system. I am certain this is not by chance. Why is there not even one developed nation practicing any other system? This shows that if a country wants to modernize, to realize a modern market economy, it must practice parliamentary democracy as its political system.

Of course, it is possible that in the future a more advanced political system than parliamentary democracy will emerge. But that is a matter for the future. At present, there is no other.

Based on this, we can say that if a country wishes to modernize, not only should it implement a market economy, it must also adopt a parliamentary democracy as its political system. Otherwise, this nation will not be able to have a market economy that is healthy and modern, nor can it become a modern society with a rule of law. Instead it will run into the situations that have occurred in so many developing countries, including China: commercialization of power, rampant corruption, a society polarized between rich and poor.

However, it must be noted that parliamentary democracies exist primarily in developed nations and emerging ones. Some of the developing countries practiced parliamentary politics early on but could not fully realize its potential, and problems developed: the government had trouble exercising its authority, society was not stable enough, military coups were staged using these problems as an excuse. This also shows that parliamentary democracy, which is modern, advanced, civilized, and mature, must have certain necessary conditions and that not just any nation can adopt and use it well.

Given current conditions in China, we must establish that the final goal of political reform is the realization of this advanced political system.

If we don't move toward this goal, it will be impossible to resolve the abnormal conditions in China's market economy: issues such as an unhealthy market, profiting from power, rampant social corruption, and a widening gap between rich and poor. Nor will the rule of law ever materialize. In order to resolve these problems, we must in concrete terms conduct political reform with this as our goal.

On the other hand, given the reality in China, we need a relatively long period of transition. The experiences of other Asian nations are worthy of our attention in this regard. For example, territories and nations such as Taiwan and South Korea have gradually made the transition from their old systems to a parliamentary system, and have had positive experiences that we would benefit from studying.

In China, for the sake of a smoother transition, at least for a while, we should maintain the ruling position of the Communist Party—while changing how the Party rules. It might still be the right approach.

This would be a good starting point: first, because it would help maintain stability in society and create a good environment for economic, social, and cultural development, and second, it would facilitate a smooth transition to a more mature, civilized, and democratic political system as economic, social, and cultural conditions change. In other words, we should not rush to copy wholesale [a new political system] all at once. However, we must march toward this goal, and absolutely should not move in the opposite direction. We must refrain from perverse actions that don't facilitate, or are even subversive to, achieving this goal.

How long this transition lasts must be determined by social developments. It is critical that the leadership of the Communist Party adhere to this belief. Then it can respond skillfully to circumstances as they arise, gradually, step-by-step, according to the right priorities.

This transition cannot rely entirely upon the ruling party's self-inclination. Public opinion and other social forces must push for it. We must not wait passively for the conditions of economic and cultural development to progress until parliamentary democracy suddenly is announced. The process must be gradual and progressive.

As social, economic and cultural conditions change, there should be constant reform and improvements in the political system, so that the changes and conditions influence and compel each other forward. As to how this transition should be made, we should pursue the improvements I mentioned earlier in how the Communist Party governs.

If the final destination is a parliamentary democracy, the ruling Party must achieve two breakthroughs. One is to allow other political parties and a free press to exist. This can happen gradually, but it must be pursued.

The second breakthrough is having democracy within the Party: that is, the Party needs to adopt democratic procedures and use democratic means to reform itself.

In the past, during the war years and the early years of the republic, there was a need to emphasize centralization and discipline. However, it would be impossible to make the transition from a revolutionary Party to a governing Party, and to lead society's transition to a system of parliamentary politics if the Party doesn't practice a thorough democratic system within itself. The existence of legitimate differences of opinion must be allowed within the Party. Even Chairman Mao said that the minority should be protected in the Party. Different opinions must be allowed to exist, and different factions should be made legitimate. In debates and competitions, different sides within the Party should all observe the same rules.

It would be wrong if our Party never makes the transition from a state that was suitable in a time of war to a state more suitable to a democratic society. This breakthrough must occur. Of course, there will be the issue of the nationalization of the military. More important, the reform of the legal system and an independent judiciary should take precedence.

Our hope is for the ruling position of the Communist Party to be maintained for a considerable period of time, so that the transition can be made under its leadership and preparation made in an orderly manner. As for how long the Communist Party keeps its ruling position, this should be determined by the consequences of society's political openness and the competition between the Communist Party and other political powers. If we take the initiative and do this well, the ruling position of the Communist Party could be maintained for a very long time. However, this ruling position must not be maintained by using the constitution to monopolize this status. Rather, the Party must be made to compete for it. I believe that this is ultimately a worldwide trend that we cannot defy.

If we act with initiative, it will be beneficial to the Party, society, and the people. Any other approach will be harmful. The trend is irrefutable, that the fittest will survive. As Sun Yat-sen said, "Worldwide trends are enormous and powerful; those who follow them prosper, and those who resist them perish."

I believe the time has come for us to tackle this issue seriously.

> *Zhao Ziyang's political career ended with the Tiananmen incident of 1989, but the debate over China's reform continued. A resurgence of the Anti-Liberalization Campaign that Zhao had feared would follow the crackdown in Tiananmen did not materialize. But the*

Party suffered serious damage to its reputation and was condemned by the world for its excessive military reaction.

Deng Xiaoping's alliance with Party elders to topple Zhao resulted in disarray in the new leadership group and brought the reform movement to a standstill. The result was a slump in real GDP growth in the two years following the Tiananmen incident, the most dramatic slowdown since 1976. Deng saw his legacy endangered and the possibility that all the gains made by the economic reforms would go to waste. He could not let this happen.

Deng's last important political action was his renowned "southern tour" of the Special Economic Zones in 1992, a move that revitalized the economic reform programs. The trip was timed to force the upcoming 14th Party Congress later that year to reaffirm further reforms. Those who had maneuvered to ditch economic reform were pushed into compliance by Deng's southern tour. They had watched the Soviet Union collapse; they had lost the trust of the Chinese people after the Tiananmen Massacre and had been powerless to improve the economy. However, the year 1992 marked the end of the debate over the transformation to a free market economy. The outcome has been the transformation of China into a twenty-first-century economic powerhouse, with a renewed insistence on authoritarian autocracy.

Still under house arrest, Zhao Ziyang died on January 17, 2005.

Epilogue

Bao Pu

To understand the extraordinary political journey of Zhao Ziyang, it is important to know exactly what he was up against when he reached Beijing's highest echelons in 1980.

The dominant players in his circle were the "Communist Party elders," men who had been swept aside by Mao Zedong for their reluctance to embrace his radical programs. Having been deprived of their political clout by Mao for nearly two decades, the elders were anxious to seize power and use their remaining years to shape post-Mao China.

The most powerful among them was Deng Xiaoping. Deng had just the right experience to manage the two factions who emerged at the top. As a political conservative, he had the support of Party elders desperate to save the Party from ruin. As a liberal on economic issues—purged not once but twice by Mao—Deng was credible among those who wanted to break from the old days of collectivization. The division among Party leaders over the direction of reform required one top leader to settle disputes. With his combination of seniority, competence, and backing from military heavies, Deng emerged as the paramount leader, filling the void in an authoritarian system that had lost its Great Helmsman.

Another influential elder was Chen Yun, who was even more senior than Deng and was a founder of the Party. He had won enduring respect for having quickly stabilized the nation's war-torn economy in the 1950s, when he was Vice Premier.

When this group came to power, it was clear what would dominate the agenda: economic recovery and an end to China's isolation from the world. In December 1978, at the Third Plenum of the 11th Central Committee, the Party issued a resolution to shift its emphasis from "class struggle" to "economic development." This brought an end to the Party's obsession with destroying "class enemies," which had persisted for thirty years. The Mao era was at an end, and the era of reform was under way.

New political stars began to emerge. Hu Yaobang took over as Director of the Organization Department in December 1977, with power over Party personnel decisions. He immediately began reinstating the victims of Mao's purges; their gratitude turned into solid political support for Deng Xiaoping, who had promoted Hu.

Another new star was Zhao Ziyang. Two years earlier, Deng had sent Zhao to his own home province of Sichuan, which was then on the brink of agricultural disaster. Zhao, who already had years of experience administering Guangdong Province, restructured Sichuan's rural economy. In just a few years, he dramatically raised agricultural production and average incomes in this province of 100 million people, where it was officially revealed that 10 million had died of starvation from Mao's Great Leap Forward. Though his policies seemed to border on "capitalist," their success made Zhao's early reputation.

Despite his many years in provincial bureaucracies, Zhao possessed the political skill of not standing out too much, which helped him rise to the top without causing much commotion or upsetting hard-liners. His quick ascendance began in August 1977 at the 11th Party Congress, when he became an alternate member of the Politburo.

Deng quickly consolidated power by naming Hu Yaobang as Chairman of the Party and Zhao Ziyang its Vice Chairman and Premier of the State Council. Deng's influence now hovered over the Party and state administrations.

Deng's two rising stars began getting to work. Hu's success rehabilitating disgraced Party members, coupled with Zhao's gains from his agricultural innovations, allowed Deng to assert his control both within the Party and among the people. He also became the first Chinese communist leader to win widespread praise from abroad. The new catchphrase in China was "reform." With the help of the Party's propaganda machine, reform became the embodiment of all hope and all things good.

There was only one problem: no one could agree on exactly what form this reform should take. The pragmatists cared little for Marxist dogma. They knew from experience that incentives and market elements worked. Party elders such as Chen Yun, however, believed that the Communist Party should remain loyal to its founding ideology and pursue Soviet-style socialism. For them economic reform just meant recovering from the disasters inflicted by Mao. Among these conservatives, there were also personal reasons for opposing reform. Li Xiannian, who had managed economic affairs for a significant term during Mao's era, saw reform as an implicit criticism of his past work and feared being marginalized. And career bureaucrats—the fabric of China's administration—who had been trained for decades to believe that "capitalism" was the supreme evil, now felt disoriented and threatened by the new political culture.

All of this meant that China's reformers would not have an easy ride. When Zhao became Premier in 1980, he was still new to Beijing's high politics. The first major issue he had to handle was the 1981 economic "readjustment," which had been launched by conservative elder Chen Yun. Zhao had no choice but to head the effort, but in that role he quickly grasped the weaknesses of the central planning system, which had managed economic affairs by assigning quotas throughout the land. He tried to move quickly with reforms.

It was a rocky period. Deng had made it clear that he wanted "no squabbling" at the top. Though the intention of his words wasn't spelled out, they clearly meant that Deng hoped to do as he wished without interference. But when Deng's beloved Special Economic Zones were starting to look overly capitalist, Chen Yun in 1982 launched a "Strike Hard Campaign Against Economic Crimes" that indirectly was aimed at neutralizing the liberal policies the zones allowed. Chen had found a way to exert his will without political "squabbling," and Deng had not detected the ploy. Under these conditions both Hu and Zhao felt compelled to go along with Chen.

By this time, Zhao knew he was operating in a political minefield but pressed ahead in his effort to modernize the economy. It didn't hurt that the idea of allowing food imports, for one, was actually proposed by Chen Yun himself, who was eager to break from the Maoist policy of total self-reliance. China quickly became one of the world's major grain importers. With the pressure off domestic grain production, the state could relax restrictions and quotas that in the past had condemned 800 million peasants to poverty. China then decided to spread to the rest of the nation the rural reforms that Zhao had launched in Sichuan and others had launched in Anhui. Though the policy was resisted by a few provincial administrators, the gains were so immediate that most regions quickly adopted them voluntarily. In contrast with Mao's ruthless campaign to force communes on rural China, the dismantling of this same system was done without coercion.

Progress continued along the coast, too. The Special Economic Zones in the east continued to develop. But because they were set up as isolated laboratories for reform, Deng was able to avoid broad and costly political debates among Party leaders about whether they passed the test of being "socialist."

With the necessary conditions for further reform in place, what was most needed was a clear sense of direction from the central leadership. As the new Premier, Zhao concluded that the main economic imperative was to tackle China's chronic inefficiency. Zhao may have been insulated within the world's largest communist bureaucracy, but he realized that, to make progress, China had to abandon its planned economy in favor of a free market. It was the triumph of good sense.

But to make this happen in a government that still had considerable conservative opposition, Zhao had to twist orthodox doctrine, invent euphemisms for his policies, and keep pressing for Deng's support while ignoring the complaints of other powerful elders. He was always vulnerable to the reality that his ideas were obvious contradictions of the Party's official line.

Opponents such as conservative ideologues Hu Qiaomu and Deng Liqun tried to exploit this vulnerability and were a constant source of irritation for reformers such as Hu and Zhao. The major force keeping these attacks at bay on the "theoretical front" was Deng Xiaoping, who couldn't care less about doctrine. When Zhao became Party General Secretary, he exercised his power to finally finish off the leftist institutions from which these attacks originated.

China's transformation to a market economy passed the point of no return sometime in the 1980s. Politically, however, the Party never abandoned its authoritarian ways. The elimination of Mao's "class struggle" was a breakthrough on one level, but it gave people a false impression that somehow the political system or the Party's leadership style had changed. In fact, the problems of authoritarian rule persist to this day. Without a change, China cannot escape them: a lack of accountability and a Party that is always above the law.

This all but ensures that the government will continue to face episodes of rebellion. The Party has fretted throughout its history about how tolerant it should be in dealing with criticism. In 1957, Mao urged intellectuals to speak out in the Hundred Flowers Campaign, then cracked down on those who did so a year later with the Anti-Rightist Campaign (which Deng carried out). In 1979, Deng continued to suppress the critics. He shut down the "Democracy Wall" movement, in which thousands of intellectuals and young people had posted calls for political freedom on a wall in Beijing. He later sanctioned a 1983 drive against "Spiritual

Pollution," meaning primarily foreign influences, and he proposed the 1986–87 Anti–Bourgeois Liberalization Campaign.

When Hu Yaobang failed to carry out that campaign, Deng dismissed him. A major force for political reform was thus gone. Hu had seemed intent on trying to create a more tolerant, open Party. But as Deng's displeasure with Hu grew, Party elders exploited the rift. With Deng's sanction, they tried to curtail the powers of other reform-minded officials. They even attempted to replace Hu with one of their own.

On this issue, however, Deng stood firm. Although he had removed Hu, he was not about to let an opponent of economic reform, someone like Deng Liqun, succeed Hu. So he promoted Zhao to General Secretary. He did consent to the promotion to the premiership of Li Peng, whose mentor was conservative elder Chen Yun. But he did not trust Li to run the economy, and so to ensure that Zhao would still call the shots in that sphere, Deng created the Central Economic and Financial Leading Group and put Zhao in charge.

It was not the first time Deng had bypassed official institutions, nor would it be the last. In January 1987, he designated an ad hoc "Five-Person Group" to take over from the Politburo Standing Committee upon Hu's dismissal. Then he appointed a "Seven-Person Group" to appoint officials in preparation for the leadership changes at the 13th Party Congress. Though Deng was able to maneuver past some of the recalcitrant elders, he had also planted the seed for future turmoil. In the end, Premier Li was not willing to submit to a reduced role. And an increasingly volatile economic situation helped him to cause trouble.

The decisive blow was an outbreak of high inflation in 1988, exacerbated by an ill-fated and (by Zhao's own admission) ill-conceived attempt to make a bold breakthrough in reforming the pricing system. The government made a fatal error by announcing price hikes before executing them. The public reacted with panic buying and bank runs. The apparent severity of the situation caused Zhao to abruptly abandon price reform.

The damage to his political standing had been done. His opponents began a concerted effort to oust him. Zhao's job became increasingly difficult. He had won impressive victories in his earlier efforts to keep reforms on track. He had neutralized the Anti-Liberalization Campaign in 1987. He had coined the phrase "the initial stage of socialism" as a theoretical basis for China's adoption of free market policies in this first phase of its evolution.

But political reform was a thornier issue. At one point Zhao did write a letter to Deng urging him "to establish a much-needed system of leadership," which suggested problems with the existing autocratic system. Deng got the letter but not the message. Deng had once spoken of the need for "political reform" and for more democracy within the Party, but that was when his political rival Hua Guofeng was the one with too much power. After Deng himself became the top leader, he never talked that way again. In general, Deng's idea of "political reform" did not go beyond administrative reforms to make the Party more efficient.

Zhao mostly accepted Deng's dominance because it helped him fend off other elders on economic matters. When Deng at one stage suggested retiring from the Politburo Standing Committee, Zhao attempted to persuade him to stay on; he needed Deng. But when Zhao prepared to present a series of political reforms at the 13th Party Congress, Deng imposed limits on them that Zhao had no choice but to accept. Deng wanted no part of the Western system: "Let there be not even a trace of tripartite separation of powers."

Zhao recognized that the Party needed to change the way it governed. Without crossing Deng, Zhao proposed a "separation of power between Party and state." The proposal was passed by the Party Congress but was later resisted by Party officials at all levels who were not willing to give up their authority. Serious political reform never got off the ground.

With the eruption of the student demonstrations of 1989, Zhao ran out of time. When Deng decided to call in the military, Zhao made clear he could not take part in such a decision. He was not the only top leader who was hesitant: Deng was unable to win over the majority of the five-member Politburo Standing Committee. So Deng, experienced in sweeping aside Party and government procedures when he needed, won the support of a prominent old general, Yang Shangkun, who guaranteed his control over the military.

After the protests were suppressed, Deng had to grapple with his own legacy. If the hard-line victory ended up killing economic reform as well, Deng would face the terrible prospect of being known as the butcher of Tiananmen who defended an indefensible regime and squandered the prestige he had gained earlier from the nation's economic progress.

And so he set out to change things. In 1992, he went on a celebrated tour of the booming cities along the southern coast. It was a clear signal to China's leaders that economic reforms should proceed—that no one should try to stop them. The move helped force the 14th Party Congress later that year to reaffirm further reforms.

By then the Soviet Union had crumbled. With that collapse hanging over their heads, China's conservatives—who had lost the trust of the people after the Tiananmen Massacre, and had ditched economic reform but shown themselves unable to improve the economy—were pushed into compliance. They had come to realize that the massacre had consolidated the Party's authoritarian rule. With a renewed sense of security, they stopped worrying and prospered.

Today, twenty years on, economic reforms have roared ahead, and capitalism—a stock market, a real estate market, private business—has taken hold. And yet, just as Zhao realized in his later years while under house arrest in his lonely courtyard house, corruption is crippling the system and undermining the people's belief in the government's ability to improve their lives. Without political reform, with no checks and balances, the market is distorted, manipulated by corrupt officials and dirty dealing. The nation is still ruled by men, not by law. While in seclusion, Zhao ultimately concluded that to make progress, China would be better off with a Western parliamentary system. But his conceptual breakthrough came only after he had been silenced.

Zhao Ziyang had no interest in being a visionary. He was a pragmatist who wanted to solve real problems. He led his country through confusion and chaos and made difficult choices for the sake of improving the lives of others. He did his duty. His legacy, recorded here, will ensure he does not fade from history.

A Brief Biography of
Zhao Ziyang

Based on a Chinese version compiled by Li Shuqiao, former secretary of Zhao Ziyang.

1919 October 17   Born in Hua County, Henan Province

1932   Joins the Communist Youth League

1933 August   Enrolls in Henan Province Kaifeng Junior High School

1935 December   Participates in Communist Party activities; organizes student demonstrations against the Japanese, a first step on his path of political activism

1936 August   Enrolls in Hubei Province Wuchang High School

1937 July   Drops out of school as Japanese Imperial Army launches full-scale invasion of China; returns to his home province of Henan, which soon becomes occupied territory and where the Chinese Communist Party (CCP) forms an organized resistance against the Japanese

1938 February   Joins the CCP

1939 January   Becomes Party secretary of Hua County, starting his career as a civilian administrator within the CCP organization

1949 March   Becomes CCP secretary of Nanyang Region, Henan Province

1951   Leaves his home province of Henan for Guangdong, beginning a long and successful career as a provincial administrator

1958–60   *Mao's Great Leap Forward campaign*

1962   Becomes second Party secretary of Guangdong Province and participates in the meeting—known as the Seven Thousand Cadres Work Conference—where party veteran Liu Shaoqi publicly disagrees with Mao on key policy issues

Experiments with halting the communes and contracting land back to private farmers as a "temporary" measure to recover from the disastrous Great Leap Forward

1965   At the age of forty-six, becomes the youngest provincial Party chief as he rises to the position of first Party secretary of Guangdong Province

1966–76   *Mao's Cultural Revolution*

1967   Temporarily detained at Guangzhou Military Command Center as part of the Cultural Revolution purge to cleanse officialdom of supporters of "revisionist" policies (policies that were moderate in contrast to Mao's)

1970   Works as a fitter at Xiangzhong Mechanics Factory of Lianyuan County, Hunan Province

1971 April   Named CCP secretary of Inner Mongolia Autonomous Region and deputy director of its Revolutionary Committee; this marks his reinstatement after being purged

1972 April   Returns to Guangdong as Vice Chairman of the Revolutionary Committee

1973 August   Becomes a member of the CCP's Central Committee

1974   Becomes first Party secretary of Guangdong Province

1975 October   Sent by Deng Xiaoping to become first Party secretary of Sichuan Province; the rural reform policy that he initiates in Sichuan is one of the first of its kind and becomes a model of success in the effort to dismantle Mao's people's communes

1977 August   Named alternate member of the Politburo, the beginning of his ascendance to top leadership positions

1979 September   Becomes a member of the Politburo

1980 February   Becomes a member of the Politburo Standing Committee (PSC)

1980 March   Takes charge of the nation's economic affairs as leader of the Central Economic and Financial Leading Group

1980 April   Becomes Vice Premier of the State Council

1980 September   Becomes Premier of the State Council

1982 September   Renewed as member of the PSC at the First Plenum of the 12th Central Committee

1984 December 19   Signs Sino-British Joint Declaration with Prime Minister Margaret Thatcher in Beijing for the return of sovereignty over Hong Kong to China on July 1, 1997

1986 October   Becomes leader of a new group with the mandate of proposing a political reform package, the Study Group for the Reform of the Political System. Other members are Hu Qili, Tian Jiyun, Bo Yibo, and Peng Chong

1987 January   Becomes Acting General Secretary of the CCP

1987 October   At the 13th Party Congress, declares that China is at the "initial stage of socialism," thereby clearing the way for further market transformations; also proposes the one and only political reform package in CCP history, attempting to change "the way the CCP governs," that is, to introduce reforms such as the separation of power between Party and state

Becomes general secretary and first vice chairman of the Central Military Commission, and remains a member of the PSC

1989 April 15   *Hu Yaobang dies, sparking the student demonstrations*

1989 April 22   Proposes a three-point approach to the student demonstrations: encourages a return to class, holding dialogues, and using the law to punish only those who have committed crimes

1989 April 26   People's Daily *publishes Deng's condemnation of the student demonstrations, which escalates tensions into a serious political crisis*

1989 May 4   Delivers speech to Asian Development Bank delegates that calls for dealing with the demonstrations "based on the principles of democracy and law"

1989 May 17   Participates in the meeting at Deng Xiaoping's house where Deng decides to impose martial law; Zhao says he would find it difficult to carry out such a decision

1989 May 19   Visits student demonstrators in Tiananmen Square and gives an impromptu speech pleading with them to leave the square, knowing that an army assault is imminent. It is his last public appearance

1989 June   An enlarged Politburo meeting is held to criticize Zhao and strip him of all his positions. This begins his sixteen years of isolation and house arrest

1997 February 19   *Deng Xiaoping dies*

1997 September 12   Sends a letter while under house arrest to the 15th Party Congress appealing to the leaders for a reassessment of the crackdown on demonstrators in Tiananmen Square in 1989

2005 January 17   Dies in Beijing

Who Was Who

An Zhiwen (1919–) was deputy director of the State Commission for Economic Reform and a member of the Central Economic and Financial Leading Group from 1987 to 1992. An was an ardent supporter of reform.

Ivan Arkhipov (1907–98) was the Soviet first deputy prime minister who in the 1950s led Moscow's efforts to lend technological aid to China. Arkhipov was regarded as a friend of China for his role in helping to draw up its first Five-Year Plan.

Bao Tong (1932–) was a member of the Central Committee and was entrusted by Zhao to formulate plans for political reform as director of the Political Reform Research Institute of the Central Committee. Bao was Zhao's secretary in the early years of his premiership. In 1989, Bao supported Zhao in opposing Deng's decision for a military crackdown on Tiananmen protesters. As punishment he was jailed for seven years.

Bo Yibo (1908–2007) was one of the most influential Party elders. Bo was vice chairman of the Central Advisory Commission from 1982 to 1987.

Chen Guodong (1911–2005) was the Communist Party's secretary of Shanghai in 1979. From 1985 to 1992, he was the director of the Party's Shanghai Advisory Committee.

Chen Junsheng (1927–2002) was the Communist Party's secretary of Heilongjiang Province. He became a member of the State Council in 1988.

Chen Xitong (1930–) was mayor of Beijing and played an important role in channeling the course of events toward the crackdown on protesters in 1989. Chen's report, published in June that year, was the only official account of what happened in the military assault. Chen was expelled from the Communist Party in 1997 and sentenced in 1998 to sixteen years in prison on bribery and corruption charges.

Chen Yeping (1915–94) was Director of the Department of Organization and became a member of the Central Advisory Commission in the 1980s.

Chen Yizi (1940–) was director of the State Research Institute of Economic Reform. In 1989, during the Tiananmen protests, Chen organized and published a statement that informed the public about Zhao's resignation and called on people to oppose the looming crackdown. Chen has lived in exile in the United States ever since.

Chen Yun (1905–95) was, after Deng Xiaoping, the most influential of the Party elders. Chen won praise for the quick and successful stabilization of China's war-torn economy and for the first Five-Year Plan, based on the Soviet economic model in the early 1950s. His practical approach was swept aside by Mao Zedong's desire for a speedy transition to a socialist economy. Chen's political comeback in the post-Mao era was marked by his insistence on planned economics in the era of reform. From 1982 to 1987, Chen was a member of the Politburo Standing Committee and chairman of the Central Discipline Inspection Commission. From 1987 to 1992, he was chairman of the Central Advisory Commission.

Deng Liqun (1915–) was the Director of the Propaganda Department from 1982 to 1987. An ardent Mao loyalist, Deng became the voice of the conservatives in the reform era and could count on the support of Chen Yun, Li Xiannian, and other Party elders.

Deng Maomao (1950–) is the nickname of Deng Xiaoping's third daughter, Deng Rong. She is the deputy director of the China International Friendship Association.

Deng Xiaoping (1904–97) was China's undisputed leader during the years of transition after Mao, from 1981 to 1997. He supported economic liberalization, and the success of the Reform and Open-Door Policy earned him enormous prestige and strengthened his power base. Politically, Deng insisted on continuing one-party rule and was responsible for the crackdown on political dissent in 1979 (the "Democracy Wall" movement) as well as the violent response to the 1989 Tiananmen protests. Deng was a member of the Politburo Standing Committee from 1977 to 1987 and chairman of the Central Military Commission from 1981 to 1990.

DING GUAN'GEN (1929–) was Minister of Railways and an alternate member of the Politburo in the 1980s.

DING SHISUN (1927–) was the president of Peking University from 1984 to 1989 and vice chairman of the China Democratic League from 1988 to 1996.

DU DAOZHENG (1923–) was the director of the General Administration of Press and Publications from 1987 to 1989. Du is an outspoken supporter of reform.

DU RUNSHENG (1913–) was a director of both the Communist Party's Research Office of Rural Reform and of the State Council Center for Development Studies from 1983 to 1989. Du is a well-respected leader in the field of rural reform.

FANG LIZHI (1936–) was first vice president of the University of Science and Technology in Hefei, Anhui Province, and a professor of astrophysics. Fang sympathized with the earlier round of student protests in 1986–87 and was removed from his official posts and expelled from the Party. He is now living in exile in the United States.

FEI XIAOTONG (1910–2005) was a professor of sociology at Peking University and the chairman of the China Democratic League from 1987 to 1996.

HENRY FOK (1923–2006), also known as Huo Yingdong, was a Hong Kong entrepreneur. Fok was a longtime supporter of the mainland government, serving as the vice chairman of the Chinese People's Political Consultative Conference in 1993.

MILTON FRIEDMAN (1912–2006) was an American economist, Nobel laureate, and influential proponent of free market economics. In 1988, Friedman was received by General Secretary Zhao Ziyang in Beijing, where he praised Zhao as "the best economist I have ever met from a socialist country." Friedman's ideas and advice played an important role in shaping economic policies in post-Mao China.

GAO YANG (1909–) was president of the Central Party School of the Central Committee from 1987 to 1989 and a member of the Central Advisory Commission.

MIKHAIL GORBACHEV (1931–) was General Secretary of the Communist Party of the Soviet Union from 1985 to 1991, the last Soviet leader before the collapse of the U.S.S.R. His perestroika (restructuring) program brought liberal changes to the Soviet Union.

Gu Mu (1914–) became Vice Premier and director of the State Capital Construction Commission in 1975. He was a member of the State Council from 1982 to 1988.

Guo Luoji (1932–) was a prominent liberal scholar who in 1979 published an article in the *People's Daily* arguing that citizens should be allowed to debate political affairs. Deng Xiaoping took it as a personal insult and a criticism of his jailing of dissident Wei Jingsheng.

HAO JIANXIU (1935–) was deputy director of the State Planning Commission from 1987 to 1998.

HE DONGCHANG (1923–) was vice president of Tsinghua University from 1978 to 1982, Minister of Education from 1982 to 1985, and Vice Minister of the State Education Commission from 1985 to 1992. In 1989, his role in presenting the student protests as a cause for alarm played into the agenda of the hard-liners.

HE YIRAN (1918–) was vice chairman of the regional government of Guangxi Zhuang Autonomous Region from 1979 to 1983.

Hu JIWEI (1916–) was a senior journalist and chief editor of the *People's Daily*. Known as one of the leading advocates within the Communist Party for media freedom, Hu opposed the military crackdown on Tiananmen protesters in 1989 and was subsequently stripped of all official positions.

Hu QIAOMU (1912–92) was Mao's secretary from 1941 to 1966. Hu was one of the most prominent defenders of Maoist doctrine in the era of reform. He was a member of the Politburo from 1982 to 1987 and a member of the Standing Committee of the Central Advisory Commission from 1987 to 1992. He was also deputy director of the Party Propaganda Department and director of the Party History Research Office.

Hu QILI (1929–) was the mayor and Party secretary of Tianjin from 1980 to 1982, and then went to Beijing where he became director of the General Office and a member of the Secretariat of the Central Committee. In 1987, he was made a Politburo Standing Committee member. In 1989, Hu opposed the military crackdown on Tiananmen Square protesters and was ousted from his positions.

Hu YAOBANG (1915–89) was Chairman and General Secretary of the Chinese Communist Party from 1980 to 1987. He reversed the internal Party purges of the Mao years, which earned him respect from Party members and the general public. Viewed by Deng Xiaoping and other Party elders as being too tolerant of the liberal trend among Chinese intellectuals in the late 1980s, Hu was forced to resign as General Secretary in 1987. His sudden death on April 15, 1989, triggered the student protests in Tiananmen Square.

HUA GUOFENG (1921–2008) was Mao's successor, and served as China's paramount leader from 1976 to 1980. Hua's legitimacy was based on having been handpicked by Mao, and he attempted to retain the Chairman's policies, an effort that was doomed to failure in the post-Mao era. Hua was swept aside by the reform-minded Deng Xiaoping.

JIANG LIU (1922–) was director of Scientific Socialism Studies at the Central Party School of the Central Committee from 1977 to 1987.

JIANG ZEMIN (1926–) was a member of the Politburo and the Communist Party's secretary of Shanghai. Jiang was promoted to replace Zhao Ziyang as the Party's General Secretary after the Tiananmen military crackdown in 1989.

KANG SHIEN (1915–95) became Vice Premier and deputy director of the State Planning Commission in 1978. Kang was also the Minister of the Petroleum Industry after 1981.

KIM IL SUNG (1912–94) was the paramount leader of North Korea. Kim was General Secretary of the Workers' Party of Korea and President of the Democratic People's Republic of Korea from 1948 to 1994.

Tsung-Dao Lee (1926–) is a Chinese American physicist and a professor at Columbia University. Lee has been well received in China for being one of the few Nobel laureates of Chinese descent.

Lei Jieqiong (1905–) was a professor at Peking University and chairwoman of the China Association for Promoting Democracy from 1987 to 1997.

Li Peng (1928–) was a Power Industry Minister and a Vice Premier before becoming Premier in 1987 as part of the shuffle that resulted from the ouster of Hu Yaobang. In 1989, as a member of the Politburo Standing Committee, Li promoted the decision for a military crackdown on the protesters in Tiananmen Square, making him one of the principal characters influencing that course of events.

Li Rui (1917–) was Vice Minister of Water Conservancy and Electric Power and in 1958 became one of Mao Zedong's political secretaries. Li was expelled from the Party and jailed in 1959 for siding with Peng Dehuai, who had expressed reservations about Mao's Great Leap Forward campaign. Li's case was overturned in 1979 and he became Vice Director of the Organization Department. Li was one of the most outspoken supporters of reform, and is known for his series of published recollections and commentaries on Mao.

Li Ruihuan (1934–) was the Communist Party's secretary of Tianjin. Li became a member of the Politburo in 1987 and a member of its Standing Committee in June 1989. Li's membership on the Standing Committee was made possible by the vacancies left by Zhao Ziyang and Hu Qili. He was moderately pro-reform.

Li Tieying (1936–) was a member of the Politburo and director of the State Education Commission from 1988 to 1993.

Li Weihan (1896–1984) was Director of the United Front Work Department from 1948 to 1964 and vice chairman of the Central Advisory Commission from 1982 to 1984.

Li Xiannian (1909–92) was Vice Premier in charge of economic affairs from 1954 to 1980, and was involved in directing the Mao-style state-controlled economic system. In the post-Mao era, Li viewed many reform policies as having reversed or implicitly criticizing his past work. He served as a member of the Politburo Standing Committee from 1977 to 1987, as President of the People's Republic of China from 1983 to 1988, and as chairman of the Chinese People's Political Consultative Conference from 1988 to 1992. Li remained a powerful conservative influence and attempted to block the reversals of Mao's policies in the economic and political arenas.

Li Ximing (1926–2008) was the Communist Party's secretary of Beijing. In 1989, Li actively promoted the hard-line approach to the student protests in Tiananmen Square. In 1993, Li became a vice chairman of the National People's Congress.

Li Yimang (1903–90) was Deputy Director of the International Liaison Department from 1974 to 1982 and deputy secretary of the Central Discipline Inspection Commission from 1978 to 1982.

Li Yong (1948–) was Zhao Ziyang's secretary of military affairs from 1985 to 1989 and later became director of the Development Commission of Tianjin.

Li Zhengting (1918–) was deputy secretary of the Central Discipline Inspection Commission from 1987 to 1993.

Liang Buting (1921–) was the Communist Party secretary of Shandong Province from 1983 to 1988.

Liang Xiang (1918–98) was the Communist Party secretary of Shenzhen from 1981 to 1995 and the governor of Hainan Province from 1988 to 1989. Liang is recognized as a pioneer in implementing reform in Shenzhen, one of the first designated Special Economic Zones.

Liao Hansheng (1911–2006) was a veteran of the army and served as a vice chairman of the National People's Congress from 1983 to 1993.

Lin Tung-Yen (1912–2003) was a Chinese American structural engineer and founder of T. Y. Lin International.

Liu Binyan (1925–2005) was an influential journalist who in the 1980s was a pioneer in exposing serious social problems. Liu was a senior reporter at the *People's Daily* from 1979 to 1987 and was exiled to the United States after 1989.

Liu Shaoqi (1898–1969) was one of the founding leaders of the People's Republic of China. After its establishment, Liu held the most senior position after Mao. Liu disagreed with radical Maoist economic policies, such as the Great Leap Forward and the rural people's communes. Purged by Mao, Liu died in isolation and humiliation during the Cultural Revolution.

Liu Zhengwen (1912–) was vice chairman of the Chinese People's Political Consultative Conference of Anhui Province from 1987 to 1997.

Lu Dingyi (1906–96) was a liberal writer within the ranks of the Communist Party. Lu became a vice chairman of the Chinese People's Political Consultative Conference in 1980.

Lu Keng (1919–2008) was a prominent journalist in Hong Kong. His interview with Hu Yaobang in 1985 angered Deng Xiaoping and became one of the key reasons behind Deng's decision to dismiss Hu.

Lu Zhichao (1933–) was the appointed leader of the Political Group of the Central Committee Secretariat Research Division headed by Hu Qiaomu. Lu also was chief of the Theoretical Studies Bureau of the Department of Propaganda.

Mao Zedong (1893–1976) was one of the founders of the People's Republic of China and the supreme leader of the Chinese Communist Party. During the post–civil war period from 1949 to 1976, Mao's goal of a rapid transformation to socialism was the nation's priority. To realize this objective, China created a system of state planning and ownership, and Mao periodically waged mass campaigns to root out opposition both outside and within the Party. After his death, the Party's reforms reversed Mao's social and economic programs, but he nonetheless remains the icon of the Chinese revolution.

Meng Xianzhong (unknown) was an official in the Communist Party's General Office of the Central Committee in the 1990s.

Yasuhiro Nakasone (1918–) is a Japanese politician who served as Prime Minister from 1982 to 1987. In that role, he normalized diplomatic relations with the Soviet Union and the People's Republic of China.

Nie Rongzhen (1899–1992) was one of ten marshals in the People's Liberation Army. He served as director of the General Staff Department of the PLA from 1950 to 1954 and as director of the State Science and Technology Commission from 1958 to 1970. Nie was credited for his leadership of the Chinese nuclear weapons and military space programs.

CHRISTOPHER PATTEN (1944–) was the last British governor of Hong Kong from 1992 to 1997. After Hong Kong's handover to China, Patten served as the European Union Commissioner for foreign relations. He is now the Chancellor of Newcastle University and the University of Oxford. As governor of Hong Kong, Patten attempted to reform the election process of the Hong Kong legislature, an effort for which he was vilified by the Chinese government.

PENG CHONG (1915–) was secretary of the Central Committee Secretariat and a vice chairman of the National People's Congress in the 1980s.

PENG DEHUAI (1898–1974) was a prominent People's Liberation Army commander who served as the People's Republic of China's first Defense Minister. In 1959, Peng criticized Mao's Great Leap Forward, which incurred Mao's wrath. Peng was purged and publicly humiliated. His fate, together with that of Liu Shaoqi, are the primary showcases of Mao's whim.

PENG ZHEN (1902–97) was an influential Party elder who was chairman of the Standing Committee of the National People's Congress from 1983 to 1988.

QIAN LIREN (1924–) was the director of the *People's Daily* from 1985 to 1989.

QIAO SHI (1924–) was a member of the Politburo in charge of the security apparatus. Qiao became Vice Premier in 1986 and a member of the Politburo Standing Committee in 1987. In 1989, though he originally agreed with Zhao's moderate approach to the student movement, Qiao abstained from taking a side at the moment that a decision was made for a military crackdown. He ultimately carried out Deng's orders.

QIN BENLI (1918–91) was chief editor of the *World Economic Herald*, an outspoken pro-reform newspaper in Shanghai. Qin published commemorative articles about Hu Yaobang in April 1989 despite Party officials' warnings not to. He was removed from office by the Communist Party secretary of Shanghai, Jiang Zemin. This highly publicized and controversial event turned out to be an unexpected boon to Jiang's political career, as just months later, after the Tiananmen crackdown, he was chosen to replace Zhao as General Secretary.

REN ZHONGYI (1914–2005) was the Communist Party's first secretary of Guangdong Province from 1980 to 1985. He was a leading practitioner of the reform policies in one of China's most progressive regions.

RUAN CHONGWU (1933–) was Minister of Public Security from 1985 to 1987 and became deputy director of the State Science and Technology Commission soon after Hu Yaobang was forced to resign.

RUI XINGWEN (1927–2005) was the Communist Party's secretary of Shanghai from 1985 to 1987. Rui was a secretary of the Party's Central Committee Secretariat from 1987 to 1989 and was an ardent supporter of reform. Rui was removed from his official post for taking a stand sympathetic to the student protesters in Tiananmen Square in 1989.

SONG PING (1917–) was deputy director of the State Planning Commission from 1972 to 1987 and Director of the Organization Department from 1987 to 1989. After the June Fourth incident, he ascended to the Politburo Standing Committee, along with Li Ruihuan, to fill the spots left vacant by Zhao Ziyang and Hu Qili.

SONG RENQIONG (1909–2005) was an influential Party elder. He was Director of the Organization Department from 1978 to 1983 and a member of the Politburo from 1982 to 1985.

SU SHAOZHI (1923–) was the director of the Institute of Marxism–Leninism–Mao Zedong Thought at the Chinese Academy of Social Sciences from 1982 to 1987. Accused of having "liberal tendencies," Su lost his position in 1987 and was exiled after 1989.

SUN CHANGJIANG (1934–) was deputy director of the Theoretical Division of the Central Party School of the Central Committee. Sun was known for his participation in a theoretical debate between Hu Yaobang and Mao's successor Hua Guofeng. The debate marked the beginning of Deng Xiaoping's ascendance to his position as paramount leader.

SUN QIMENG (1911–) was one of the founders and chairman of the China National Democratic Construction Association from 1983 to 1997.

Tian Jiyun (1929–) was Vice Premier from 1983 to 1993 and a member of the Politburo starting in 1987. Tian was an outspoken supporter of reform.

Tsiang Sho-Chieh (1918–93) was a professor of economics at the University of Rochester and Cornell University, and director of the Chung-Hwa Institute for Economic Research in Taiwan during the 1980s. Tsiang was a promoter of a free market economy.

Wan Li (1916–) was the Communist Party's first secretary of Anhui Province in 1977. He was known for his early successes with rural land contracts in Anhui. Together with Zhao, who had similar achievements in Sichuan, Wan was instrumental in dismantling Mao's people's communes. Wan was a Vice Premier from 1983 to 1988 and a major supporter of reform. He became chairman of the National People's Congress in 1988.

Wang Daming (1929–) was Deputy Director of the Propaganda Department from 1986 to 1987 and chairman of the eighth Beijing local Chinese People's Political Consultative Conference from 1993 to 1998.

Wang Daohan (1913–2005) became deputy director of the State Import-Export Commission in 1978. In 1980, Wang became the Communist Party's secretary of Shanghai.

Wang Heshou (1909–99) was second secretary of the Central Discipline Inspection Commission and was known for his involvement in many of the internal Party cases of great historical significance, including those of Lin Biao, Jiang Qing (Mao's widow), and Liu Shaoqi.

Wang Jian (1954–) was a researcher at the Economic Institute of the State Planning Commission. He was known to Chinese scholars for an article published in *Economic Daily* in 1987 in which he proposed a strategic economic development model that relied heavily on international trade that was later widely perceived as having been adopted by Chinese leaders.

Wang Jikuan (1931–2007) was a consultant for the State Council's Center for Economic Technology and Social Development Studies in the 1980s.

Wang Meng (1934–) is a prominent writer. He was the Minister of Culture from 1986 to 1989.

Wang Quanguo (1919–) was the Communist Party's deputy secretary of Guangdong Province from 1975 to 1979 and secretary of Hubei Province from 1982 to 1983.

Wang Renzhi (1933–) was the Communist Party's Director of the Propaganda Department from 1987 to 1992. He had a reputation for siding with Party elders and undermining reform.

Wang Renzhong (1917–92) was Vice Premier of the State Council. Wang headed the investigation of Zhao in the aftermath of the 1989 events.

Wang Ruilin (1930–) was Deng Xiaoping's secretary starting in 1952. Wang became director of the General Office of the Central Military Commission when Deng was its chairman, and later deputy director of the Communist Party's General Office of the Central Committee.

Wang Ruoshui (1926–2002) was deputy chief editor of the *People's Daily* and a well-known liberal scholar. Wang's articles on "the alienation of socialism" triggered a public debate in the early 1980s that amounted to one of the first intellectual movements to challenge the Party line in the post-Mao era.

Wang Ruowang (1918–2001) was on the board of directors of the Chinese Writers' Association and deputy chief editor of *Shanghai Literary Magazine*. Wang was jailed for fourteen months for his participation in the 1989 protests before being exiled to the United States in 1992.

Wang Weicheng (1929–) became Deputy Director of the Propaganda Department in 1987 and was later director of the Legislative Commission of the National People's Congress.

Wang Zhen (1908–93) became China's Vice President in 1988. He was a powerful Party elder who often tried to resist reform. In 1989, Wang actively promoted the military crackdown on the students in Tiananmen Square.

Wei Jianxing (1931–) was the Communist Party's Director of the Organization Department from 1985 to 1987, then Minister of Supervision from 1987 to 1992.

Wei Jingsheng (1950–) is a Chinese dissident. In 1978, Wei was a leader of the Democracy Wall Movement, during which he wrote a poster, titled *The Fifth Modernization*, calling for democracy. Perceived by Deng Xiaoping as a critic of his authoritarian rule, Wei was sentenced to fifteen years of imprisonment in 1979 and became one of the best-known Chinese dissidents. Wei now lives in exile in the United States.

Wen Jiabao (1942–) was director of the General Office of the Central Committee from 1986 to 1992. Wen became a member of the Politburo Standing Committee in 2002 and China's Premier in 2003.

Gordon Wu (1935–), also known as Hu Yingxiang, is a Hong Kong entrepreneur, and the founder of Hopewell Holdings Limited.

Wu Xiuquan (1908–97) was Vice Minister of Foreign Affairs and Director of the Communist Party's International Liaison Department from 1958 to 1975.

Wu Xueqian (1921–2008) was a member of the Politburo and Vice Premier of the State Council. Wu was Minister of Foreign Affairs from 1982 to 1988.

Wu Zuguang (1917–2003) was a prominent playwright who was regarded as liberal among Chinese writers.

Xiao Hongda (1918–2005) was director of the General Office of the Central Military Commission and deputy secretary of the Central Discipline Inspection Commission from 1987 to 1992.

Xiong Fu (1915–95) was Deputy Director of the Propaganda Department and the director of the Xinhua News Agency. From 1978 to 1988, Xiong was the chief editor of *Red Flag*, the official magazine of the Party's Central Committee.

Xu Jialu (1937–) was a professor of Chinese literature at Beijing Normal University and vice chairman of the China Association for Promoting Democracy.

Xu Jiatun (1916–) was the Communist Party's secretary of Jiangsu Province and later became chief of the Xinhua News Agency in Hong Kong, then China's defacto official political presence in the territory. Xu has lived in the United States in exile since supporting the prodemocracy movement in Beijing in 1989.

Xu Shijie (1920–91) was from 1988 to 1990 the Communist Party's secretary of Hainan Province, one of the coastal regions designated as a Special Economic Zone during the reform era.

Xu Xiangqian (1901–90) was the general chief of staff of the People's Liberation Army from 1949 to 1954. Xu served as Vice Premier and Minister of Defense from 1978 to 1981.

Yan Jiaqi (1942–) is a political science scholar known for his 1979 proposal to abolish the lifelong leadership position held by the Chinese Communist Party and the state. Yan was a researcher at the Central Committee's Political Reform Research Institute, headed by Bao Tong. Yan has been living in exile since the Tiananmen crackdown.

Yan Mingfu (1931–) was Director of the United Front Work Department of the Central Committee from 1985 to 1990. He was removed from his official post for not actively supporting the Tiananmen crackdown in 1989.

Yang Shangkun (1907–98) was a member of the Politburo from 1982 to 1987 and vice chairman of the Central Military Commission. He became President of the People's Republic of China in 1988. Yang played a key role in 1989 by submitting to Deng Xiaoping's decision to pursue a military crackdown on the Tiananmen protests. Yang was instrumental in mobilizing the army to carry out the order.

Yang Wenchao (unknown) was a secretary for Zhao Ziyang in the early 1990s.

Yao Xihua (unknown) was from 1987 to 1989 the chief editor of *Guangming Daily*, a newspaper influential among the intelligentsia.

Yao Yilin (1917–94) was Vice Premier from 1979 to 1993 and director of the State Planning Commission from 1980 to 1983. Often siding with conservative elders such as Chen Yun, Yao ascended to the Politburo Standing Committee in 1987. As one of the five members of the Politburo Standing Committee, Yao actively supported the military crackdown in Tiananmen in 1989.

YE JIZHUANG (1893–1967) was Minister of Trade and Minister of Foreign Trade in the early days after the founding of the People's Republic of China.

YE XUANNING (1938–) is the second son of China's esteemed Marshal Ye Jianying. He was director of the Liaison Division of the People's Liberation Army's General Political Department from 1990 to 1993.

YONG WENTAO (1932–97) was the Communist Party's secretary of Guangdong Province and Guangzhou Municipality from 1965 to 1966.

YU GUANGYUAN (1915–) was a prominent economist in the 1980s and vice president of the Chinese Academy of Social Sciences.

YU QIULI (1914–99) was Vice Premier from 1975 to 1982, and director of the General Political Department of the People's Liberation Army from 1982 to 1987. A veteran of the State Planning Commission, Yu was its director from 1975 to 1980.

YUAN MU (1928–) was director of Premier Li Peng's office and director of the Research Office of the State Council. Yuan became the official spokesperson during the Tiananmen crackdown in 1989.

ZENG XISHENG (1904–68) was the Communist Party's secretary of Anhui Province. From 1959 to 1961, he promoted the policy of contracting land to farmers instead of forcing them into people's communes. He was purged in 1962 for opposing Mao's wishes.

ZHANG GUANGNIAN (1913–2002) was a prominent poet and literary critic, known for his 1955 *Chorus of the Yellow River*.

ZHANG JINFU (1914–) was director of the State Economic Commission from 1982 to 1988 and secretary of the Central Committee's Economic and Financial Leading Group.

ZHANG SHUGUANG (1920–2002) was the Governor of Hebei Province and Secretary of the Party Committee of Inner Mongolia Autonomous Region in the 1980s. Zhang became a member of the Central Advisory Commission after 1987.

ZHANG WEI (1913–2001) was vice president of Tsinghua University and member of the Degree Commission of the State Council from 1980 to 1987.

ZHANG XIANYANG (1936–) was an outspoken liberal intellectual who was in charge of the study of Lenin and Stalin at the Chinese Academy of Social Sciences. Zhang was expelled from the Communist Party in 1987.

ZHANG YUEQI (1938–) was both deputy director of the General Office of the Central Committee and Zhao Ziyang's secretary from 1987 to 1989.

ZHAO JIANMIN (1912–) was governor and Party secretary of Shandong Province and a member of the Central Advisory Commission from 1987 to 1992.

ZHENG BIJIAN (1932–) was a special adviser to General Secretary Hu Yaobang in the 1980s. In 1992, Zheng became Deputy Director of the Propaganda Department.

ZHOU ENLAI (1898–1976) was one of the founding leaders of the People's Republic of China. Zhou held the position of Premier from 1949 to 1976. Zhou's mostly pragmatic and moderate approach, in contrast to Mao's radicalism and ruthlessness, earned him enormous admiration among the populace. His death set off the "April 5th Incident" of 1976, the first large-scale public demonstration in the People's Republic of China.

ZHU HOUZE (1931–) was Director of the Propaganda Department from 1985 to 1987. His moderate stance was not tolerated by the Party elders, and he was removed from his post after Hu Yaobang's ouster. Zhu served as deputy director of the Rural Development Center of the State Council from 1987 to 1988.

Acknowledgments

T he editors would like first of all to express their sincere gratitude to Bao Tong, whose efforts were instrumental in making this publication possible. With his inside knowledge of China's recent reform efforts, Bao Tong—who was once Zhao Ziyang's top aide—provided us with insight at almost every stage of this endeavor. Bao Tong, who is the father of Bao Pu, one of the book's translators and editors, spent seven years in prison for siding with Zhao in opposing the Tiananmen crackdown. At his home in Beijing, he remains under constant surveillance.

We would also like to thank Adi Ignatius's wife, Dorinda Elliott, a Chinese speaker who was *Newsweek*'s Beijing bureau chief during the period described in this book. She provided valuable counsel and editing ideas throughout the development of this project. Without her sustained fascination with China and her ability to cross cultural divides, this material would have had a more difficult time finding its way to the English reader.

We're grateful for the wise and elegant contribution of Roderick Mac-Farquhar, the Leroy B. Williams Professor of History and Political Science at Harvard University and the author of many books on China, most recently *Mao's Last Revolution* (coauthored with Michael Schoenhals, Harvard Universtiy Press).

We have been impressed at the speed and competence of the team at Simon & Schuster. Our wonderful editor, Priscilla Painton, and publisher, David Rosenthal, were enthusiastic from the start about a project they could only refer to as "Untitled" by "Anonymous" as it moved through the publication process. Aileen Boyle, Irene Kheradi, Lisa Healy, Linda Dingler, Michael Szczerban, and Daniel Luis Cabrera brought their usual rigor and high standards to the making and marketing of the book, and made sure it was handled with care.

Lastly, we want to thank our friend and literary agent Rafe Sagalyn, who helped us shape an idea into a book.

There are many who must remain unnamed who have worked behind the scenes from inside China. They took unimaginable risks to safeguard, preserve, and transport Zhao Ziyang's secret tapes to safety outside the country. We only hope that this publication gives them gratification and that in the future their own stories can be told.